RISING FROM
THE ASHES

RISING FROM THE ASHES

Development Strategies in Times of Disaster

Mary B. Anderson
Peter J. Woodrow

LYNNE
RIENNER
PUBLISHERS

BOULDER
LONDON

Published in the United States of America in 1998 by
Lynne Rienner Publishers, Inc.
1800 30th Street, Boulder, Colorado 80301

Library of Congress Cataloging-in-Publication Data
Anderson, Mary B., 1939–
    Rising from the ashes : development strategies in times of
disaster / by Mary B. Anderson and Peter J. Woodrow.
    Originally published: Boulder : Westview Press : Paris : UNESCO,
1989. With new pref.
    Includes bibliographical references.
    ISBN 1-55587-800-8 (pb : alk. paper)
    1. Disaster relief. 2. Community development. 3. Disaster
relief—Developing countries—Case studies. 4. Community
development—Developing countries—Case studies. I. Woodrow, Peter
J. II. Title.
[HV553.A58   1998]
363.34'8'091724—dc21   97-45940
                                                                CIP

Printed and bound in the United States of America

        The paper used in this publication meets the requirements
  ∞   of the American National Standard for Permanence of
        Paper for Printed Library Materials Z39.48-1984.

    5 4 3 2 1

Contents

Preface

In the years since *Rising from the Ashes* was first published, the number of international nongovernmental organizations (NGOs) working in disaster situations has risen dramatically. The amount of aid provided to people in crises by the NGOs has also increased, as agencies of both the United Nations and bilateral donor governments have more and more come to rely on NGOs as their "operational partners" in the field.

We believe that these trends reflect two positive realities. The first is that compassion continues to motivate individuals and societies to reach out to people in crisis and to offer direct support that alleviates their suffering. The second is that, overall, NGOs still offer a reliable and caring conduit for aid to reach real people in real need.

At the same time, in many donor countries NGOs are under attack by journalists and other critics who have seen the negative impacts of well-intentioned emergency assistance. While these adverse effects are not new—in fact, it was our awareness of them that prompted the project that produced this book in the 1980s—they have become more widely acknowledged. And many of today's critics imply, or overtly call for, an end to international aid. Because aid sometimes does harm, they contend, it would be better not to provide it.

It is our unequivocal position that international aid is a good thing and that it should continue. While it is true that aid can cause harm, it is also obvious that withholding aid would also do harm. The goal of this book, and of other projects in which we are now engaged, is to gather the powerful lessons of past aid experience. These lessons can guide the design of urgent relief efforts so that they will, with greater certainty, save lives and alleviate suffering and leave their recipients stronger and better able to cope with future crises.

The decision to republish *Rising from the Ashes* responds to a continuing demand from field-based aid workers and from those who manage aid systems. As more people become directly involved in humanitarian assistance, we have received repeated requests for a reprinting of the lessons gathered and analyzed here. We are delighted that colleagues have been willing and able to make this happen.

Deserving of particular thanks are Carolyn Makinson of the Mellon Foundation, Perry van der Meer of the International Rescue Committee, and Lynne Rienner of Lynne Rienner Publishers.

As this volume goes back into print, we feel compelled to offer one further comment about its use. In recent years, many disasters have been the result of political, intergroup violence rather than the perturbations of nature. We both find in our current work that the Capacities and Vulnerabilities Analysis presented here can be adapted to provide a deeper understanding of these conflict situations and, thus, to prompt better aid to their victims. However, one particular adaptation is critical in the circumstances of civil war. While in non–conflict-related disasters, it is always right to support local capacities, in a conflict environment, some indigenous "capacities" are directly involved in perpetuating hatred and pursuing war. More careful analysis is critical under these circumstances, and our earlier suggestion for disaggregating among groups as one identifies capacities is reinforced by experiences of providing aid in conflict areas. An additional category for understanding differences in society should now involve identifying which capacities provide the basis for future unity and peace, and which represent the strengths of some people who are intent on using them for division and dominance.

With this addition, we again welcome readers to use the analyses and stories provided here to prompt creative and effective support to sufferers of future disasters that truly recognizes, builds on, and strengthens their capacities to create secure and just societies.

Mary B. Anderson
Peter J. Woodrow

Acknowledgments

Most books represent the involvement and ideas of more individuals than those whose names are listed as authors. This is abundantly true in this case. We are indebted to many people.

These people include the several dozen individuals who actively assisted us during each of thirty field visits and the staff people from the headquarters of over fifty NGOs in Europe and North America who collaborated on the project. Also included are the numerous individuals in research centers, international donor agencies, UN agencies, universities, and NGO consortia who participated in our explorations.

The number is so large that we tremble at the challenge of naming individuals, lest we leave out too many. Yet we must name some.

First, Dawn P. Trainor, who, with patience, humor, and skill, supported, thought, and worked with us when we were in the field or at home, and who, when all was said and done, got the manuscript into publishable form in spite of our frequent changes of mind and incessant editing.

Hussein M. Adam, senior project associate, brought valuable ideas and his unique perspective to the entire project process. He also served as an informal ambassador and inveterate networker for the effort.

Our "core group," which included Peggy Antrobus, Tim Brodhead, Goran Hyden, Noel McGinn, and Donald Schramm, provided days of enthusiastic grappling with issues and useful guidance to the project. Thus, they share with us responsibility for the framework and structure of both the research and this book.

The IRDP Advisory Panel, including representatives of each of the NGOs that participated in the project, was a rich source of experience and challenge. Their participation has been a crucial part of the process of developing the ideas in this book. While many people have been engaged with us from the NGOs, there are a few who served beyond the call of duty: Robert T. Snow of Oxfam America and later American Jewish World Service; Nancy Nicalo of Church World Service; Jacques Cuenod of ACORD and later ICVA; and Gunnar Hagman of the Henry-Dunant Institute.

Several others worked with us as researchers and writers in the process of developing the case histories: Mohamed Hassan Farah, Hady M. Ly, Roberto Muj Miculax, Mark Nieuwkerk, Ronald Parker, Ann K. Qualman, Donald Schramm, Robert Thomson, Daniel Torrealba, and Christopher M. Harris, who also worked with us as a research assistant. Additional research assistants, Arun Joshi, Thomas LeBlanc, and Julie Lineberger Cincotta, contributed a range of skills to the project. They organized our library, did independent research, wrote helpful "think" pieces, answered telephones, handled correspondence, and, in general, helped the office and project run.

The project would not have been possible without generous grants from several funding sources. We intentionally sought broad support and were pleased to receive assistance from the following funders: the Canadian International Development Agency, the Exxon Education Foundation, the Ford Foundation, the Office of Foreign Disaster Assistance/U.S. Agency for International Development, PACT (Private Agencies Cooperating Together), the Royal Norwegian Ministry of Development Cooperation, the Swedish International Development Authority, UNICEF, and USA for Africa. Relief and development agencies that contributed with grants or in-kind assistance include: ACORD, Africare, American Friends Service Committee, CARE, Catholic Relief Services, Church World Service, Foster Parents Plan International, Oxfam America, Save the Children Federation, Swedish Red Cross, and World University Service Canada.

We also received assistance in the field in the form of transport and hospitality from the following Southern NGOs: SURERD (Somalia), Ethiopian Red Cross, Centro de Estudio Sociales Solidaridad (Peru), Equipo del Desarrollo Agropecuario de Cajamarca (Peru), Lutheran World Service-India, International Institute of Rural Reconstruction (Philippines), Norfil Foundation (Philippines), Social Action for Rural and Tribal In-Habitants of India, and Social Work and Research Center (India).

Our intellectual and managerial home was the Graduate School of Education at Harvard University. We gratefully acknowledge the support afforded by Dean Patricia Alberg Graham, by other deans, and by the directors of various assisting offices. We also appreciate the faculty, staff, and students who encouraged us with ideas and enthusiasms of their own.

Finally, we are indebted to Greg Bates, who gave days and nights providing technical assistance and solving the important detailed problems of preparing the typescript for this book. Thanks also to Helen Snively for patient and meticulous proofreading, to Jerry Alexander for his generous professional services in making maps, and to Katherine Shorey for her creative rendering of graphs and charts.

—M. B. A.
—P. J. W.

RISING FROM
THE ASHES

Introduction

Help!

Disaster strikes. When word reaches the outside, people rush to help the victims. By the time aid arrives from outside, however, the "victims" are helping themselves. For sudden onset disasters, such as hurricanes, earthquakes and floods, survivors at the scene rescue the injured, salvage materials and begin to rebuild. In slow onset crises, such as drought and famine, "victims" pursue a myriad of survival strategies long before outside aid givers are even aware of their difficulties.

Still, disasters *do* strike, suddenly or slowly. Disasters can be defined as crises that overwhelm, at least for a time, people's capacities to manage and cope.[1] They rightly invite a compassionate response from those not victimized. Outsiders who give aid may be from no farther away than the next village, or they may live on other continents and have no experience of either the people or the societies they want to help.

Aid: Help?

The relationship between aid givers and receivers has received much attention. It is complex. Aid, intended to help, can often harm. Motivations of the giver are honorable, and suspect. The *impact* of aid on the recipient is sometimes helpful, sometimes as damaging as the original disaster.

The subject of this book is "outsider" aid (whether international or from nearby), and the purpose of this book is *to help the givers of aid learn how to give it so that it supports the efforts of people to achieve social and economic development.*

1. Frederick Krimgold in: *Overview of the Priority Area Natural Disaster*, United Nations, New York (15th October 1976).

The focus of our concern is the nations of Africa, Asia and Latin America where there is widespread poverty and in which the people and governments are engaged in a development process. While there is disagreement about whether or not the actual number of disasters has been increasing, there is evidence that the number of people suffering from disasters is increasing, and the majority are from these regions of the world.

Fortunately, many people are horrified by the continuing and widening gap between those who live secure lives and those who continually suffer from poverty, inadequate food, ill health and limited opportunity. Over the years, a sizable organizational apparatus has grown up which represents the institutionalization of their concern. It involves the bilateral and multilateral aid agencies including the UN agencies, the international development organizations, and the non-governmental organizations (NGOs) from Africa, Asia, Latin America, Europe and North America.

This latter group, the NGOs, play a special role in disaster response and development programming. Varied as they are, they work "on the ground," close to the local people, providing relief and development assistance. Most believe that this closeness increases the likelihood that their assistance will really support local development. However, most also see a division between their relief work and their development work. They have established certain principles for development work which they frequently abandon in the face of the perceived urgency of a disaster.

The result has been that opportunities for harnessing emergency work for development have been missed. Too often, disaster responses in the form of relief aid have not contributed to long-term development and, worse, actually subverted or undermined it. *There is no reason why this should continue to be the case.* If the number of times external agencies intervene in disaster responses is actually increasing—and it is—then the necessity for designing relief interventions so that they contribute to long-term development becomes all the more important. Relief efforts directed at "getting things back to normal" will do just that and no more, leaving people as vulnerable to the next crisis as they were to the last.

The Question and an Answer:

The question is: how can agencies provide emergency aid that meets immediate needs and, at the same time, contributes to and supports long-term development?

In an effort to find practical answers to this question, a number of NGOs joined together to collect lessons from their past project experience that would help them improve the developmental impact of their emergency aid. The International Relief/Development Project (IRDP) was a collaborative effort among NGOs for exploring the relationships and linkages between relief and development and for deriving lessons for future project design and implementation.

The IRDP developed thirty case histories based on selected project experiences of these collaborating agencies. The cases examine experiences in providing emergency relief in disaster situations and analyze the impact of the relief work on long-term development in the countries where the disasters occurred. The cases cover a range of experiences in many countries, across disaster types and involving different NGOs.[2] The lessons and guidelines for program design presented in Part I of this book are derived directly from these cases. Short, illustrative examples drawn from the cases are interspersed in the text of this book. A selection of complete cases is presented in Part II.

The guidelines and lessons presented in this book also build on the work of many people who have been working, thinking and writing on these topics in recent years. In fact, we note a significant convergence of thought and approach among many people who work on disaster response, refugee programming, development, NGO assistance and even in other more distant fields. There are clear areas of difference among these writers' approaches and between some of them and us. Still, certain elements are common to us all. First, there is a re-examination in process of the purposes and mechanisms of aid and of how and why it has, so far, not been more successful in really aiding the poor people of Africa, Asia, and Latin America. Second, there is a heightened sense that, to provide effective assistance, donor agencies must learn more about the recipients. They must have a clearer knowledge of, and respect for, them. Finally, there is greater exploration of the relationships between management, management styles (especially NGO) and developmental outcomes. For reference to the people who have most influenced us, see Appendix B.

If You Read On, What Will You Gain?

As noted above, the purpose of this book is to help NGOs and others figure out how to provide emergency assistance so that it supports long-term development. Its lessons are applicable as well to the design of development projects (which, alas, also sometimes fail to support development), especially those in areas vulnerable to disasters.

It is *not* a manual or a how-to-do-it book. It *is* a book which tells how some people have successfully linked relief work with development in past projects and which suggests, therefore, ideas and approaches for others to use in the future.

This book is divided into two major parts. Part I presents the lessons learned and guidelines derived from the thirty case histories and through

2. A complete list of the IRDP cases is provided in Appendix A.

discussions and meetings with the NGOs which participated in the process. Part II presents eleven of the cases themselves, selected to represent the breadth of NGO experience in disaster relief.

Within Part I, the first chapter describes the purposes of the book and presents a framework for analysis which provides a "map" for understanding and analyzing the project histories. It sets forth the tool of Capacities and Vulnerabilities Analysis by which it is possible to predict before the fact, or assess after the fact, the extent to which relief and development projects actually support or subvert development. Capacities and Vulnerabilities Analysis emerged and was refined through the IRDP process of analyzing field projects.

Chapters 2-7 examine a series of decisions and choices in disaster relief programming. This does not pretend to be a comprehensive treatment of all the important things to be considered in development. Rather, these chapters present and discuss the set of issues that came up repeatedly in the NGO experiences, identifying pressures and dilemmas confronting NGOs, summarizing the "lessons learned" from the thirty case histories, and presenting a set of principles or criteria for judging and handling these issues in future projects. As the reader will find, this section examines some of the "received wisdom" about emergency response and finds that sometimes it is neither received nor wise.

The Conclusion to Part I turns to a discussion of the relationships between principles, policies and practice—within a relief or development agency, within the wider NGO community, and between NGOs, governments, and donors. The agenda for further work on the linkages between development and relief includes a need to "close the gap" between widely accepted developmental principles, the policies adopted by agencies, and the systems for putting such principles and policies into practice in the field. This book represents one effort to close the gap, and, by doing so, to support the development efforts of people around the world.

Within Part II, three sets of cases are offered. The first set of three cases examines projects which provided relief, but in an innovative and developmental manner. The second set of cases involves situations where ongoing agency development work was interrupted by a disaster, causing the agency to change to relief work. The final four cases illustrate creative approaches to work with refugees or displaced people.

Lessons Learned and Guidelines for Program Design

Introduction to Part I

Thinking Development in a World of Disasters

Concepts and Tools for Program Design

The commitment to development is clear and unshakable among nongovernmental organizations. However, when circumstances require them to respond with immediate humanitarian relief, development goals are often lost or at least deferred while emergency efforts prevail. The informed analysis, sensitive implementation, and regular evaluation characteristic of development work are all but abandoned in the face of the crisis. With regret, agencies feel that they cannot maintain their commitment to development while disaster response is demanded.

The International Relief/Development Project has tried to provide a way for NGOs to hold fast to development aims while proceeding to address immediate needs in the wake of disasters. The basic approach, developed through the study of NGO field relief projects, is presented in Chapter 1. Capacities and Vulnerabilities Analysis provides a way to sort information about a disaster situation and to set priorities among program options. This "analytical framework" is the lens through which a wide range of issues is examined throughout the balance of Part I.

Decisions and Choices in Program Design and Implementation

A number of key issues in disaster relief programming appeared again and again in the projects and programs examined by IRDP. In Chapters 2-7, we report what we have learned through the case histories about these issues, showing how Capacities and Vulnerabilities Analysis can be applied in project design and implementation. The issues examined are grouped under six headings:

First Decisions in Programming

The Context of Programming

Dimensions of Programming

People and Programming

Approaches to Programming

Cooperation and Accountability in Programming

In the first of these, we begin by examining the first decisions that NGOs make about disaster response—namely, the decision of whether or not to provide assistance and, if so, whether to develop a full relief program or to join together with local NGOs as partners to provide relief. In the next section, we look at the strong influence, on all programming, both of the political context and of the policy context in which agencies provide assistance. We end this discussion by analyzing the importance of information to project design and operation. Who needs to know what, and when do they need to know it? What are the purposes of information and how can it be used to increase a project's developmental impact?

Under "Dimensions of Programming," three other design issues—the speed, size and duration of responses—are discussed and myths about them debunked. The chapter on "People and Programming" discusses issues about *whom* the projects are focussed to help. We suggest applying the term "participants" to describe those people to whom aid is provided because they are the real actors in any development effort. We then focus on two "special" groups often named as recipients of emergency assistance: women and refugees.

Issues of importance to the NGOs themselves as they hire staff and plan the content and mechanisms of projects are treated in the section on "Approaches to Programming." Finally, two areas of concern to almost all NGOs with whom we worked are discussed in "Cooperation and Accountability in Programming."

While we do not deal explicitly with disaster preparedness, mitigation and prevention, in a basic sense these are what this book is all about. Awareness of the relationships between disaster response and development is fundamental to preparedness and mitigation. In the final analysis, because local capacity is increased through development to the point where it can cope with crises that occur, even disaster "prevention" is possible.

Chapter 1

A FRAMEWORK FOR ANALYZING CAPACITIES AND VULNERABILITIES

What Is This Analytical Framework?

The analytical framework is a tool to help NGOs design and evaluate relief projects. It is difficult, when comparing varied experiences, to take account of the specifics of each situation and, at the same time, to develop generalizations that are valid in multiple situations. Relief work is complex, involving many people, many agencies and many governments at the international, national, regional and local levels. Also, disasters are caused by both natural and human factors, and the range of possible responses is large. Many variables must be taken into account in designing disaster responses and maximizing their developmental impact.

How can we deal with such complexity and diversity of experience and still generalize enough to help future project planners? The comparison of diverse experience is greatly facilitated by a simplified (but not simplistic!) framework for analysis. Such an analytical framework should provide a straightforward system for considering the factors that are critical to the design and implementation of effective relief projects.

An analytical framework sets out *categories* of factors to be considered and suggests a sequence or order in which to consider them. The categories must be comprehensive enough to cover all the important variables, but few enough that they are easily remembered. In essence, this framework helps us to "map" a complex real situation, to highlight the crucial factors, and to illustrate the *relationships* among factors that matter most to project effectiveness.

We begin with a straightforward presentation of the categories of the analytical framework. Then, five factors that add important dimensions to the analysis reflecting the complex reality of project contexts are introduced and discussed. Finally, the application of the framework to the design or evaluation of projects is discussed, especially as it can inform and guide the many decisions that NGOs face about whether and how to give aid.

Vulnerabilities and Capacities Analysis

The analytical framework is based on the dual concepts of capacities and vulnerabilities. We explore vulnerabilities in order to understand why a disaster happened and what its impact has been, why it affected a particular group of people, and how to estimate the risks of future disasters.

It is important, here, to make a clear distinction between vulnerabilities and "needs." Vulnerabilities refer to the *long-term factors* which affect the ability of a community to respond to events or which make it susceptible to calamities. Needs, as used in a disaster context, refer to immediate requirements for survival or recovery from a calamity.

For instance, those who suffer from mudslides in an urban area may have *needs* for temporary shelters and medical attention. They may *need* help with housing and infrastructure reconstruction. On the other hand, the *vulnerabilities* in the situation include many long-term trends and factors, some of which directly contribute to the suffering caused by the mudslide: crowding, siting of homes on unstable land, use of poor housing materials, etc. Other vulnerability factors do not relate directly to danger from mudslides, but do affect the ability of the community to respond to and recover from any serious crises: rural to urban migration because of lack of rural employment opportunities, lack of government enforcement of building codes or other services, absence of strong community organizations, and pervasive poverty, itself.

Vulnerabilities precede disasters, contribute to their severity, impede effective disaster response and continue afterwards. Needs, on the other hand, arise out of the crisis itself, and are relatively short-term. Most disaster relief efforts have concentrated on meeting immediate needs, rather than on addressing and lessening vulnerabilities.

Vulnerabilities analysis[1] can help prevent two pitfalls of relief work. First, it calls into question any post-disaster attempts simply to "get things

---

1. "Vulnerability Analysis" is applied by others to procedures for assessing vulnerability to natural hazards such as earthquakes, floods, typhoons or droughts. Here we use the term in a broader sense.

back to normal," because, by raising awareness of the factors that contributed to this disaster, it shows that "normalcy" involved vulnerabilities that, if not changed, may lead to future disasters. Second, it alerts relief workers to the potential for unwittingly contributing to future vulnerabilities by their interventions. Much of so-called "development" actually increases vulnerabilities. Examples include construction of high-rise buildings in earthquake zones without using earthquake-resistent techniques or building commercial or residential units on flood plains.

To avoid increasing vulnerabilities, it is necessary to identify capacities in order to know what strengths exist within a society—even among disaster victims—on which future development can be built. Acknowledging the capacities of the affected population is essential for designing and implementing disaster responses that have developmental impacts. Every society has both strengths and weaknesses, capacities and vulnerabilities. When a crisis becomes a disaster (i.e., it outstrips the capacity of the society to cope with it) then the society's vulnerabilities are more noticeable than its capacities. However, for agencies wanting to help with recovery and systemic development beyond recovery, understanding both is essential.

Not all crises become disasters and not all people suffer equally from any given disaster. Why do disasters occur where and when they do, and why do they happen to some people and not to others? The answer lies in an examination of vulnerabilities. People become disaster "victims"[2] because they are vulnerable. Because people have different degrees of vulnerability, they suffer differently.

The most visible area of vulnerability is physical/material poverty. Poor people more often suffer from crises than people who are richer—because they have little savings, few income or production options, and limited resources. Less obvious, but equally important, are two other areas of vulnerability that may also contribute to victimization. One of these is the social/organizational realm—how a society is organized, its internal conflicts and how it manages them. The other is the motivational/attitudinal area—how people in the society view themselves and their ability to affect their environment. Societies may be either vulnerable or have capacities in these areas, and these vulnerabilities or capacities are as important as their material resources, or lack of them.

For example, even poor societies which are well-organized and cohesive can withstand, or recover from, a disaster better than those where there is little or no organization and people are divided. Similarly, groups who share strong ideologies or belief systems, or who have strong

2. Victim is in quotation marks here because the term itself encourages the notion of helplessness or lack of capacities. This will be discussed further in Chapter 6.

Figure 1: Capacities and Vulnerabilities Analysis Matrix

	Vulnerabilities	Capacities
Physical/ Material What productive resources, skills, and hazards exist?		
Social/ Organizational What are the relations and organization among people?		
Motivational/ Attitudinal How does the community view its ability to create change?		

Development is the process by which vulnerabilities are reduced and capacities increased.

experiences of successfully cooperating to achieve common social goals, even when struck by disaster, may be better able to help each other and limit some kinds of suffering than groups without such shared beliefs.

The three areas of vulnerabilities and capacities are represented in the matrix presented in Figure 1. The analysis always refers to factors at the *community* level, rather than at the individual level. The internal lines in the matrix are dotted because the categories overlap and there is constant interaction among them.

Physical/Material

We begin with the physical/material realm, not because it is the most important (experience shows that it often is less important than the other two areas), but because it is the area on which most outside disaster assistance is concentrated. When a disaster strikes, it is the physical destruction or suffering that compels the attention of outsiders. Although disaster "victims" suffer physical deprivation (food, shelter, medicines), they always have some physical/material resources left. These may be recoverable goods or only the skills they carry with them. These capacities are the point of departure for developmental work.

To understand physical vulnerabilities, we ask what were the ways in which the group (who became "victims") were physically vulnerable. For example, are they disaster victims because of their economic activities (as when farmers cannot plant because of floods or nomads lose their grazing lands because of drought) or because of their geographic location (homes built on flood plains, in cyclone areas, or on mountains prone to mudslides)? Or, are they simply too poor and possess too few resources for long term sustenance?

The physical/material category includes land, climate and environment, people's health, their skills and labor, infrastructure, food, housing, capital, and physical technologies.

Social/Organizational

To explore the social/organizational vulnerabilities and capacities, we ask what was the social structure of the people before the disaster and whether it served them in the face of this disaster. What has been the impact of the disaster on social organization? This category can include the formal political structures and the informal systems through which people get things done, such as making decisions, establishing leadership, or organizing various social and economic activities.

Social and organizational vulnerabilities are obvious when there is prejudice or conflict within a society. Divisions according to race, religion, ethnicity, language, class, or caste can weaken the social fabric to such an extent that people are more vulnerable to crisis. The most obvious and devastating disaster resulting from social vulnerability is war when conflict becomes overt. Millions in today's world suffer social, as well as physical, disruption as refugees.

On the other hand, people, even disaster "victims," always have social coping systems: family, group, community, and/or area-wide organizations; systems for distributing goods and services; inter- and intra-family decision-making patterns. Efforts to overcome a disaster should recognize and build on these. Furthermore, by becoming engaged in assessing its own capacities, a community can build community cohesion through joint action.

Motivational/Attitudinal

To understand the motivational/attitudinal realm, we ask how the community views itself and its ability to deal effectively with its physical and social/political environment. What were people's beliefs and motivations before the disaster happened and how did the disaster affect them? Do people feel they have the ability to shape their lives? Strength or weakness in this realm can make a significant difference in a society's ability to rebuild or improve its material base or its social institutions.

A community is psychologically or motivationally vulnerable when people feel victimized, fatalistic or dependent. Sometimes religion (or ideology) and superstition can underlie such vulnerability. Sometimes religion provides common faith and strength. The indicators of capacities and vulnerabilities in the motivational/attitudinal realm vary with context and culture.

When people share a sense of purpose, a feeling of empowerment, or an awareness that they are agents of their own lives and futures, they can produce more and create a more satisfying community. IRDP staff met several community people, involved at the village level in responding to a disaster, who identified a key capacity in the motivational category as "fighting spirit." In fact, a crisis can be the catalyst for extraordinary efforts by communities. Relief and development workers have often noted that people are more open to change and to considering new ways of doing things in the wake of a disaster. People's sense of capacity and competence also constitute the basis for any attempt to overcome a disaster and to build better and stronger economic and social systems. Any agency wanting to help with disaster assistance should encourage and support these capacities, rather than undermine them by its relief efforts.

Our discussion to date has put vulnerabilities before capacities. This is because vulnerabilities are most obvious in times of disaster. However, it should be clear by now that capacities assessment is critical for designing projects to have a positive developmental impact. For this reason, and to emphasize this point, hereafter we refer to the analysis as Capacities and Vulnerabilities Analysis.

Additional Dimensions: Complex Reality

Five factors must be added to the analysis in order to make it reflect complex reality and, therefore, to increase its usefulness. These five dimensions are: A) disaggregation[3] by gender; B) disaggregation according to other differences; C) constant change; D) interactions among the analytical categories; and E) scale/levels.

Gender Disaggregation

In all societies, men and women have different social and economic roles. A gender-based division of labor exists in all situations, whether the society is modern or traditional. In some situations the differences are deeply embedded in culture or religion and constitute a significant part of culture; in others, change is occurring rapidly and gender roles are in flux. In all cases, examining the three categories of capacities and vulnerabilities for women and for men makes sense if one is to find the best programmatic intervention for supporting development.

For example, in refugee camps where women are not present, it has been observed that camp managers have difficulty arranging some of the basics of camp life such as food distribution and preparation—an activity traditionally managed by women. Relief programming that did not take account of that fact would encounter difficulties.

After ascertaining the physical/material capacities and vulnerabilities in any society, we should ask *who* has access to and control over these resources. What skills and expertise do women have? What skills and areas of coping are especially identified with men?

Similarly, social/organizational structures often exclude women's participation. Relief or development efforts that are designed to encourage community participation may rely entirely on existing decision-making structures, only to discover that women, on whom some project activities depend, have been left out. Also, a community's sense of its ability to achieve its goals or affect change may differ between men and women.

Disaggregation According to Other Differences

A community can also be analyzed according to other ways it is divided: by rich, poor, and poorest of the poor; by ethnic, political, or

---

3. *Disaggregation* refers to the analytical process of breaking things down into discrete categories—the opposite of *aggregation*, or putting things together.

Figure 4: Analysis Changes over Time

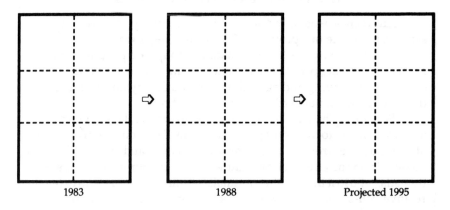

1983   1988   Projected 1995

TIME AND CHANGE FOR A NEW NOMAD COMMUNITY

When the project began, the participants were almost totally destitute. They were nomads living in the Sahelian area of Mali who had lost all of their animals and had no land or other resources with which to make a living. In an experimental program, the government provided small plots of land and a few animals to each family. An NGO provided organizing assistance and small amounts of funds to the new village.

Five years later, the situation was quite different. Agricultural activities were regular and productive. Herds had been built up again. A diversified economy was taking shape. Schools and other permanent buildings were built.

Ten years after the project started (and several years after its official close), a severe drought once again hit the region. The new capacities and reduced vulnerabilities of the village nomads led them to try new strategies for survival. They relied on skills learned through the project to earn money in towns to the south.

An analysis of this community over time reveals how capacities and vulnerabilities changed markedly. An agency wishing to assist these people would need to adopt different approaches at different times. The agency that did assist them could see where its work had decreased vulnerabilities and increased capacities and where, in a few cases, some people's vulnerabilities were increased.

Interactions

As important as the dynamic over time, and related to it, is the fact that there is constant interaction among the six categories of the analysis. Reductions in physical vulnerabilities may be accomplished by an increase of capacities in the social realm, and, at the same time, cause a shift from a sense of dependency to a sense of effectiveness in the motivational realm. A strong leader can inspire people and help them organize themselves to increase their physical resources.

Any intervention by an agency *will* have an impact in all six categories as a chain of interaction occurs. Failure to recognize and attempt to predict these interactions can be a programmatic mistake. At worst, negative impacts on capacities can result; more often, opportunities to support and encourage existing capacities are lost. Both slow down development.

As already mentioned, the categories are not entirely discrete—they overlap and interact. It is not always possible—and certainly it is not necessary—to place a factor in one cell of the matrix.

INDIRECT EFFECTS FROM SELF-HELP WORK

Parts of Mexico City were devastated by the earthquake in 1985; 75 percent of the housing was destroyed. An outside NGO came with offers of assistance to one community that was among the poorest and lacked community organizations—if the people would organize themselves into self-help groups.

In the course of rebuilding their homes, they came to know and trust each other. From home building they moved on to other areas of joint enterprise, such as a cooperative laundry and a bakery which increased their productive capacity. In this case the community was mobilized to address a physical/material problem (housing), but the project was designed so that new social/organizational capacities were created, resulting in additional successful efforts to build the physical/material realm (productive assets).

Scale/Levels

The Capacities and Vulnerabilities Analysis can be applied to small villages and local neighborhoods, to larger districts, to whole nations, and even to regions. As the scale of application increases, the factors examined become less precisely defined, but one can still assess both disaster proneness and development potential at each level.

There are also interactions across levels that affect programming. A small community contained within a larger entity faces limitations on its independent ability to reduce vulnerabilities and increase capacities. Smaller political units are affected by policies and political events at regional, national and international levels.

In the physical realm the point is obvious. A village downstream from others who use the same river cannot adequately, by itself, protect against flood or drought. A community in a war zone may have strong internal cohesion, but it will be susceptible to the impact of the surrounding conflict, nonetheless.

**Figure 5: Capacities and Vulnerabilities Analysis
Applied at Different Levels**

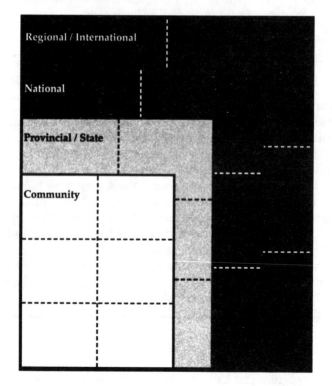

How to Use Capacities/Vulnerabilities Analysis

Capacities and Vulnerabilities Analysis is not prescriptive. It does not tell what to do in any given situation. It is only a *diagnostic tool*. But, as a tool it has power—power to organize and systematize knowledge and understanding of a situation so that we can recognize important factors affecting people's lives, and more accurately predict the impact of our own interventions on their internal resources. It may also help to avoid costly errors in programming. It is applicable at many points and stages in disaster response.

Decision Tree

The "decision tree" presented in Figure 6 identifies the points of decision for an NGO considering its response to a disaster. Each of the "decision points" is pictured as a matrix:

At each of these decision points, an agency should ask the basic developmental question: How will our intervention affect capacities and vulnerabilities? At these points, Capacities/Vulnerabilities Analysis helps an agency assess the likelihood that its intervention will have a developmental effect, and at every point, the analysis provides a way of thinking about what choices to make.

While consideration of capacities and vulnerabilities occurs throughout the decision tree, the chart also shows a specific point, once the agency has decided where it will work, at which a thorough Capacities/Vulnerabilities Analysis of the local participant population should be done as part of the planning process. The people, themselves, should be involved in information gathering and interpretation for the Capacities and Vulnerabilities Analysis. This is a powerful way to help them increase their understanding of their own situation, and, therefore, their capacities to effect desired change.

The Decision Tree is drawn so that choices that require less NGO involvement are on the left and those that require more NGO involvement are on the right. It shows the usual decision paths undertaken by an agency when responding (or not responding) to an emergency. However, the process is never as linear or neat as the diagram seems to imply. An agency might choose one path—say, to establish its own programs. After further information gathering and work, it might decide to go back and choose another route—perhaps to work with a newly-discovered local partner.

Figure 6: Decision Tree for Agency Intervention

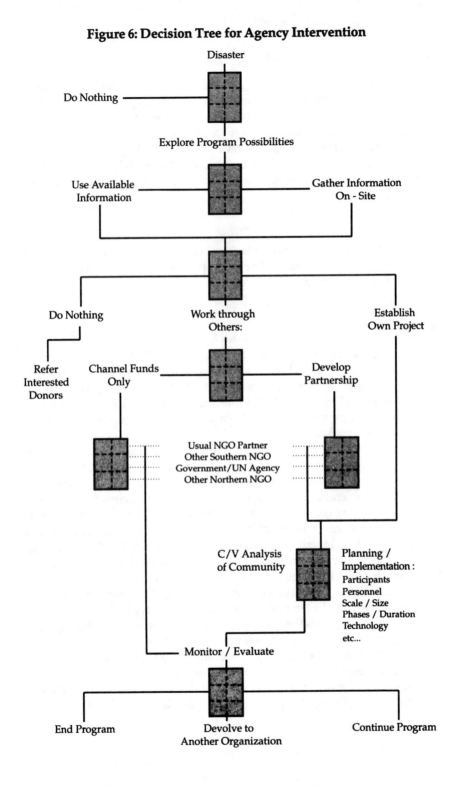

Project Assessment

Capacities and Vulnerabilities Analysis also provides a tool for assessing the relative merits of a range of possible project activities (lower right hand side under PLAN in the Decision Tree). In every post-disaster situation, people have immediate needs that can be identified. For complex disaster circumstances, many useful methods of "needs assessment" have been devised. However, the question we pose is not just what the emergency relief needs are, but *how* they might be met in ways that contribute to development in the long term.

For instance, in a famine, the most striking immediate needs are for food and acute medical care for the severely malnourished. But some of the long-term vulnerabilities in the situation might include soil degradation, water table depletion, damaging land use and access patterns, isolation from transport systems, and inadequate systems for preventive health care.

Figure 7 depicts how an agency can think about the relationship between the needs it has identified in a disaster, its options for programmatic response, and the probable developmental impact of the range of proposed programmatic responses. Each program that is being considered can be assessed according to how it will affect the capacities and vulnerabilities of the community. The question is (for example): How can food and medicine (to meet immediate needs) be provided in a way that addresses the long term vulnerabilities and builds capacities (for long-term development)?

Figure 7: Program Options Tested
Against Capacities/Vulnerabilities Analysis

Immediate Needs for:	Range of Program Possibilities	Impact on Capacities and Vulnerabilities
Emergency Food	A. Feeding centers with Western MDs	⇨
	B. Village distribution and local medics treat severe cases	⇨
Medical Care	C. Village distribution and local health educators train mothers in ORT	⇨

Chapter 2

FIRST DECISIONS IN PROGRAMMING

The early choices that an agency makes in response to a disaster are crucial. They establish the overall shape and direction of the program. The first decision is whether to provide assistance or not. The dynamics of decision-making under conditions of urgency are explored below in the section on "The Decision to Intervene."

The other major, and early, decision for outsiders is whether to work through another local agency or to establish an independent program. The considerations involved in this decision are discussed in the section on "Partnerships."

THE DECISION TO INTERVENE

Policies vs. Pressures

NGOs feel compelled to respond to disasters for both good and bad reasons. Committed to humanitarian principles, they naturally work to alleviate human suffering and provide assistance to those in need. Even development agencies who "never" do relief work find themselves drawn to a compassionate response in times of emergency.

But, NGOs are pressured to respond to disasters by more than straightforward humanitarian concern. Our discussion begins from the perspective of Northern NGOs as they decide whether and how to provide relief aid. While the "scenes" in which the pressures are played out may differ for local or Southern NGOs, some of the pressures we examine are familiar in those settings too.

For example, the news carries compelling stories of suffering and need. The telephone rings as people ask where they can send donations. Other agencies announce their actions. The newspaper deadline for listing the agencies accepting donations is at 4 p.m.! Staff members in the country of the disaster report poignant stories of suffering and ask for authorization to spend funds. Headquarters telex the field, requesting a disaster response program design as soon as possible. Organizations feel that their survival demands engagement in relief work. Agencies may feel they have to respond to disasters in order to keep their names before the public and to compete for funds for international work. It is a fact of life that development funds are harder to raise than relief funds. In the United States, several recent big relief operations (Kampuchea and Ethiopia) have provided opportunities for agencies to build their lists of regular donors. This has been true even for agencies that do not usually do relief work.

It is important to recognize the multiple pressures that NGOs experience as they decide whether or not—and how—to respond to a disaster because these affect (and often distort) the potential for designing a response that will have a developmental impact. This is true both for foreign or Northern NGOs and for indigenous or Southern NGOs. In the sections of this book that follow, we examine how the lessons learned through IRDP can help an agency resist inappropriate pressures and/or educate its public and donors so that they do not apply pressures that undermine development.

Northern agencies experience pressures to engage in emergency relief work.

Scene One:

- *The telephone rings:* It's a call from the government aid agency (AID, ODA, SIDA...). "We are getting pressure from Congress (Parliament...) to spend money on this crisis in Palmania. What are you folks going to do? Any chance you can put a proposal in? We're trying to move about $2 million in the next three weeks!"
- *The telephone rings:* It's a member of the Board of Directors. "I've been reading in the papers about the massive flooding in Palmania. One of the worst areas is right where I worked as a Peace Corps volunteer in 1965. Sounds like people are in terrible shape and there's a lot to be done. I've talked with Joe Love [Board Chairman] and he and I agree that we [the agency] ought to be doing something. I expect you are already drawing up plans...."
- *The telephone rings:* It's a colleague from another agency with which your agency has worked closely in the past. "We have decided to respond to the crisis in Palmania, but we'd like to put together a

consortium. Together we could raise several million dollars. Would you folks like to come in with us?"

- *A meeting is called:* Your agency's country director for Palmania is called to a meeting of all NGOs working in the country with the minister of foreign affairs and the director of the Department of Aid and Cooperation. "We appreciate all the work you agencies have been doing for development. In the face of the widespread effects of the flooding, we would like every one of you to cease regular operations and help with relief and reconstruction efforts during the next year."

- *A telex arrives:* It is from a local Palmanian NGO (PARD: Palmanian Aid for Rural Development) which was originally started by your agency. "Conditions desperate. Estimate 75 percent of houses destroyed and 60 percent crops lost in our project area. Many people homeless and without food. Your continued support greatly needed. Request $500,000 funding plus emergency shelter supplies and 1000 MT grain ASAP."

Then the following discussion might well occur at a meeting at the headquarters of the Northern NGO.

Scene Two:

The Executive Director; Bruce, Overseas Program Director; Jack, Emergency Desk Chief; Anne, the Regional Director; Alia, the Desk Officer for Palmania; George, Director of Finance and Fundraising; and Pat, Public Appeals Coordinator, meet as the Emergency Response Planning Team.

- *Executive Director:* Perhaps we can start with a report from the field. Anne, what have you regional people got?
- *Anne/Regional Director:* We've got telexes from the field from our Country Director reporting strong requests for help from the government. Our friends at PARD have also telexed asking for help. The newspapers have been calling asking if we will respond. It's been quite a day! We are asking for volunteers to come in to help answer calls, but we don't know what to tell people yet. We've asked the field to make a proposal for a program but haven't heard back.
- *George/Finance Director:* It's clear to me that we have to get an ad in the *Capital Herald* immediately. Pat and the public appeals folks have already worked up a format with some great photos picked up from the wire services of people huddled on rooftops and floating houses.
- *Alia/Palmania Desk Officer:* But wait a minute! We haven't even figured out if there is something useful we can do. Despite all the drama in the media, people coming out of Palmania have been saying that local NGOs and government agencies are handling the emergency very well.

Maybe there will be a role for us later but right now the crisis is being handled. Our field staff report that local people are in charge. I thought our policy was to support the decisions of our resident field staff.

- *Pat/Public Appeals Coordinator (ignoring her):* We're planning a special mass mailing to all of the people that responded to the Kampuchea and Ethiopia emergencies. We expect about a 25 percent return from them, which is great. This will be smaller but we can still probably expand our donor base.
- *Bruce/Overseas Program Director:* I suggest we slow down here and think carefully about what we're doing. Our program development policies say that we will only respond to emergencies in countries where we are already working. Of course, we are working in Palmania, but the most devastated zones are in areas of the country where we have never worked, with a completely different ethnic group and culture. In the past, we have also said that we would not get involved in food aid. Food seems to be a major part of this program. Also, PARD's work in rural areas has not been particularly supportive of local people. They've been taking over operation of local cooperatives without training the coop members to run them themselves. I'm not sure this is one in which we should get directly involved.
- *Executive Director:* Joe Love, the Board Chairman, has been talking to other Board Members, some of whom were Peace Corps workers in Palmania.
- *Alia* (under her breath): Yeah, I know....
- *Executive Director* (continuing): There's strong support there for action. I've talked with the executives over at our sister agencies at World Savers and White Knights; they're going ahead full steam. I don't think this is one we can miss.

These scenes reflect a confusion of pressures and policies that is common when people must make decisions under disaster conditions. How can an agency make a good decision about whether and how to intervene—adhering to its developmental principles and policies—and not get deflected by the very real pressures that operate on it? A sorting of the pushes and pulls in this kind of decision-making helps ensure that development considerations are held in focus.

A relief agency depends heavily on the funds it raises for emergency responses and is, in a real sense, vulnerable if no disasters occur! Most agencies—whether identified as relief or as development agencies—are "vulnerable" to the pressures exerted by their board members and major donors for certain kinds and locations of programming. To increase their ability to provide assistance that supports development, agencies need to reduce their own vulnerabilities to pressures that force programming they know will increase dependency. At the same time, they must increase their

THE ARMERO DISASTER: NGO INVASION

In November 1985, the Nevada del Ruiz volcano erupted near the town of Armero, Colombia. Melting snows pushed tons of mud down the mountain valley, totally levelling the town and killing 22,000 of the 30,000 residents. The survivors lost relatives, homes, possessions. Their organizations were devastated and they suffered psychological trauma. Media coverage of dramatic attempts to rescue people trapped in the mud, especially one little girl named Omayra, rivetted world attention. Donations for Armero relief flooded into NGO offices around the world. Within weeks, many agencies came to Armero from all over the world to provide relief assistance to victims. During the next year, millions were spent on relief and reconstruction efforts for the 8,000 survivors. There were so many agencies and so few survivors that competition among NGOs for "beneficiaries" was intense. While survivors were able to "shop" for the most advantageous package of benefits (housing, grants, loans) for their families, it was a situation guaranteed to cause these survivors to learn to depend on relief aid rather than to rebuild for themselves.

capacities to a) educate the public about the relationships between relief and development; b) develop fundraising strategies that attract donors who understand the importance of supporting local efforts; c) assess the impacts of their programming on local capacities and vulnerabilities; and d) select and train staff, provide funds, and plan programs that recognize and support the capacities of the program participants.

An agency may do a Capacities and Vulnerabilities Analysis on *itself*, at any point, to ascertain its ability to provide aid developmentally. Specific capacities to do developmental programming at specific locations, such as language facility, familiarity with local culture or experience with local groups, may help an agency decide whether or not to intervene with emergency aid.

Scene Three:

If an NGO had adopted policies and approaches that reflected its commitment to relief work that supports capacities and reduces vulnerabilities, the scene played above might look quite different. For example:

• *Executive Director:* We've called this meeting because, clearly, Palmania has experienced a terrible disaster. The flooding is bad and people are suffering. Let me remind us all, our policy is to provide relief aid only in ways that support local efforts and capacities. Anne, what have you

could follow this with offers to help, over the long term, in efforts to reduce vulnerability to future repetitions of the disaster.

If, on the other hand, an agency decides to do nothing because staff have decided that the area is "hopeless" and nothing worthwhile can be done, then this decision is not supportive of local capacities which staff assume to be non-existent. Vulnerabilities are assumed to be overwhelming and there is no possible action to reduce them.

Collaborating with Local NGOs

An agency can choose to work through other agencies, either by channeling funds or by developing a partnership which includes programming dimensions. A decision to work with a Southern partner agency is, in and of itself, a decision to rely on local capacity. However, the developmental impact of this decision depends on the nature of the collaboration. This is discussed further in the next section of this chapter.

To apply Capacities and Vulnerabilities Analysis to a decision to channel funds through or to work with another agency, one would ask the basic questions about the nature of the response that the *other* agency

---

SUPPORTING LOCAL NGOs

As Kampucheans were crossing the border into Thailand in 1980, many international agencies responded by helping to set up refugee camps. Thai NGOs also wanted to help. They felt kinship with these refugees and knew that they had certain skills for working with them that European and North American NGOs did not have.

But, at each planning session with the United Nations High Commission for Refugees (UNHCR), the offers from the Thai NGOs to help were passed over. They did not have the experience in refugee camp management that UNHCR officials felt was needed. Thousands of refugees were arriving each day; UNHCR felt it could not take a "risk" with these untried local agencies.

One Northern NGO saw what was happening and considered it a special opportunity. It called a meeting of many local NGOs and set into motion a process of collaboration in refugee work. The Northern agency, with several Thai NGOs as its partners and subcontractors, put in a proposal to UNHCR to manage one of the holding camps. They stipulated that they would insist on the involvement of the Thai NGOs, and that they would take a developmental approach to work in the camp. UNHCR accepted this arrangement.

Today, the Thai NGOs which were involved in this response compete for and win contracts from UNHCR for refugee camp work.

proposes. Does it rely on and support local capacities and help local people reduce vulnerabilities or not?

The Establish-Your-Own-Program Option

A Northern agency may also decide to set up its own program in a disaster area. Chapters 4 through 8 of this document discuss the issues of design and implementation of disaster projects and programs and examine the ways Capacities/Vulnerabilities Analysis can be applied to each issue. These issues are relevant to all programming, whether undertaken by a Northern or a Southern NGO.

NORTH-SOUTH PARTNERSHIPS IN DISASTER RELIEF

Issue #1: Building North-South Partnerships

Many Northern NGOs, instead of becoming directly involved in emergency program implementation, are now funding relief efforts implemented by Southern NGO partners.[1] Such cooperative relationships take many forms. What are the best arrangements for partner relationships that support development of Southern NGOs? Reliance on a local agency does not, inevitably, result in support and encouragement of local capacity. Sometimes outside agencies only *use* a local agency to front for their own activities. The message conveyed is pure lack of confidence: "You need us to get things right; without our money, technical assistance, and staff you would be incompetent."

How can Southern NGOs assess potential Northern NGO partners? How can Northern NGOs assess potential Southern NGO partners?

What is the developmental approach that a Northern agency can take to support the work of a Southern NGO? The process should start with a respectful assessment of capacities. What has the local NGO done? What is it already good at doing—development work or relief programming? Who is its constituency? Some local organizations have experience and capacity in certain areas but weaknesses or lack of experience in others. A Northern NGO can support the local organization by building on existing capacities and helping it increase its competence in new areas. Both partners should assess what is needed to make that happen.

A program agreement between a Southern NGO and a Northern NGO can legitimately include budget items for the organizational

1. Some Northern NGOs have "logical" partners—especially among religious organizations and "spin-off" local organizations associated with or founded by secular Northern NGOs.

development of the Southern NGO. Training in organizational skills could be provided directly by the Northern partner staff (if *they* have the appropriate skills or experience) or by a third party.

A partnership agreement between a Southern and a Northern NGO might include any combination of the following elements: funds, technical assistance, personnel (exchange or secondment), materiel, information/reporting, training.

Questions for Partnership Agreement

1. Who has responsibility for doing what, when and how?
2. What processes will be followed for program planning, implementation, and decisions on changes in program? Who will be involved?
3. What are the expectations for results, implicit and explicit?
4. What reporting is required: on expenditures, on program?
5. How will evaluation be performed, by whom, using what criteria? And, most important,
6. How will decisions be made about all of the above?

NGO-GOVERNMENT ALLIANCE

Sometimes people criticize NGOs for being not only *non*-governmental, but *anti*-governmental. There are, however, a number of cases where NGOs have worked closely and successfully with Southern governments.

In one such example, a Northern NGO worked with the Forestry Department of a Sahelian country that was devastated by drought. In the bush area bordering the desert many trees had died. Villages lost their major source of income and fuel. The project worked under the Forestry Department to develop a cadre of village level extension agents to work with village people promoting replanting.

Forestry Department staff, including a project director, were seconded to the NGO project. The NGO and government department worked together to make sure that the extension system could be sustained by the Forestry Department after the NGO left.

Southern NGO Considerations

What should a Southern NGO ask about a potential Northern Partner? A suggested list:

1. Does the Northern NGO offer anything that will increase your ability to work effectively?
2. How much of a relationship does the Northern NGO want? Does it want to give a grant or to have involvement in program design? Is this a one-time or short-term relationship, or are there possibilities for further collaboration in the future? Is this the relationship you want?
3. What is the "style" and development philosophy of the NGO? Is its political or religious agenda compatible with your own? Do their people treat your people with respect?
4. What are their reporting requirements? What kinds of information does the partner agency need in order to report to its donors and constituents? What burden does this place on you?
5. Where does the Northern NGO get its funds—from government agencies, from private foundations, from the general public, from a specific constituency, such as a religious group? How does this affect what activities it can fund and how can it fund them?

Issue #2: Levels of Development and Accountability

When Northern NGOs work with Southern NGOs, new complexity is introduced. Levels involved include 1) the community, 2) the Southern NGOs, and 3) the local and national government agencies. Each of these levels represents important areas where Northern NGO assistance can increase or undermine existing capacities. They also represent areas of potential competition for resources and attention. For example, to what extent does time and effort spent in capacities development of a Southern NGO (by both Northern and Southern partners) divert resources from the support of local community people?

As Southern NGOs become more and more visible in the development process in their countries, governments have begun to feel that the NGOs compete with them as initiators and sustainers of development at the local level. At the other extreme, concerns are raised that relatively small and experimental NGO projects remain small and experimental. They are not integrated into government programs and policies. In some cases, NGOs do not help improve sustainable government services, but set up parallel systems in health, education, agricultural extension, etc. This not only represents a choice to support a Southern NGO instead of local government; such efforts often also rely on continued outside funding. The issue is not whether it is better to support an NGO or a government, but how to support *sustainable* capacity.

As Northern NGOs work with and through Southern NGOs, questions are also raised about accountability. Even though removed from project operations, Northern NGOs bear responsibility for the outcomes of projects they fund. If an emergency project funded by a Northern NGO and implemented by a Southern NGO is anti-developmental, the Northern NGO is responsible too. Partners must agree on the criteria for monitoring and evaluating projects. Such an agreement should include how to fulfill primary accountability to project participants and secondary accountability to donors (government, private foundation, or general public).

This chapter has discussed how Northern and Southern NGOs can establish their relationship to encourage and support local capabilities. The agreements they make must be based on respect and on a common commitment to promote development. And Southern NGOs should be sure that they can truly benefit from a partnership—that it will help them strengthen their abilities to work—before they agree to such an arrangement.

Chapter 3

THE CONTEXT OF PROGRAMMING

Aid, especially relief assistance, is often given in highly politicized contexts. It cannot be neutral or apolitical, even though agencies often claim, or try to achieve, neutrality. However, in spite of politics, aid can be developmental, but only if NGOs acknowledge and understand the political context and establish appropriate procedures for working under different types of regimes. Aid is also influenced by the policy context set by the international donor community. This community should, therefore, assume as much responsibility as the operational agencies for the impact of their policies on the developmental quality of relief assistance.

To sort out the contingencies and pressures of the political and policy contexts in which they work, as well as to design and implement projects, NGOs require adequate information. However, IRDP studies showed that they seldom gathered, or used, information appropriately or developmentally. These issues are all discussed in the following section.

THE POLITICAL CONTEXT

Issue

Relief and development work do not happen in a political vacuum. In fact, emergency relief situations are often among the most politicized in the world. How can relief and development agencies function developmentally in these highly politicized circumstances? And, on the other hand, what is the political role of relief or development?

Pressures and Dilemmas

"Politics" make life and work difficult for NGOs trying to work with people to improve their material and social conditions. For the outsider, political nuance—often with life-threatening or -preserving consequences—can be dizzyingly subtle and complex. Relief and development agencies often work in highly polarized settings where there are political factions and factions within factions, all with involved histories and alliances. They must sometimes work within and at the behest of systems which do not appear to promote (and may even undermine) the developmental interests of project participants. Even when a host country is stable and unified, political considerations can impose what seem to be constraints on NGO work, whether outsider (Northern) or local (Southern).

Relief assistance has often become a political football, especially in times of conflict. The delivery of food, medical care, or other resources can

---

THE POLITICAL CONTEXT IN ETHIOPIA

Northern agencies were confronted with a dilemma in Ethiopia in 1984-85. Many lives were in the balance, but relations with national institutions were particularly delicate. How could a humanitarian agency respond compassionately and yet avoid conflict with government policies?

Agencies chose different paths:

1. Some groups focussed their work with insurgent groups, mostly from Eritrea, offering relief and development assistance to the needy in these areas.

2. Some groups began work inside Ethiopia, within the government's purview, but then found that they had to challenge government actions and policies. Several were asked by the government to leave and cease relief work.

3. Other NGOs found ways to work with government agencies and local officials that they felt did not violate their own principles. They believed that, by emphasizing contacts and cooperation at the local level, they were able to support developmental relief efforts.

4. Several NGOs were able to work on both sides, providing relief and/or development assistance inside Ethiopia and with refugee or insurgent groups.

All four approaches had both developmental and political ramifications.

be used to manipulate people. Outside agencies can become an unwitting party to the use of aid for political purposes.

Lessons Learned from IRDP Cases

1. Aid is always part of the political environment, is influenced by it and exerts an influence on it. Developmental relief assistance, therefore, is never really apolitical or neutral.

2. It is possible to do developmental work in conditions of social and political upheaval, and within countries where the regime in power imposes limits on NGO work. It is even possible to do developmental grassroots work in countries where the political situation is extremely volatile and polarized.

3. The process of political change within Southern societies is not the responsibility of Northern interveners. Outside agencies should not attempt to impose a particular politics or ideology on the people with whom they work. It is, in the end, up to the people of any society to determine their own political directions. Outsiders can support local people in the process of increasing their own capacities, including their knowledge of options and their capacity to influence government policies and the shape of their government.

4. In situations of extreme political division, outside agencies may usefully divide the work among themselves, some working on one side, others on the other, of a conflict. Or a single agency may work on both sides of a conflict to maintain a stance of impartiality.

Application of Capacities and Vulnerabilities Analysis

Every agency that operates from a principled commitment to the alleviation of human suffering will find itself confronted by hard political choices. Capacities and Vulnerabilities Analysis must include assessment of the importance and impact of political factors on a proposed relief project. As an agency works with local people to design ways to reduce vulnerabilities and increase capacities, the interplay between history, social movements, ideology, conflicts, environment, and economy must be kept in mind.

People in political conflicts suffer. They often need resources and assistance that outside agencies can offer. Are they to be denied assistance because others criticize actions or policies of their governments? Agencies who care about both the immediate and long-term needs of these people have a range of options. They can emphasize support of local capacities or reduction of long-term vulnerabilities.

Assistance agencies that take an explicitly political approach—such as solidarity groups or those that make public political statements—consider that their efforts act to reduce long-term vulnerabilities. Their intent is to create a climate of world opinion which questions actions or policies they dislike.

Agencies that work on the ground with local people emphasize the support of local capacities. They can provide two things: a) needed resources and b) some political protection. Material resources can, however, always be misappropriated. When assistance supports local initiatives to solve local problems, it is less susceptible to misuse than assistance that provides sizable material resources from outside. Also, agencies that work at the grassroots level have a greater possibility of contributing to genuine development of local capacities than those that work at higher administrative levels away from the people. In the longer run, any increase in local capacities has a fundamental political impact. Both approaches are needed if vulnerabilities are to be reduced and capacities increased.

In the final analysis, it is not up to outsiders to solve the political problems of any society. Local people must develop their own capacities for achieving the political economy they want. Outsiders can help in a limited way, but only if they fully acknowledge the political context of their work, prevent misappropriation of their resources and focus on the support and development of local capacities.

THE INTERNATIONAL POLICY CONTEXT

Issue

As they operate in political contexts, agencies also operate in a "policy context" set by the international disaster response and development communities. This context affects their own agency-specific policies and programming approaches.

International agencies (such as the U.N.), the large bi-lateral and multi-lateral donor agencies, governments, and inter-governmental consortia directly involve themselves in disaster response by establishing policies and procedures for providing relief assistance. Their policies can make it more difficult for an agency to promote development or they can set terms for action that encourage agencies in developmental work. Areas in which the general context influences agency actions include policies on funding, project phasing, partnership arrangements and inter-governmental relations.

Pressures and Dilemmas

Bi-lateral and multi-lateral donor agencies are subject to the perceptions and intentions of their various legislative and governing bodies (ODA to Parliament, AID to Congress etc.). This authority often enacts regulations that serve the interests of the donors more than those whom aid is intended to help. For example, funding policies can include provisions for "tying" aid so that goods and services are procured from certain sources. Or bi-lateral donors sometimes direct their support of NGO projects only in countries which are considered political allies. The dilemma is, how can the interests of the policy-setting agencies be joined with the promotion of development?

Lessons Learned from IRDP Cases

1. The agencies which set the international policy context can encourage or discourage developmental field work. Thus, these agencies should examine how their policies affect capacities and vulnerabilities and accept as much responsibility for encouraging development as the implementing agencies.

2. In particular, funding policies of bi-lateral and multi-lateral donors affect the work of implementing agencies and, often, limit its potential positive impact. Policies which limit development should be changed.

Application of Capacities/Vulnerabilities Analysis

Capacities and Vulnerabilities Analysis has implications for agencies and organizations that set the broad relief policy context. Each of their policies should be assessed in terms of its impact on NGO work as it, in turn, affects local capacities and vulnerabilities. For example, when donor agencies strictly specify the time span and uses of disaster response funds, as opposed to "development" funds, they limit the developmental potential of disaster work in two ways. First, the message conveyed by such a policy is that relief is not held to developmental standards. (It is assumed that relief aid cannot be developmental.) Second, the policy actually places limitations on the uses to which funds can be put, forcing the programming priority to be on giving certain goods and services to "victims," rather than on finding alternatives by which people can acquire what they need.

Similarly, agencies sometimes restrict the duration of relief work. Because judgments about how to ensure developmental impacts require more flexibility regarding duration, these policies can limit, or undermine, developmental effects.

On the other hand, international policies can encourage developmental impacts of assistance. Some international agencies establish incentives for NGOs to form partnerships with local counterparts, thus encouraging local capacities development.

The donor and policy-setting agencies design their policies and regulations so that implementing agencies are primarily accountable to the donors for the use of funds and for programming decisions. There is nothing intrinsically wrong with this *if* the standard to which they hold the operational agencies is the *developmental* standard; i.e. what is the impact on participants' capacities? The policy-setting agencies should examine each of their regulations and requirements, assessing its consistency with this standard—*if* they truly seek to support development.

INFORMATION IS POWER or
WHO NEEDS TO KNOW WHAT?

Issue

NGOs need information before they intervene in a disaster situation. Most agree that, without certain basic information, they cannot make a responsible decision about what kind of help to give. Most agencies assume they need information on: a) the extent of the damage done by the disaster; b) the immediate needs of the sufferers; c) what the affected government and other agencies are doing in response; and, in some cases, d) other pertinent facts about infrastructure, administrative arrangements, laws, climate, political context, culture, etc.

But how much, and what kind of information is necessary for making good intervention and programming decisions?

Pressures and Dilemmas

Some people urge the NGOs to gather extensive baseline data on areas and populations before beginning programmatic work. Others say that suffering demands quicker action; hence, they urge rapid needs assessments in order to target agency responses to areas of greatest need. Agencies are held, simultaneously, to standards of efficiency and practicality by some people and to academic standards of anthropology, political science and economic planning by others.

Every individual agency feels compelled to gather its own information for fear that it will be "caught out" with an ill-planned program. The media watches relief programs closely. The donor public insists on assurances that their funds are used well. Agencies are wary of relying on information gathered by others as a basis for their own decisions.

But information gathering is expensive in both time and money. How can NGOs know, in advance, what they will need to know? The goal is to gather the "right" information quickly; too often the "wrong" (or unnecessary) information is gathered too slowly.[1]

Lessons Learned from IRDP Cases

1. Much of the information that agencies need is either already available, or is easily obtained, by using local people to gather it. (After all, local people usually already "know" what the situation is. Only the outside agency needs this information.)

2. Involving project participants in gathering and organizing data can empower local people and increase their understanding of and ability to cope with their own situation.

WITH WHOM SHALL WE WORK?

An Agency in the Philippines intended to assist the poorest of the poor. But it was difficult for the newly-arrived field staff to make judgments about people's needs. It looked to them as if everyone were very poor. They called community meetings and asked the groups of *barrio* members to rank themselves, and their neighbors, into three groups. The first group was made up of those who were really well-to-do. The second group included families who were middle-income and the third group was of the poor. The *barrio* families, trying to classify themselves, decided that a fourth designation was needed—the very poorest of the poor.

They engaged in interesting discussions to try to figure out which of them fell into which group and why. By the time they finished agreeing on who was in the four groups, they were ready to get on with community activities. People also knew what was expected of them—they did not vie for resources with those who were poorer; they took responsibility for meeting their own and others' needs.

---

1. For a helpful discussion of these issues, see various articles by Robert Chambers, including "Shortcut Methods of Gathering Social Information for Rural Development Projects" in Michael Cermea, *Putting People First: Sociological Variables in Rural Development*, Oxford University Press, 1985.

3. Some agencies fear inadequate information so much that they seriously overdo their data collection. This can be expensive, redundant, ineffective, and anti-developmental. If the agency also fails to use the information gathered (as experience shows is often the case), then much effort and expense is wasted.
4. Information gathering sometimes becomes an end in itself. The purpose—to promote effective programming—is forgotten.

Application of Capacities/Vulnerabilities Analysis

Capacities/Vulnerabilities Analysis prompts a two-pronged examination of the information problem. First, we look at the *content* of information: what needs to be known. Second, we look at the *process* by which decisions are made about what and how much information is needed and how it is gathered.

INFORMATION FOR WHAT? FOR WHOM?

An agency operated a project for displaced people in Somalia. After several years of frustrating work, the staff decided to do a major baseline survey, not just of the resettlement area, but of the entire district. The information was to be used to reorient the project.

A consultant was brought from Europe. He constructed a detailed questionnaire for a house-to-house survey and outlined precise information to be gathered. The original plan was that he would conduct the survey himself, but the local staff of the agency rebelled, saying that they wanted to do the data gathering. Six of the local staff members spent four months gathering information from the community.

The consultant returned to work with them to analyze the results and write the report, which ran to over 200 pages. The report contained detailed information on agriculture, livestock, marketing, commerce, institutions, services and natural resources, and a discussion of development potentials for the area.

The local staff are proud of what they have learned about data collection and analysis. They "own" this survey and its results. However, they acknowledge that most of what they learned they already knew from working in the community. The report, in English, is of limited use to local officials and the people of the area have no idea of what is in it or why it was collected.

Content

When planning relief responses, most agencies focus on finding out what the needs of disaster "victims" are. It is true that aid agencies should have a clear understanding of what is needed because they should *never* supply something that is not needed. However, needs assessments provide only part of the information that is necessary for planning relief that supports development. Agencies need also to know about existing capacities and vulnerabilities.

Different information is needed at different points in the chain of disaster response. What agency headquarters staff need to know in order to make an initial commitment differs greatly from what field staff need to know in order to implement a project on the ground. It is difficult to know how much information is necessary at each stage of project design and implementation. The basic rule for an NGO beginning an emergency response is: assume that there are some important local capacities and set into motion a process for finding out what these are. Thus, for making a decision to intervene, headquarters might want to know if the mechanisms exist for identifying local capacities. Staff involved in field level programming, on the other hand, should identify specific capacities for making decisions and performing jobs involved in the relief effort. For example, what are the existing systems for allocating and distributing goods? If we rely on these, will the process include those most in need?

Similarly, because current needs arise from some deeper vulnerability (e.g., people are hungry today because land is depleted over time through overuse and deforestation), an agency should soon begin gathering information about the long-term trends and deeper causes of the immediate danger. When this is known, programming can begin to do more than meet immediate needs.

Information is a critical element in control. Priorities, programming styles, and project outcomes can be determined by who knows what. One major thrust of information-gathering should be to ensure that local people are gaining information about (and, hence, control over) their own circumstances—the causes of their problems and what they can do about them. Even short-term supply of needed materials can be done in a way that helps people diagnose the causes of their problems and begin to plan ways to overcome them. This leads us to consider the process of information gathering.

Process

The very process of gathering and organizing information can empower people and increase their understanding of their problems. They can identify cause and effect; they can identify options for action. However, while local people know things, they do not always have the skills for organizing and analyzing what they know. NGOs can provide training or other guidance to help people use effectively what they know or find out.

When NGOs hire outsiders to gather data about an area in which they want to work, they may end up with very good information about capacities, vulnerabilities and needs. However, increasing the knowledge of outside agencies does nothing, itself, to help those meant to benefit. An NGO that turns to local people and relies on them to provide needed information takes an opportunity to reinforce local capacity and to enlarge it.

The essential point is that information has *no* value in and of itself. More detail is not always better. Everyone does not need all information. Each agency does not have to gather its own information. The knowledge that information gives is only useful as it helps in the design and implementation of aid efforts that promote development. To learn only of "victims' needs" is to miss out on the essential information about capacities and vulnerabilities without which a relief effort will not be effective developmentally.

THE SILENT SURVEY

Community development workers went to a village that was a possible site for project work. Instead of asking direct questions of villagers, they conducted a "silent survey." They sat in the village tea shops and other gathering places and listened to the villagers talk about their lives. After three days of doing this, they met with the village council and presented an analysis of the major concerns of the village, asking for confirmation or correction of the findings. The village elders were so impressed with the insights of the community development workers (essentially, how well they reflected the experience and concerns of the villagers) that they immediately approved a first project initiative.

Chapter 4

DIMENSIONS OF PROGRAMMING

How fast (or slow)? How big (or small)? How long (or brief)? These quandaries confront an agency that attempts to plan and implement a developmental relief program. The general public and many relief agencies have believed that, in a disaster response, speed is necessary and "more is better." In recent years, NGOs have also been exhorted to take on a long-term commitment in areas where they work. The three sections below examine these myths and offer a way to look at them through Capacities and Vulnerabilities Analysis.

THE MYTH OF SPEED

Issue

Agencies believe that emergencies always require speedy response from outside. They feel that they must rush to disaster scenes to be helpful.[1]

More important than speed is *timeliness*.

To be timely is to be there *when needed*. Timeliness requires that agencies anticipate crises and their impacts. Timeliness also requires that agencies look before they leap, and sometimes move rapidly and sometimes slowly.

---

1. NGOs, of course, recognize differences between sudden- and slow-onset disasters. However, even in slow-onset disasters such as drought and famine, there is a crisis stage when the international community decides that an urgent response is needed.

Pressures and Dilemmas

The pressures to act quickly are real. The international community becomes aware of a disaster because people are suffering and, because of the suffering, they feel they must respond urgently and quickly. In addition, agencies which prove that they have rapid response capacities may get more donations.

Lessons Learned from IRDP Cases

1. The need for speed is a myth.
2. The most propitious time for external agencies to be helpful is seldom, if ever, in the *immediate* aftermath of a disaster. Most immediate needs of disaster victims are met by local people, organizations, and government bodies. Survivors help the wounded; they rescue them, care for them, tend their less serious wounds. They immediately begin the process of rebuilding. NGOs which do not have a program or staff in the area simply cannot move material or people into place within hours after a disaster.[2] And it is within these hours, and the next few days, that rescue and evacuation activities are critical and injuries must be treated.
3. Even when an agency works in a country already, it may be better not to rush to assist in an emergency. If local people and government are effectively handling their rescue and relief operations, then an outside NGO need not take a role.
4. IRDP cases show that there is one quick response which can be helpful—namely, giving funds to a local, operational agency to do something it could not do without such funds, such as: hire an extra staff person; buy food from the next town; or rent a truck to take people to medical care, etc.

Application of Capacities/Vulnerabilities Analysis

The danger of speed is that, in a rush, an agency will focus entirely on victims and their needs, problems, and suffering and fail to note capacities. Capacities-building requires consultation and involvement; this does not take vast amounts of time, but it does necessitate an approach which assumes that local people, not outsiders, are "in charge."

When compulsion for speed means that an NGO assumes all responsibility for the management and logistics of relief, this is apt to override

2. There are very few exceptions. Agencies whose sole purpose is to move quickly to provide medical supplies might be one.

existing local capacities. We have often seen women sitting in lines and waiting to be handed food—when we know that in most societies women are the managers of food systems, including its preparation and allocation. "Victims" can *always* be engaged in some aspects of relief delivery. This involvement often results in more efficient and equitable distribution than a logistically-oriented external NGO would be able to accomplish.

IN THE IMMEDIATE AFTERMATH, THEY ARE DOING FINE

Can we help?

The floods covered two-thirds of Bangladesh. People were stranded on roofs and high ground and needed food, clean water, and some medicines. Reports flowed out to other parts of the world about these needs. Concerned people wanted to respond.

One report went like this: "It is a terrible and widespread natural calamity. But, of course, Bangladeshis know that flooding is due each year, and the government and local agencies had prepared for such an event. Food is available locally, having been stored in past good years in water-tight warehouses, mostly on high ground. The thousands of small boats that people in Bangladesh use to get around have been organized by local NGOs and other agencies to carry this food to stranded people. They are taking drugs and water too. Of course, it is difficult for them to reach the most remote areas, but they have a better chance of doing so than airplanes which still cannot land anywhere in the country since the runways are under water.

"I'd say the Bangladeshis have the immediate crisis well under control. But, we can help in the aftermath. There will be a lot of work to be done, dredging canals, cleaning up housing, redigging ditches, repairing wells. Bangladeshis can do all of this, but if we help, it can be done more quickly and with less cost to local enterprise. I would say we should get resources together to help support this work, when the floods recede. When our airplanes can finally get in, we also might help replenish the food supplies, so they will be ready the next time the floods are so severe."

Another NGO director reported on the same events as follows: "It is the worst disaster I've ever seen. Women and children are huddled on rooftops with no help coming. Shortages of food and clean water are severe. We must get help to these poor people immediately. Bangladesh is such a poor country. It does not have the resources to deal with such a disaster."

Timeliness and the support of existing capacities are the goals of emergency relief. Suffering demands urgency, but planning and the support of capacities do not have to give way to the compulsion of speed.

SCALE OF PROGRAM

Issue

When suffering is great, the more agencies and the larger their responses, the better. Yes? Or no? More is not always better for development. Too much aid can overwhelm local resources and introduce expectations that are unrealistic and unsustainable.

Complicating the issue is the fact that the scale of a project needs to be decided *in relation to:* a) the size of the emergency; b) the size and experience of the operating NGO; c) the time over which the intervention will occur; d) the size of the group affected by the disaster. When a large NGO provides assistance in a mammoth disaster over several years (as in a long-term famine for example), a large program may be necessary, appropriate and developmental. However, if a large agency provides a lot of aid in a very short time, especially in an emergency which is geographically confined such as a mudslide or volcano, the sheer volume of aid in relation to the numbers of project participants may be inappropriate and anti-developmental. When there is lots of money to spend, the urge is to spend it. Houses are designed that rely on imported building materials, large and expensive staffs (expatriate and local) are hired, technologies are imported, new agencies are started which depend on external funding, and so on.

Scale varies according to other factors. For example, a small agency can provide the channel for sizable funding in a program that requires very few staff over an extended time. Or, many staff can work across a wide area providing almost no material aid.

Too small is as non-developmental as too large. There have been small project efforts that have made some people genuinely better off, but the impact in the face of widespread poverty and suffering is so insignificant as to be almost immoral. Poverty demands a serious response.

How can an agency assess these issues of scale?

Pressures and Dilemmas

The pressures to become large and to give more aid are great. When the press excites public sympathy surrounding a disaster, an agency may be inundated with donations earmarked for this emergency that push it toward extensive programming.

NGOs often grow at the time of a disaster when they increase staff to handle extra donations and extra programs. Success is equated with growth; it "proves" that the agency is "effectively meeting real needs."

Government donors tend to rely on NGOs that can absorb large amounts of aid rather than having to parcel it out among a number of smaller efforts (and to monitor its use among them).

When suffering is great, human beings respond compassionately, wanting to do as much as possible. Concern for establishing the line between enough and too much is overridden by sympathy.

The pressures to do too little are not so obvious. Where they exist, they are often internal to the organization and arise from two motivations. The first is to do high-quality work, which is seen to be possible only when each detail is carefully controlled. This dictates smallness. The second is to protect the agency from negative publicity that can come from high visibility.

Lessons Learned from IRDP Cases

1. IRDP learned by omission one lesson about scale. To locate projects about which to write cases, we asked the NGOs to nominate what they considered their most successful projects in terms of developmental impact. Only one large-scale project was nominated. We conclude that, in most NGO experience, smaller relief projects are more apt to be developmental than large ones.

2. There is asymmetry in the relationship of the size of the intervention and its potential developmental impact. The larger the intervention, the greater the potential for a negative developmental impact, and it is not true that the potential for a positive impact is also greater. Very small interventions can have significant developmental impacts, but their negative effects are limited by their size. Thus, when in doubt (and one should be in doubt!), it is better to do less than to do more, and the larger the project planned, the greater the risks to the local population that it will leave them worse off than before.

Application of Capacities/Vulnerabilities Analysis

Capacities and Vulnerabilities Analysis helps in assessing scale. Development theory includes a notion of "absorptive capacity," i.e., the ability of a society to absorb and use aid or technical assistance. One capacity to be assessed is the capacity of project participants to utilize and control aid. Assistance should be scaled so that it does not overwhelm local capacity but supports it. Local participants must be in charge.

One other danger of large-scale projects is identified by vulnerabilities analysis. Large-scale assistance may prompt expectations that it will continue. People redefine their "needs" at levels supported only by outside aid. As a result, participants increase their dependence on outside aid. This dependence is a form of vulnerability.

On the other hand, because vulnerabilities often reflect large and deep-seated problems, any project designed to reduce vulnerabilities probably needs either to be large or to have a real potential for replication. For example, deforestation, river silting, and war are big problems and require, big solutions. Still, efforts to replant forests, regenerate soil or dredge rivers can add up if there is cooperation among villages.

The size of a relief effort should be decided in relation, first, to the extent of life-threatening needs. (If people die of hunger, then capacities are not increased.) But, in both the immediate and the long term, scale must also be judged according to the local capacities to learn from and take control of the assistance. If local people can assume management of the resources offered by an aid project immediately or over time, then their capacities will be increased by this aid.

DURATION OF PROGRAMMING

Issue

How long should NGO relief activities last? Emergency work has been seen as short-term work. More and more, however, NGOs have become convinced that to have a developmental impact, they must do longer-term programming and plan longer projects. Does this mean that short-term work cannot be developmental? Or does staying longer actually increase dependency?

Pressures and Dilemmas

Pressures to extend projects or to plan longer projects come from many sources. An agency doing a good job in an area naturally wants to keep up the good work. An effective project becomes a good public relations focus, it raises money, and it adds to the agency's reputation for effectiveness.

Participants in projects often urge agencies to take on other tasks. They do this because of appreciation for good work in the past, and also because they want to continue to enjoy the benefits (employment, access to resources) that the project offers. There is always more to be done. A sense of unfinished business, or of additional opportunities, keeps some agencies in areas after they might usefully have left.

Finally, inertia may keep an agency involved in an area. Continuing to do what you have been doing is easier than pulling out and facing criticism for "abandoning" the people.

Lessons Learned from IRDP Cases

1. There is an important distinction to be made between an NGO's long-term commitment to people with whom it works and long projects. While commitment to people should not be turned on and off, long projects do not, of themselves, increase the likelihood of development.

HOW LONG WILL YOU STAY? WHO SETS THE TIMETABLE ANYWAY?

An agency in northeastern Thailand worked in disaster response rural development. The staff were very careful not to let local people become dependent on them. From the first days of their work in villages, they made clear the timetable of their involvement and everyone knew that, three years later, they would pull out. Staff often reminded the villagers of this, and, as the ending time came near, they again informed the village councils of the closing date.

Most villages were ready and were glad to work out a situation where the villages were classified into three groups: a) those that were completely on their own, having started a number of activities that they could sustain; b) those that would have a continuing relationship with the agency staff, being able to ask for advice every now and then, but who really did not need frequent visits or attention; and c) new villages where the agency had not yet worked, where resources and attention would be focussed next. Villages in groups "a" and "b" also agreed to help with the new villages.

But one village had special difficulties. They had been relocated numerous times as the war came close and receded in their area. They simply needed more intense help. The agency staff met with the villagers. The issue was: How long did they think they needed extra help? Much discussion ensued. The villagers said they would be ready in six months. The agency staff agreed.

Six months later, the villagers told this story to a visitor. They said how grateful they were for the commitment of the agency which showed when they were willing to continue to supply help after the deadline. They also told how proud they were of their own ability to meet their self-designated deadline. They were now a "b" village.

2.   The essential principle governing decisions regarding the duration of projects is the same old principle of supporting capacities and lessening vulnerabilities. The question, "How long is long enough but not too long?" must be answered in terms of its impact on local people's capacities and vulnerabilities.

3.   Long projects, whether they are focussed on relief or development, can actually undermine any developmental impact they intended to have. This is because project participants become dependent on the outsider's advice, leadership and/or resources.

4.   Thus, to prevent dependency, it is best always to be clear about the intended length of a project. Local people should know, from the beginning, how long a project will last and what will be the measures or benchmarks that will signal completion. They should also know their role in making these judgments and decisions.

5.   It is usually clear when to end a project that is designed to develop specific local capacities through training. This is because it is possible to know when people have learned what was to be taught.

6.   There are clues or warning signals about when one has stayed too long in an area and, when these are spotted, even if they occur months before the intended closure of a project, they should be noted and dealt with.

SHORT-TERM PROJECT
WITHIN LONG-TERM COMMITMENT

A Northern agency worked on a resettlement scheme with nomads in Mali who suffered from drought in the early 1970s. The project was planned as a five-year effort, with specific objectives to be achieved in that time. As the Northern agency phased out, various local and government units were to take over responsibility.

The agency withdrew its formal relationship with the project in 1980 as planned. However, the community asked for continued assistance with some specific additional efforts, so while the agency staff person began to work with other nomad groups in the area, he also continued to visit the old project site as needed. A strong and friendly relationship continued. During the drought of 1983-85, the Northern agency again helped this area in small ways, but the nomad community was essentially on its own. The main focus of the agency's work shifted to other groups of nomads. But, everyone knows that its commitment continues.

Application of Capacities/Vulnerabilities Analysis

Development is an ongoing process. NGO projects, whether relief or development, should fit within and encourage that process. The *length* of a project is not as important as whether it is developmental. The decision to end a project should also be gauged by developmental criteria.

While development certainly takes more than the usual two- to three-year project life span, it is not at all clear that long-term projects have a greater developmental impact than shorter projects. In fact, when staying a long time involves taking over more aspects of a community's development, the longer-duration projects and programs may be anti-developmental. Long involvement can, clearly, increase dependency of local people on an outside agency. Sometimes the most developmental approach can be very short-term.

The length of a project should be just that length that provides the most encouragement and support to local people to take responsibility for their own development and does not stray over the line into perpetuating dependency on the outside agency.

Warning Signs

There are some warning signs that a project may risk increasing local vulnerabilities by staying too long and/or decreasing local capacities. These are:

1. The project is run by a staff of local people who rely on the income earned through the project to support themselves and their families, but who have no options for other employment. An agency faced with this can:

    a. help find local, or other, sources of continued funding for the activity which will be in the control of the local staff;

    b. train the staff so that they are able to move into other realistic opportunities when the project closes; and/or

    c. reduce staff through attrition far enough in advance of closure that the disruptions and guilt are lessened.

2. People increasingly come to project staff (either local or ex-patriate) to ask advice; they seem unable to make individual or group decisions without this consultation. They cannot settle disputes without consultation.

While having local people begin to consult with project staff is one sign of acceptance, trust, and project success, such consultations should be assessed as to whether they make sense or not. Is the decision one that the

---

TIME TO MOVE OUT

In the Philippines, the rural develooment project began by placing workers in each of eight villages. These workers lived with and identified with the people they sought to help and were gradually accepted by them as friends and neighbors. One worker was named as godmother to forty-three children born in her area!

But after four years, these workers noticed a change. True, they were respected and included in their villages, but they also had become *too* important as village leaders and decision-makers. They observed that the village people made no real decisions and took no actions without first consulting them.

The NGO decided it was time for these field workers to move out of their villages. The village workers helped organize a system of volunteers who took on many project activities while they continued to visit the villages regularly. They were right. When they removed themselves from everyday contact, they found that villagers took on plans and projects with vigor and independence.

---

staff really can help on? Do they have some abilities that are needed in the consultation? Could local people have done as well (or better) without such consultation? How much time are such consultations taking? Are they prolonging and postponing decisions, or are they really facilitating them?

Is staff tempted to, or—heaven forbid—do they actually, make decisions about the issues? Do they become partisans or advocates for one position in the community or do they encourage those who hold that position to develop their own arguments and strategies? An agency faced with this can consider the following options:

1.   Change the project style; refuse to decide, only encourage others to take responsibility.
2.   Be careful not to feel responsible for preventing "mistakes" which may occur if you don't take charge.
3.   Withdraw staff to some distance, maintain some contact and support.
4.   Close the project.

Staff should be rewarded by agencies for skillfully ending projects early. Agency resources would go farther. Staff could be paid for the months left of their contracts if they complete a project early. They might do an evaluation of the project, work in the home office, do public speaking, or go on leave if there were no other productive work to be done.

Faster is not always better. More is not always better. Longer is not always better. Speed, size and duration of project aid must be thought about, by NGOs, as they relate to capacities and vulnerabilities. If faster, bigger and longer mean that an NGO is taking charge and deciding issues that should be in the purview of local people, the impact can be anti-developmental. Timely responses that are scaled to encourage local initiative and control and that represent long-term commitment (if not long projects) have a better chance of being developmental in their impact.

THREE GENERATIONS OF "DEVELOPMENT" ASSISTANCE

In one town in Colombia, an agency had been working on development efforts for three decades. During this period, the town had experienced devastating floods, earthquakes, and fire. The agency's child sponsorship strategy had continued, steadfast, through it all.

A staff person from the agency reported proudly: "We have several families who have been with us for three generations. We first assisted the grandparents, then the parents; now the third generation is receiving our assistance!"

While this is a community with vast needs and difficult development dilemmas, if working with one individual family for three generations cannot help them pull themselves out of poverty, something is wrong with the development strategy. The long-term commitment of the agency to the area has not promoted self-reliance.

Chapter 5

PEOPLE AND PROGRAMMING

With whom should a project work? The poorest of the poor? Those "ready" for a dramatic leap in development? Women and children? Refugees? What are the criteria for making such choices? The three sections of this chapter explore the general question of project participants and then look at two important issues: incorporating gender considerations in programming and engaging refugees in their own development process.

PROJECT PARTICIPANTS

Issue #1: What's In a Word?

Language is powerful. The terms used to refer to people affected by a disaster reveal attitudes about them. Aid agencies have called them "victims," "survivors," "recipients," "clients," "beneficiaries," and the "target population." Each of these terms implies different things. Some imply that these people are less than fully competent to cope with their own lives and futures. Others imply admiration for or accountability to them. However, all imply that the aid giver is the active party.

No one ever develops anyone else. People and societies develop themselves. External agencies can help, but the people who live in the situation must take ultimate responsibility, and they gain the advantages or suffer from the mistakes of their, and donor's, actions. They are, fundamentally, the "participants," not just in projects or programs, but in development.[1]

Issue #2: Choosing Among Potential Participant Groups

How does an agency choose whom to work with among the groups affected by a disaster? Often, the people most severely affected are those who are already marginal in the society. They are poor, have little political power and live on the "edges" of communities. They are the most vulnerable people in "normal" times. Richer and/or more powerful groups, while they have more to lose in an economic sense, also have more resources for dealing with cataclysm. For example, those who remain over the years in refugee camps are the poorest families, with few options or supports such as family members abroad or marketable skills.

DISASTERS AS OPPORTUNITIES FOR EMPOWERMENT AMONG THE POOREST

An NGO had just finished training its field staff. They were ready to go to their villages where they would undertake a long-term grassroots development effort in rural Luzon. Then the Mayan volcano erupted and the villagers, with whom the field staff were to work, were evacuated to shelters. The more well-to-do members of the community did not go to shelters; they had families or other resources which allowed them to find alternatives in nearby towns.

The NGO staff moved into the shelters with the volcano "victims." They began to get to know each other, at such close quarters and with time on their hands. Staff began to organize villagers to consider their problems and solutions. Since the better-off community members who usually held positions of leadership were not in these shelters, new leaders began to emerge. New ideas about priorities emerged, and groups who had not previously worked together began to cooperate on plans. By the time they left the shelters and went back to their villages, the groundwork for grassroots development had been laid.

---

1. For the most part, in this document, we call people involved in disaster programs "participants." However, for emphasis, we occasionally refer to them as "victims," but always in quotation marks.

Pressures and Dilemmas

Many considerations go into the choice of project participants, ranging from ideological to practical. In recent years, relief and development agencies have stated their priority for working with the poorest of the poor. Journalists focus attention on the most dramatic cases of need. Governments request assistance for people in specific geographic areas, ethnic groups, or classes/castes. Some agencies feel a natural concern for people with whom they have worked in the past or who are of the same religious affiliation.

GETTING THE MIX RIGHT: ADDING TO THE POOL IN COLOMBIA

An agency established a project to assist victims of the Nevada del Ruiz volcano eruption and mudslide that killed thousands of people in the town of Armero in 1985. After an emergency period of assistance to survivors in tent camps, NGOs helped set up a new community to provide housing assistance. Some of the "camp dweller" families chose to live in the new town.

Meanwhile, the relief community had realized that those who had survived the mudslide and lived in the camps were the most "marginal" people of Armero, those who had been living along the hillsides at the edges of town. In many ways they were the least successful and least educated people. They had few skills and no experience of cooperating with each other. Another group of Armero survivors was slightly better off. They chose not to live in camps, but "floated" to relatives or nearby towns.

When the new housing settlement first began, the agency ran into severe difficulties dealing with these "poorest of the poor." They were suspicious of the project that required them to organize into self-help groups in order to build their own houses from the materials provided by the NGO. The NGO finally decided to engage some of the "floaters" who had expressed an interest in joining the project. These new participants entered the project with enthusiasm and initiative. Gradually, their involvement convinced the poorer groups that they would also benefit from full participation.

Lessons Learned from IRDP Cases

1. The most important consideration is not so much *whom* is chosen as project participants, but *how* they participate.
2. In some cases, a mix of participants can improve project effectiveness. Some projects that were working only with the poorest and the least-educated or -skilled people were struggling to get people to engage in development. When better-off people got involved as participants, they became "role models" and mentors for the very poor. More progress was made by all participants.
3. The IRDP cases show that a Capacities/Vulnerabilities Analysis reveals significant information about *how* to work with any group, tailoring program design to its particular capacities.

Application of Capacities/Vulnerabilities Analysis

To work developmentally with disaster-affected people, agencies must identify people's capacities and build on them. Some groups have very few capacities. Others have many. Strategies for working have to vary from regaining lost capacities or building essential new ones, in some circumstances, to providing minimal support to able community people in others.

For example, some refugee groups have almost no physical resources, have lost most social structure and organization, and have become completely despondent. It is difficult, *but not impossible*, to work developmentally with such a group. Strategies for doing so would certainly start at a different point from those working with groups who have suffered only a temporary setback in a relatively stable situation.

"VICTIMS" HAVE UNEXPECTED CAPACITIES

An agency that had not been working in Ethiopia prior to 1984 decided to respond to the famine. They were asked by the government to deal with food shortages in one large district. Wanting to avoid unhealthy and disruptive feeding camps, the staff encouraged people to stay in their villages, promising to bring food as close as possible to them.

"As close as possible?" wondered the famine-stricken villagers. The leaders organized their "surplus labor" (farmers idled by the drought) to build new roads so that relief trucks had access to their villages. Over 200 kilometers of roads were built by disaster "victims."

Also there is a need for public education about *recipients* of relief and development aid. "Victims" are portrayed by the media and sometimes by NGOs as having no capacities and therefore needing "our" help. Agencies need to emphasize the capacities of the people with whom they work, convincing potential donors that their contributions are important *because* they not only meet immediate needs but do so in a way that promotes development.

CHOOSING AMONG THOSE WHO NEED AID

A devastating cyclone ripped through a community and decisions had to be made about who would receive assistance to rebuild or repair the houses. There was not enough aid for everyone. Rather than choose "beneficiaries" themselves, an agency's staff asked village committees to decide. Some committees made their choices by lottery, feeling it only fair for everyone to have an equal chance. There was no disgruntlement in these communities at all.

Other communities set up meetings to discuss, together, who needed the help the most. Some people who, at first, had been insistent to the agency staff that their need was extreme, began to change in such community meetings. As they heard and thought about other people's stories of need, they began to feel some pride in volunteering to withdraw from the pool of recipients. They started to acknowledge that, in fact, they were not as badly off as others, and that, with some effort, they could find ways to fix their houses themselves.

A footnote to this happy story: An international agency sent one of its expatriate staff into the area, just after these decisions had been made. She was unfamiliar with disaster settings and was horrified to see houses completely flattened as she toured. On several occasions, she leapt from her Landrover to interview the families whose houses were down, and she promised, on the spot, that her agency would give them aid to rebuild. In her two-hour tour, she seriously undermined the community process of decision-making that had been underway. She "gave" aid randomly, depending on the route her driver took. The villagers told later visitors that some of the more well-to-do families in the area got aid through her interventions, while others who really needed the help were dropped from the list of aid recipients because of the limited resources.

WOMEN AND GENDER CONSIDERATIONS

Issue

It is now widely acknowledged that project interventions have had different impacts on women and on men. The approach has often been to treat women as disadvantaged or as having special needs not met by usual project design.

This approach, however, is limiting. We also know that women have specific important capacities. They perform many essential productive functions in all societies. They are active economic producers of goods and services, they are transmitters of culture, and they manage the central social unit—the household.

The issue is: How do we design and implement projects that integrate women and acknowledge the differences between men's and women's economic and social roles in ways that support the development of everyone's capacities?

Pressures and Dilemmas

Since the United Nations Decade on Women, all international agencies have committed themselves to taking women and development seriously. There is pressure on NGOs, and others, to include explicit statements about women in their project designs and proposals. Funding agencies consider project impacts on women before they support project proposals.

While most people agree that it is important to ensure that project efforts have equitable impacts, there is still confusion about exactly how to do this. There is growing criticism that just taking account of project *impacts* on women is not enough—more important is integrating women into overall development as active agents. NGOs are wondering how to do this. In addition, some agencies worry about promoting gender concerns in ways that also respect local cultures.

Lessons Learned from IRDP Cases

1. Women are disproportionately represented among those groups whom disasters strike.

2. Capacities and vulnerabilities differ between women and men. They have different coping mechanisms and different vulnerabilities. These differences arise from the differences in their work and social roles.

3. It is not necessary to plan special programming or events to include women in projects effectively. What is important is plan-

ning project activities so that they increase the capacities of women as well as men and decrease the vulnerabilities of women as well as men. For example, this might involve extra efforts to recruit women into existing training courses, rather than providing special women's training.

A SURPRISING OUTCOME FOR LITTLE GIRLS

One agency working in the northern drought-devastated communities of the Sudan wanted to work intensively with mothers. They decided, therefore, that they had to hire women to do this work. They needed to have good records kept; they were doing an epidemiological survey at the same time. So, they hired young women who were all graduates of grade eight in an area where most females received much less schooling.

Two years later, they were surprised to find that little girls were being sent to school by their families. Why? The people explained, "When we saw those girls with eight years of schooling getting good jobs, we realized that maybe our daughters could get hired for wages if they had an education. This is the first time we thought it made any sense to send them to school."

Application of Capacities/Vulnerabilities Analysis

In every country of the world there is a gender-based division of labor and social roles. For example, men may own land and tools and women may not. Or women may have traditional forms of cooperative labor while men do not. Village councils may be primarily involve men; women may not be free to participate. Each of these circumstances translates into differences in capacities and vulnerabilities.

Also, when a disaster strikes, women and men feel its effects differently. Both are concerned about family welfare and survival. However, if women are primarily responsible for water collection and household gardens, a drought will increase their work load immensely. Deforestation increases the workload of fuel collectors, usually women.

Recovery strategies and efforts to deal with the causes of drought and deforestation should always include the primary users of the basic resource—in these cases women. Programming around emergencies and development should always acknowledge differences in gender roles and work with the appropriate group for the most effective impact.

AFFIRMATIVE ACTION IN THE BUSH

After a cholera epidemic everyone agreed that community health workers were needed to work on sanitation, hygiene, and nutrition education house-to-house in the refugee camp in Eastern Sudan. There was *not* agreement about who should serve as the health workers. The NGO staff met with the Camp Council of (male) sheiks.

- *NGO Director:* We propose to put up notices asking young women with at least primary education to apply for the job.
- *Sheik 1:* No. No...it is not appropriate for young women to take this job. We can find young men to do this.
- *Sheik 2:* Girls will not be able to do this job. Besides, men must earn money for their families.
- *Female expatriate NGO staff nurse:* We think that women with some education will do a good job. Women cook and clean in the houses. Another woman will understand their problems.
- *Sheik 1:* But we have many young men without jobs in the camp. We must find a way to make them productive. They can no longer move with the livestock while we are in the camp.
- *Local NGO staff person:* Let's see, this house-to-house work will take place during the day. The men are often away from home during that time. Right? Hmmm. I suppose you will not mind if a young man comes into your homes to talk with your wives and daughters about sanitation and hygiene while you are away.
- *Sheik 2:* Oh, I see....
- *Sheik 1:* Perhaps it's time for women to take responsibility for educating each other about these topics. I suggest that women be recruited and given a test. Then the NGO and the Camp Council can meet to make a final selection.
- *NGO Director:* Sounds good to me.

THE UPROOTED:
REFUGEES AS A SPECIAL CASE?

Issue #1: Refugee Services

Refugees are often regarded as a special case because of the degree of disruption they experience. They suffer major increases in vulnerability—physical, social, and attitudinal. Refugee situations, by their nature, are politically complex and difficult. Refugee emergencies are usually human-caused, involving situations of conflict. They always involve movement across international borders.

Often refugees move from one area of scarce resources to another area of even scarcer resources. The decisions and policies of the "host" government have a fundamental effect on the kinds of programming that are possible with refugees. Self-reliant development is often not an option, and dependency seems almost inevitable. Also, the future is uncertain: refugees do not know if they will go home, resettle where they are, or go to a third country. And they do not know when the decision about their future will be made.

Issue #2: Refugee-Affected Groups

Refugees are not the only ones affected by the movement of large numbers of people across international borders. Wherever the refugees are placed, there are immediate effects on local people and local economies. At times the effects are from increased demand from the refugees themselves. In other circumstances, the most significant effects are due to the influx of large numbers of refugee workers and government or military officials. In any case, local people are often dislocated, suffer from the distortions of their economy, and become resentful when refugees receive better services than they do.

Pressures and Dilemmas

One of the main quandaries felt by agencies working with refugees is the push and pull of the different groups with a stake in the situation: at least two countries are involved from the start—plus the UN, relief agencies, political factions within the countries, sometimes rebel factions or movements, host government officials, local people, and other NGO staff people. Of course, the refugees themselves have the largest stake of all in the programming in a refugee camp and the long-term outcomes negotiated above and around them. NGOs work with refugees under the strictures of host government policies and, most often, under the auspices and direction of the UNHCR. They must work within these, yet still be responsive to and supportive of the goals of the refugees themselves.

Lessons Learned from IRDP Cases

1. In spite of the special circumstances surrounding refugee situations, NGOs can still work with them in ways that support long-term development. That is, lessons learned about working with other (non-refugee) groups who have experienced severe changes in their economic base or who have migrated to new environments apply directly to work with refugees as well.

2.   Refugees always have identifiable capacities—skills they brought with them, social structures that remain intact, leaders still respected, "survivor" instincts which motivate people. These provide the basis for development work.

3.   Training and education are important elements of developmental programming among refugees. Even if refugee groups cannot achieve physical/material self-reliance, they can move steadily (or readily) towards self-government and active engagement in acquiring "portable" skills that can be taken with them no matter where they go.

4.   Systems for active refugee participation in planning, implementation and evaluation of refugee programs will ensure reliance on and support of refugee capacities.

5.   A key factor in refugee programming is the response of the host government. In one case, refugees who crossed an international border were allocated land, housing, and tools. Within six months they were a self-reliant community, fully integrated into the local economy and political system. In other cases (unfortunately the more usual ones), refugees are placed in closed camps with few or no productive resources or employment opportunities. NGO developmental strategies have to vary depending on host government policies.

6.   Agencies working with refugees should always also work with local people in areas affected by refugee influxes, to maximize the developmental impact of their work.

7.   The international assistance community should give more attention to the development of innovative income-generating/employment schemes for both refugee and refugee affected populations.

CONTRASTING HOST GOVERNMENT RESPONSES

Ethnic Somali refugees from Ethiopia were welcomed as "brothers" by the government and people of Somalia (although land and other resources were scarce). On the other hand, Eritrean and Tigrayan refugees from Ethiopia met a more complex response in Sudan. Sudan welcomed refugee groups. However, employment and land scarcity in Sudan led to charges and counter-charges among domestic political forces with the refugees caught in the middle.

ORGANIZATIONAL SKILLS AMONG REFUGEES

In 1979 world news organizations carried stories of thousands of Boat People struggling across the South China Sea on leaky boats, prey to storms, pirates, and the winds of international politics. The implication was that these destitute people were helpless victims who needed everything done for them. The reality was quite different.

As soon as Vietnamese refugees came ashore, whether in Malaysia, Thailand, Indonesia, or the Philippines, they organized themselves. They made lists of families by name, age, boat, etc. They chose leaders. Within camps, they established zones, set up clinics, appointed security units. They created a hierarchy of authority and responsibility for camp life. In short order, they replicated the administrative and social organization of a Vietnamese city.

A key factor, in those years, was that the Boat People came, in large measure, from the more wealthy and educated sectors of the former South Vietnamese society. People engaged in medicine, law, government administration, business, and other professions dominated the group, mixed with smaller numbers of farmers and fishermen. To work developmentally with these people required acknowledgement of the high degree of skills present among the participants—a very different situation from many other refugee settings.

Application of Capacities and Vulnerabilities Analysis

Most refugee programming in the past focussed on things to provide to refugee groups. Recently, agencies concerned with refugees have begun to encourage refugee participation in their own community development. The trend is toward broadening the concept of refugee work beyond concern with physical safety and supplies, to include program efforts in social organization, training at many levels, revitalization of refugee culture, self-government, and self-direction.[2]

The IRDP cases show that, as in other relief situations, the most effective strategy for work starts with refugee capacities. Some aid workers have assumed that any capacities that existed in the refugee group were lost in their flight from their homes. Experience repeatedly shows that this is not the case.

---

2. See work by the Refugee Policy Group in Washington, D.C. on refugee participation, recent publications by UNHCR's Technical Support Service and Social Service Unit, and recent work under the auspices of the International Council of Voluntary Agencies on a "Development Approach to Refugee Situations."

Refugees are, by definition, "survivors" who exhibit a great deal of initiative for manipulating (in the best sense of the word) the refugee assistance system to the benefit of their communities and families. Refugees are often surprisingly strong in their motivational/attitudinal capacities—perhaps the most important element in effective strategies for participation and action.

Work with Refugee-Affected Groups

Applying Capacities and Vulnerabilities Analysis also leads to Lesson Learned #6 above: NGOs working with refugees in camps should also work with populations in the surrounding communities who are affected by the influx of refugees into their area. This is true for several reasons.

Refugees often receive benefits and services that raise their wealth or security above that of local people. This causes resentment among local populations who find their own resource base stretched by the arrival of

---

LONG-TERM DEVELOPMENT WORK OUT OF AN IMMEDIATE CRISIS RESPONSE

A Northern agency and several local NGOs joined together to meet a refugee influx crisis in Thailand. They jointly managed a holding center for refugees until a more satisfactory and permanent place could be found for them. In running the holding center, the agency staff had, as they put it, "travelled through the local villages, stopping for supplies, innumerable times." These stops alerted them to the needs of these villagers.

They began to look for ways to combine their work in the refugee center with work with the local villages. These villages were deeply affected by the influx of refugees—land and other resources were squeezed, and international funds were flowing in to support the refugees, causing the local people to resent the relative "wealth" of the supposedly "victim" group.

Even while the holding center was in operation, the NGOs began to buy supplies, as often as they could, from local farmers and merchants (rather than from the capital city as most other international agencies were doing). They actually organized joint work groups of local villagers and camp residents to build a pond, which supplied water to both groups. Finally, agency field staff lobbied their own NGOs to take on serious and long-term work with the local villages. A new indigenous NGO was ultimately born which continues basic, village-level development work in this region.

new groups and, at the same time, receive few benefits from their presence. Some NGOs have found ways to link refugee programming with development efforts among nearby groups, and thus have lessened resentment and have promoted economic activity among the local people. Such involvement can create, spread, or multiply effects in the local economy, thus making everyone better off. If the policies permit refugee movement in and out of camps, refugees are more likely to find employment in an expanding local economy.

IRDP cases explored examples of camp/local community involvement. They included arrangements to: 1) buy food and other goods for the camp from surrounding farmers; 2) hire local people to work in construction and other roles within the camp; 3) engage both local people and refugees in digging a water retention system from which both groups could draw for their supplies; and 4) create infrastructure which serves everyone, including roads, electricity, schools, and health clinics. Each of these serves the refugees and affected populations and increases the developmental impact of the agencies' work.

In the past, failure to address the needs and development aspirations of people in refugee-affected areas has seriously increased refugee vulnerability due to resentments, conflicts over scarce resources, and exploitation of the issue by domestic political forces. Resources generated to deal with a refugee emergency can, therefore, quite legitimately be applied to refugee-affected groups. If funds are restricted, NGOs should locate additional resources to expand their work to include affected populations. Otherwise an opportunity is missed for reducing local vulnerability and increasing capacity, while, at the same time, aiding the process of refugee development. In most cases, NGOs responding to refugee situations should insist that they not take on work with refugees, without at the same time taking on significant work with local people. In some instances a division of responsibility among implementing groups may be workable, but a mechanism for linking approaches should be developed.

While refugees experience special problems because of their refugee status, the approaches that NGOs can take to work with them should still emphasize and build on refugees' capacities. Linking work inside refugee camps with assistance to local, refugee-affected populations will result in a magnified developmental impact of refugee assistance.

Chapter 6

APPROACHES TO PROGRAMMING

This chapter will deal with important choices in *how* a program is implemented. Who should be hired to operate a relief project? What should their skills be? What is the role (if any) of the outside expert? How can education and training be built into programs—for staff and participants? What forms of reciprocal learning are required by development? The issues and dilemmas of expatriate participation, the use of local staff, the role of technology, the generation of knowledge and systems for learning are each dealt with here.

PERSONNEL
(When a Northern NGO Intervenes)

Issue

The staffing of any relief effort is a key factor influencing its developmental impact. Who should be hired to work on emergency programs? What qualifications do they need? What roles should they play? For how long should they be hired? Northern and Southern NGOs both must make these choices. But while Southern NGOs usually hire local people as a matter of course, Northern NGOs often bring in expatriates as well, making the choices about staff roles, relationships, responsibilities and length of service more complex.

Pressures and Dilemmas

In disaster response, agencies are pressured to "staff up" quickly. There are pressures to hire people with knowledge of the country or with knowledge of the languages of the disaster-struck area. There are other pressures to find people with previous disaster response experience and/or with certain technical skills (see section below on expertise). It is always a dilemma to find people who have the required qualifications and who are available when needed.

In addition, Northern NGOs feel pressure to hire expatriates for a number of reasons, some justified, some not: to make reporting easier from the field; to ensure "objectivity" in the distribution of program benefits; to be able to say that "our people are there"; to provide public education after their tour of service is over; because part of the organization's mission is to provide Third World experiences for Northerners; because there are people available who have valuable experience with relief programs. Finally, some agencies historically use well-intentioned volunteers for field work in emergencies.

Lessons Learned from IRDP Cases

1. Staff respect for local capacities is a far more important determinant of the developmental impact of relief projects than any other staff qualifications (such as previous disaster experience). When knowledge of the country or language helped staff assess and appreciate capacities and vulnerabilities of local people, then these were useful.
2. The projects that tended to have stronger developmental impacts relied more on locally-hired staff than on expatriate staff.
3. In some projects, expatriate staff served certain important functions that helped overall project effectiveness, e.g., as a "buffer" from political pressures for national staff.
4. Local national staff who did not believe in the capacities of the people with whom they worked were no better at supporting development than any expatriate, and expatriates who worked from deep respect and confidence in the capacities of local people were extraordinarily important in ensuring the developmental impact of emergency work.

Application of Capacities/Vulnerabilities Analysis

There are always local people with capacities for planning, implementing, monitoring, and evaluating NGO disaster programs even when, in the midst of a crisis, it appears that people are traumatized and unable to work. As an agency comes to the point of hiring staff, it should do an assessment of local human resources at two levels. First, what can the project participants do for themselves and, second, what tasks need to be done by paid personnel? Whenever people can do something for themselves, they should do so and project interventions should support this.

Agencies can support local capacities by hiring nationals to operate their emergency programs. However, just employing local people does not guarantee that a project will be developmental. *How* people are used and the ways their skills are recognized and improved affect how their capacities develop. Conversely, a decision to place expatriate staff in an emergency project does not necessarily imply a failure to support local capacities.

There are several important principles in operation in staffing decisions. These are intertwined with Capacities and Vulnerabilities Analysis.

One issue is that of the definition of *qualifications* for any job. What is implied by the choice of qualifications set for candidates for a job? Two key principles underlie the definition of qualifications. These are accountability and dependency.

A SUCCESSFUL BALANCE OF EXPATRIATE WITH LOCAL LEADERSHIP

One agency's relief effort in Ethiopia was directed, at the national level in Addis Ababa, by a citizen of a European country of mixed African/European extraction who had grown up in Ethiopia. The project coordinator, at the field level, was an energetic Ethiopian with years of experience working with NGOs. Under him on the organizational chart were an American doctor who supervised the public health program and another American who supervised the food distribution program. The rest of the staff were all Ethiopian.

This arrangement had several advantages. It exhibited clear commitment to Ethiopian leadership and control of the program. At the same time, the presence of highly qualified expatriates "protected" the project coordinator from political and social pressures. If he chose to, he could always point to the presence of the foreigners as he denied favors or refused to bend policies in ways that would harm the program. At times he even asked one of the Americans to represent the agency at local NGO coordination meetings. He said that, while he and the American might make the same points, expatriate staff from other agencies might take the American more seriously.

Agency statements about job qualifications contain an implicit, if not explicit, notion of accountability. When qualifications stress competence and experience in narrative and financial reporting according to the agency's procedures, this implies that accountability to the headquarters (and, possibly to donors) is of utmost importance. Similarly, accountability to headquarters is implied when local staff are hired for their abilities to speak and write in the language of the donor agency.

If, on the other hand, an agency feels that primary accountability of any project activity should be to the local participants, the criteria set for staff choices would be different. They would include such things as local language competence and knowledge (for both expatriate and local staff), sensitivity to area mores and customs, appreciation of local culture and history, and, most of all, proven ability to work with, rather than for, people.

Criteria for selection of staff are also critical as they affect the potential for dependency creation. When agencies stress certain kinds of technical competence, especially among expatriate staff, they run the risk that these staff will provide only technical expertise during the project but not leave behind any technical competence among the people with whom they work. In fact, they may set up systems in the project area which require the continued input of outside expertise and increase dependency on outside help. When agencies insist that staff show their qualifications as teachers or trainers of the techniques they know, then the chances that their work will increase local capacities improve. Below, in the section on "Expertise," we discuss this in more detail.

There are several other important considerations for agencies hiring local and expatriate staff. For hiring local staff, these include:

1. The political, historical, social, and cultural context of the country. Differences and power relationships between urban educated and rural poor, between classes, ethnic groups and religious groups, and between men and women are key. Decisions about *who* to hire to staff projects should be made, as far as possible, with the goal of supporting the participants' capacities both locally and *vis a vis* other dominant groups in their own societies.

2. Both traditional and changing roles of men and women in the society and economy should be noted. Agencies should usually not hire women only for programs that focus on women. Nor should they assume that male and female staff have equal access to men and women participants. When possible, opportunities should be exploited for supporting the capacities of both men and women, and this often requires strategies that take account of differences in gender roles. (See section on "Gender" in Chapter 5.)

3. Emergency programs provide opportunities to train local people in skills that increase their capacities to deal with subsequent crises and/or development efforts.

4. It is important to establish clear expectations about length of employment from the beginning of a relief (or development) effort. Local staff may become dependent on the outside agency's continuing in the project area for their and their families' survival.

For hiring expatriate staff, the basic rule is to do so in ways that support local capacities development. Some IRDP cases show that this was most effective in cases where:

1. Expatriates were placed in training or other specialized roles.

2. Their assignments were relatively short-term and they could "work themselves out of a job" quickly.

3. They had appropriate language skills and familiarity with the culture and politics of the country in question.

4. They filled "number two" positions, where indigenous people held key decision making and leadership positions.

The basic qualification for any staff—local or expatriate—should be their ability to recognize, support and increase the effective capacities of the people with whom they work. Staff must realize that they cannot "do development." They *can* promote the efforts of local people to develop themselves.

EXPERTISE

Issue

What is the role of expertise in development or in disaster response? Some kinds of technologies and specialized knowledge are important for development. However, thirty years of international aid experience show that technology and knowledge do not, in and of themselves, bring development. It is the people's development of their own "expertise" that underlies genuine development.

Pressures and Dilemmas

The pressures to hire experts to respond to disaster situations and, for that matter, in development projects arise from several sources. First, when there are clear and identifiable problems that "we know" are susceptible to certain technical solutions (we know how to build dams, earthquake

---

THE DESIGNATED DEVELOPMENT PERSON

There was a refugee emergency. One agency sent several expatriate staff. The assignment of one of these people was to think only about the development implications of the program. He was not to become involved in responding to the emergency. He monitored the emergency program being implemented by his colleagues, making sure that developmental aspects were included. While the emergency was at its peak, he also started to plan for developmental activities. Because he was "free" from the urgency of the emergency, he had the energy to think about the development aspects of all of the work.

---

resistant houses, treat cholera, etc.) then we feel we have a responsibility to offer this technology. Second, though it may be more developmental to help people discover such things for themselves, it is wasteful and time-consuming to insist that each society reinvent its own wheel. Knowledge and technology should be free goods; human societies should benefit from each other's discoveries. Third, many host countries insist that NGO staff be "experts." They do not want generalists; they believe the best aid they can get should include "modern and sophisticated" knowledge and technologies.

Lessons Learned from IRDP Cases

1. Technical expertise is sometimes irrelevant, or damaging, to the development process. It certainly cannot have a developmental impact if it is not offered developmentally.

2. There is no "technological fix" that will bring development. (Even proponents of "appropriate technology" sometimes assume that, if we only get the technology "right," then development will follow.)

3. For technical expertise to be useful in development terms, it must be accompanied by *developmental expertise*. People who are experts in a sector—agricultural economics, hydroelectricity, animal husbandry, brain surgery—may get agricultural price policy on track, establish an effective electricity grid for an area, improve cattle stock, or save a life. But they may leave people as dependent on outside knowledge and expertise as when they arrived.

THE EXPERT TEACHES/LEARNS
WITH LOCAL "VICTIMS"

One NGO staff person we know is an expert on earthquake response and knows a lot about earthquake-resistant housing. He was called to come urgently after a Latin American earthquake. Many houses had been demolished. People were stunned by the damage to their property. They looked to the outside expert for help.

He began his assistance in this way. He asked people to join him in a walk around the area and to show him the damage. Everyone was eager to join this "walk" because they knew that he represented an agency with funds to help them rebuild their houses.

They inspected houses, some completely fallen and others still intact, some damaged with parts still standing. He asked people, "Why do you think that house, or that part of a house, survived? Why did this house fall down?" They told him theories based on their knowledge of past earthquakes.

By the time the walk was over, they were ready to sit down and discuss earthquake-resistant housing designs based on their own building materials, local terrain, and local construction techniques. Our "expert" learned new things, and the housing that was built fit the local environment better than a design he had brought in his hip pocket, drawn on a blueprint in New York City.

Developmental experts have the ability to create the conditions in which people themselves acquire expertise or generate new knowledge, appropriate to the context. These activities also imply sharing knowledge, but doing so in a way that involves the "recipients" in applying, shaping, using it.

An outsider can make a contribution by teaching what s/he knows from experience elsewhere. But s/he can make a greater contribution by increasing the capacity of local people to learn from their own environment and experience. This involves devising methods of experimentation and learning that are appropriate to the cultural context and that can become permanent systems for discovery and communication of knowledge.

Application of Capacities/Vulnerabilities Analysis

Capacities/Vulnerabilities Analysis provides a way of thinking about expertise and technology. Many groups with whom NGOs work in disasters and development have little technical expertise and minimal technologies. Nonetheless, through capacities analysis, it is possible to

---

GENERATION OF KNOWLEDGE IN THE BUSH

A large refugee settlement was established in Eastern Sudan where, for centuries, the main enterprise had been animal herding. In the area surrounding the refugee settlement, large-scale commercial farms grew sorghum. But the refugee families each had only a small plot to grow food. No one knew how to use the small plots most efficiently to support the families.

One agency had been working with the refugees on agricultural production. They realized that the refugees were using inappropriate methods adopted from commercial farming and that the "right" ways to proceed with this soil type and rainfall pattern were unknown—even to "experts" from Khartoum. Agency staff and refugees decided to collaborate on trial plots to test varieties of sorghum, beans, and other vegetables.

Each village set aside an experimental plot while the aid agency found appropriate seeds for the trials. Village "agricultural agents" were selected to take charge of the trials as part of their training. During a full season, the agency and the village learned together what seed worked best with what mix of nutrients and weeding methods. New information was generated, relying on the skills of the local people as experimenters and the outside "experts" as collaborators.

---

identify the local knowledge base and traditional wisdom that constitute critical local expertise. We have often seen that when outside experts fail to take account of specific local circumstances, projects have not had the intended or expected impact. Sometimes such efforts increase vulnerabilities among the participant populations.

This happens in two ways. First, local resources can be undermined by inappropriate technologies (local pest-resistant crops are lost, land is devoted to high-yield cash crops requiring ecologically damaging pesticides and fertilizers, etc.). Second, local people are encouraged to adopt production patterns that require continuing inputs of external expertise, technology, or imported materials.

Developmental assistance should combine external and internal expertise to increase local capacities without, at the same time, increasing local dependence on external technologies or supplies.

EDUCATION AND TRAINING

Issue

At the heart of any development effort (whether in emergency response or in a long-term intervention) is the learning that occurs through it. What is taught and what is learned and by whom? All NGO projects carry an educational component, whether implicitly or explicitly. They teach through the actions of their aid programs—and not always what they intend. Project participants always learn something from their interactions with NGOs in the field. The question is how to ensure that the learning which occurs through a project supports development.

Dilemmas and Pressures

Agencies want to avoid "teaching" dependency or destroying motivational capacity while, at the same time, efficiently meeting urgent needs. In the midst of a crisis, where needs are desperate, it can be difficult to balance these pressures.

Outsider aid providers *do* sometimes know things that are useful. How can agencies provide this knowledge without overwhelming local initiative and learning processes? But every aid action has an implied message, as well. How can agencies avoid becoming tied in knots examining these?

Lessons Learned

1. Agencies must be aware of the implicit messages and teaching in their actions—not just what they intend, but how others perceive them.

2. Training and education are probably the most valuable tools for development and they can be applied in almost every situation, regardless of the level of disruption.

3. Disasters open up special, short-term opportunities for training and learning, in particular, learning about vulnerabilities (and capacities). In the aftermath of a disaster, people are open to examining their past behavior and learning new ways of doing things which offer greater security.

4. The learning process in disasters is two-way—for the project participants and for the relief/development worker. Many situations call for generation of new knowledge which is specific to the local circumstances, but builds on expertise gained elsewhere.

Relief/development workers are in a position to help people increase their capacity to learn from their own experience and, at the same time, to increase their listening and learning skills for use in other places.

Application of Capacities and Vulnerabilities Analysis

The discussion below will deal with two areas: implicit teaching and explicit or intentional teaching.

Implicit Teaching

The messages that "teach" project participants have powerful effects on their motivations and attitudes. The roles of aid "giver" and "receiver" carry an imbalance which, if not handled carefully, can undermine the psychological capacity of the less powerful party. Actions which imply that disaster "victims" are incompetent, or somehow to blame for their predicament, teach incompetence—and increase vulnerability.

Teaching and learning go on all the time. Whether participants learn that they are competent, or that the aid giver is competent, or that each has different competencies, depends on their sense of self, coupled with the messages conveyed through the actions and attitudes of the aid giver. One leading Ethiopian, soon after the famine response of the mid-1980s, was quoted as saying that the tragedy of that disaster lay not so much in the numbers of people who starved, though that was indeed tragic, but in the fact that Ethiopians learned that the "solutions to all our problems come from outside Ethiopia."

Project participants, through their interactions with an operating agency, learn about themselves and about how others perceive them. They learn about problem-solving. They learn about management styles, priority-setting and decision-making. They learn about communication.

Intentional Education and Training

Probably the most powerful opportunities for increasing the developmental impact of relief aid are in the realm of education and training. Such opportunities exist even in a crisis. Education may occur through formal courses (in either basic or special skills) or informal training.

The content and method of training also affect the unintentional learning. For example, *what* is taught delivers a message about the expectations for learning. Pitching the subject matter to a basic level may be appropriate for certain audiences. However, if it is too low, and content is minimal, the message is one of low confidence. "You are not capable of learning anything very sophisticated or complex." If the content is too elaborate, the result may be to confuse the students and to undermine their confidence about their capabilities. Teachers throughout time have faced

THE ATTITUDE IS THE MESSAGE

The first approach of outside aid givers to a group of disaster "victims" carries an implicit message (this also applies to approaches to national governments).

One message may be, "You've just had a tough time. We are sorry. May we help you? How?"

Or, it may be, "You are suffering. We are sorry. We shall help you. Without our help, you would suffer a lot more."

Or, "You are weak (and incompetent) to have suffered so badly from this event. Clearly you must be lacking in the skills, knowledge and resources that would have prevented this suffering. We are sorry. We shall give you help. You certainly need it right now and, since you are in such bad shape, you will probably need it for a long time. Without our help, we are not sure you would survive. But, with our experience, knowledge and resources, we can probably solve your problems, difficult and intractable as they are."

the challenge of setting learning goals that stretch people but which they can achieve.

Training/education occurs in many ways. The most intense is in one-to-one relationships. These can be consciously arranged apprenticeships focussed on teaching specific skills (carpentry, accounting, management) or they can be informal, day-to-day, collegial interactions through which each person learns from the others what they know best. Classes and courses of study on subjects identified as important by those to be trained always support and encourage the capacities of local people.

Sometimes aid projects can invigorate and strengthen capacities when they call on local people to become the trainers of others. In refugee camps, people with primary education have, with some support and incremental training, become school teachers for children. A carpenter can teach others to build looms; a woman who weaves can teach others to weave. The chain of training spreads specific skills and allows some people to develop teaching skills as well.

Disasters as Educational Opportunities

Disaster situations, because they disrupt normal life, often create opportunities for people to learn new things. One of the first effects is to heighten awareness of the problems that led to the disaster: the vulnerabilities of the community to natural hazards or human conflicts. For instance, in the wake of an earthquake, people are ready to learn techniques for earthquake-resistant building. After severe floods people will give attention to dredging waterways or constructing dikes.

LEARNING HOW TO LEARN

An agency works in a refugee camp at Qorioley in Somalia, assisting both refugees and local villagers with projects in agriculture, forestry, income generation, and community development. Knowing that they needed good information about the area if they were to conduct good programs, the agency staff got Somali community development workers to conduct surveys to gather information about project participants. These community development workers were not taught directly about interview techniques. Instead, they were asked simply to go talk with refugees and villagers. Afterwards, they met with staff to discuss what they had learned and how the information gathering was going. Through these discussions, they learned together the best methods for surveying in that cultural context.

In some situations, simply because they cannot work at their usual occupations, people have time to study. Refugee situations provide this; so do other events where people live in evacuation centers over an extended period of time.

Disasters also disrupt normal expectations. For instance, women may receive training in non-traditional areas. People are looking for new options; they are ready to acquire new skills and try new things. Latent talents (especially leadership and problem-solving skills) may emerge precisely because the events of a crisis bring them out.

Generation of Knowledge: A Joint Enterprise

Education is not a process of putting "knowledge deposits" in other people's minds. Education is a process of engaging people in discovery and thought. That is why "outsiders" who give aid must have development expertise as much as any other specialization or expertise. One of the principal skills of the development expert is the willingness to be a learner him/herself, to be "ignorant but teachable" in the local context. This implies the skill of respectful and careful listening.

SURPRISE! NEW CAPACITIES

The project was supposed to work with agricultural development among nomads in a resettlement village in Mali. Training programs concentrated on teaching farming techniques—unknown to nomads in their traditional culture. After several years, the community was feeling proud of all they had done.

But the town still seemed temporary. The leaders decided they needed permanent buildings for the school, teachers' residences, the health clinic, and the cooperative store. The agency that had been working with them agreed to help with the material supplies and the logistics of transport. They also arranged for skilled masons and carpenters to come to supervise the building projects. To keep costs low, villagers provided regular crews of volunteers to work under the supervision of the professionals. In time, the buildings were completed.Several years later, another severe drought hit the community. Many families moved temporarily to the south where jobs and food could be found. They found that the building skills they had learned through building their own village facilities were in demand. Thus, they had developed an alternative means of earning their livelihoods.

Chapter 7

COOPERATION AND ACCOUNTABILITY IN PROGRAMMING

Who cares about the outcomes of relief projects? Who should care? Is close coordination of NGO relief efforts always a good thing? Can it be anti-developmental? Who should be involved in determining criteria for success and evaluating the experience of a particular project? The two sections below explode some myths on these issues and offer new perspectives.

COORDINATION WITH OTHER AGENCIES

Issue

In disaster situations, particularly large disasters, many agencies respond. The agencies often have different philosophies and practical approaches. Do these differences cause conflicts that undermine the potential for a developmental outcome? *Should* the work of all the agencies be coordinated?

Who's In Control Here, Anyway? A Dialogue

An enthusiastic NGO staff person meets up with a Wise Sage—a Sage who has vast experience and wisdom about how NGOs operate in the field.

- *Sage:* I have pondered long, wandering among the disasters of the world. I conclude that coordination among relief agencies is not always a good thing.
- *NGO: (Startled by the suddenness of the pronouncement)* But! But...the accepted wisdom among NGOs is that coordination is *essential*. We've

THE NEGATIVE IMPACT OF
CLOSE COORDINATION

An agency was invited by a local government to work with people in a resettlement community some years after the community had been formed. The government said, "We want you to begin to work with these people developmentally. Up to now, we have simply been supplying them with the land, tools, food supplements, services, and technical assistance they need to survive. It is time that they begin to function on their own. We have begun a system of gradual cut-backs of the food rations we have been supplying."

"Good," thought the agency. "We are a development agency—not relief, and this is what we know how to do best."

But it was very difficult. To attract participants to its project work, the newly arrived agency saw that it would need to "compete" with the other agencies already at work in the area. Thus, they offered some incentives to join their program. They provided land for farming (which was allotted to their project by the local official administrative structure). They offered special land preparation services (they had to do this because all other agencies in that area provided this for "their" project participants), and they provided extra back-up staff to handle some of the ongoing agricultural work. They hired guards to protect project equipment.

Things went well. Incomes of project participants rose dramatically because there was real demand for the output of this project. So, the agency told its participants, "Now is time for us to pull back. You can begin to cover your own land preparation expenses, and pay for some of the other services we've been providing. This is good for you. This will lead you toward self-reliance."

But the people balked. Why should they pay? No one else in the region paid their NGO for such services. They went "on strike."

The agency looked back and thought about how it could have avoided this situation. When it began to do its work in this area, it accommodated to the terms of work already set by the existing aid agencies. If it had defined its terms differently from the beginning it might have attracted different people, but it might also have been able to create a different attitude and approach to development in the area.

been trying for years to get agencies to cooperate in the field to avoid duplication of effort or conflicting policies. Duplication is wasteful and conflicts undermine all our efforts.

- *Sage: (Patiently)* Yes, well, it is good to avoid conflict. But, the real question is what is most developmental in the situation? Coordination may lead to greater control and more efficiency on the part of the NGOs and this may be desirable in some circumstances and for some people. But there are times when NGO coordination inhibits development of local capacities, among government coordinating bodies and among local people.
- *NGO:(Exasperated, disbelieving)* Doesn't better coordination help that process—of building capacities?
- *Sage:* Sometimes it may. But not always. Development sometimes requires pluralist, varied approaches. Differences in agency approaches may be helpful in reaching different groups and supporting different capacities. Genuine development is seldom neat or tidy. There are really two issues here.
- *NGO:* Oh? Only two...
- *Sage: (Ignoring the sarcasm)* The first issue is control. Who is in charge of coordination? Whose purposes does it serve? Is it intended to ease the relationships between NGOs and make their logistical arrangements run smoothly? Or is it intended to ensure the highest possible involvement of local participants in planning and decision making?
- *NGO:* I suspect you might have something there. But, give me an example.
- *Sage:* Have you ever seen a circumstance where NGO coordination bodies have taken over government functions because the NGOs thought that government was too weak or disorganized to get anything done?
- *NGO:* Yeah. Or too corrupt.
- *Sage:* Wouldn't it be better if the outside agencies chose to support the development of coordinating mechanisms that were in the control of local people, or local government, and were effective?
- *NGO:* If they could...
- *Sage:* It is a lamentable fact of life that more and tighter organization at higher levels actually inhibits initiative at lower levels.
- *NGO:* I'll think about that. What's the second issue you said was important in coordination?
- *Sage:* If a relief approach is anti-developmental, then coordination of it will only make its impact worse. For example, if most agencies (and government) are involved in a handout scheme which promotes dependency, then coordinating these efforts so everyone is fitting the handout model will do more developmental harm than good. In such

circumstances, an NGO that came into this situation would want to stay free of "coordination" so that it could attempt to work with local people on a different basis. In the final analysis, anyway, it is up to the local people to develop their capacities for organizing, coordinating and controlling the range of activities in which they engage with NGOs.

• *NGO:* OK, OK, I see your point. But, now, really (he leans toward the Sage and speaks confidentially), don't you think there are *some* coordination functions that are always good, regardless of who is in charge and even if there is no agreement about developmental goals?

• *Sage:* (Considering a few minutes while our NGO friend squirms. Then, with a wink and a smile) Sure. I would include the following in such a list:

* Undertaking joint training programs for local staff and/or orientation and language training for expatriates.

* Sharing learning and evaluation of the overall assistance effort.

* Exchanging information about needs and more thorough analysis of groups of potential participants.

* Eliminating duplication and building complementarity in programming within particular sectors (health, agriculture, etc.)

MONITORING AND EVALUATION

Issue

To whom is a project accountable and on what terms? Should a relief project be judged on the efficiency of its operation, how well it gets its assistance to people in need? Who must be satisfied? Donors? National governments? Project participants? Should relief also be judged for its impact on development? How? By whom? Who owns the information from monitoring reports or evaluations and for what should this information be used?

Pressures and Dilemmas

Relief projects have typically been structured so that accountability is to the donor agency. Criteria for evaluation have usually been restricted to logistical concerns and for "end use" of goods, not for their developmental impacts. Organizational survival has dictated that NGOs respond to these demands and criteria.

The most common question posed by the donor public is "Is the aid getting through to the people who need it?" Monitoring systems "target" aid to families in most need, often using criteria set by the donor agency (e.g., all families with at least one child under the seventy percent height-for-weight nutritional standard). While such objective standards are useful for measuring progress and making sure that scarce goods are distributed where they are needed most, they also remove control and responsibility from the community and local leaders. On the other hand, an agency cannot abdicate responsibility for evaluation of project impact by choosing to work through local social systems. Traditional patterns of power and control are often not equitable; if an agency depends on local distribution mechanisms it may perpetuate the systems that made certain people vulnerable in the first place.

Lessons Learned from IRDP Cases

1. It is critical to begin to apply developmental criteria to the evaluation of relief projects, as well as judging their efficiency in delivery of goods. They are *never* neutral in their developmental impact.

2. Projects can be made accountable to project participants without "sacrificing" reasonable reporting to donors, governments, and the general public. Local people can also become active in monitoring and/or evaluation procedures. In fact, the monitoring and evaluation process, itself, becomes developmental if all parties are involved.

3. There is an education job to be done with the public, news media and donor agencies to gain support for using developmental criteria to evaluate relief work, and for using funds donated for emergency relief to support development elements of emergency programming.

Application of Capacities/Vulnerabilities Analysis

Emergency relief projects always have an impact on local people's capacities and vulnerabilities, either positive or negative. The impact of material goods is widely recognized. Goods that are provided as relief aid lessen immediate vulnerabilities. However, if they lower market prices for local goods, are siphoned off by some people for their own enrichment, and/or cause people to prefer them to locally produced goods, then they can result in increasing future vulnerabilities for some sectors of the society.

IF YOU WANT REPORTS—YOU WRITE THEM!

The Ethiopian Red Cross established a large, multi-sectoral "disaster prevention" project in Wollo province, with major funding support from the Red Cross Societies of Sweden, Japan, and the Federal Republic of Germany (FRG). Rather than appoint expatriate project staff to take on day-to-day responsibility in the project, representatives of the donor Red Cross Societies became project monitors. It was their responsibility to gather information and write reports back to Sweden, Japan, and the FRG, freeing Ethiopian staff from that task.

When, on the other hand, food is followed by plows and seed and technical assistance, there may be an increase in local capacities for raising food.

There *may* be an increase in capacities or there may *not* be. This depends on how the plows and seed and technical assistance are offered, who decides where and when they are offered, where they come from, their appropriateness to agricultural conditions, who learns from their introduction—all issues of control and participation discussed in previous sections of this book.

Since emergency relief aid has an extraordinary potential for promoting or undermining local capacities, monitoring and evaluation of projects should take account of its impact on both capacities and vulnerabilities—that is, on development.

Often, NGO evaluations of both relief and development projects are made by outside consultants and then written up and sent off to the NGO headquarters and donor offices in the North. But, local people are the "experts" in judging how a relief effort has affected their lives. Outside groups may provide support for collecting and analyzing the information, but the process of engaging project participants in the monitoring or evaluation of project activities provides an opportunity for increasing the capacities of the participants. Through reflection on successes and failures, they can improve their analytic and diagnostic capabilities and they may learn more about what does and does not work. They will increase the bases of information from which they judge outcomes and make new plans. Through this, they increase their capacities to manage activities.

NGOs may well want and need evaluations designed to answer certain questions of interest to donors, but they should not miss the opportunity to use the evaluation process to increase participants' capacities and they should insist that their donors be as concerned with the developmental impacts of their work as with their logistical efficiency.

Chapter 8

CONCLUSION

Closing the Gap Between
Principles, Policies and Practice

We have said: No one ever "develops" anyone else. People and societies develop themselves.

But, aid from "outsiders" can help. Northern and Southern NGOs, international donors, concerned individuals, development professionals, relief specialists—all can make a difference.

We know, and are humbled by the fact, that some aid makes a *negative* difference. It harms people more than it helps them. The suspicion continues that donors give aid simply to salve their consciences about their own inordinate wealth or for other self-interested reasons.

But, *we* hold that outsider aid symbolizes central and important human concern and empathy. In terms of humaneness, the world would be poorer without it. It is, therefore, incumbent on us to find ways to ensure that aid is truly supportive of development. It is essential that every act of assistance contribute to the goal of enabling people to gain self-sustaining economic and social security. It is also essential that we see this goal as immediate and attainable, not as some "pie in the futuristic sky" dream which we really have no genuine hope of or responsibility for achieving.

This book is about successful "outsider" efforts to support people's development, on their own terms and in ways that they—the participants—control and sustain. In this section, we have taken past project experience and extracted lessons for action that are developmental. The lessons are neither surprising nor counter-intuitive; all the findings are based in simple common sense. This is reassuring. Had we discovered some startling new revelations, we would have had to be suspicious of our methods for gathering and analyzing data.

However, even though the principles and lessons of aid programming sound familiar, this does not mean they are being put into practice. We have found many gaps, in relief and development work, between principles, policies and practice. Principles represent the beliefs and commitments of an agency and underlie its work. Policies apply the principles to all aspects of agency programming. Practice represents the systems and arrangements agencies adopt to ensure that policies get implemented on the ground.

All assistance agencies state their commitment to developmental principles. Fewer have systematically translated these principles into policies which govern all aspects of their work. Even fewer implement programs, particularly relief efforts, in developmental ways in all situations.

We have learned some approaches to closing these gaps from looking at varied agency experience through the IRDP process. We have examined policy options and illustrated effective practice in the sections that have gone before. In this chapter, we offer additional insights—this time from the perspective of NGO management. How can NGOs articulate their principles in ways that effectively translate into operational policies that, in turn, can be implemented on the ground in various field situations? What mechanisms exist for closing the gaps between strongly held values and their practical application under the real stresses of field conditions in emergencies?

Principles

All agencies, as we noted above, express through their own publications their commitment to developmental principles. From IRDP, however, we suggest three basic principles that should be adopted by all agencies concerned with integrating relief and development.

A Relief Principle

Relief work should be held to development standards. Thus, every disaster response should be based in an appreciation of local capacities and should be designed to support and increase these.

A Development Principle

Development work should be concerned with long-term sustainability. Thus, every development program and project should anticipate and be designed to prevent or mitigate disasters. Thus, they should identify and address the vulnerabilities of the people with whom they work and ensure that these are reduced over time.

Relief/Development Principles

1. *Both relief and development programs should be more concerned with increasing local capacities and reducing vulnerabilities than with providing goods, services, or technical assistance. In fact, goods, services or technical assistance should be provided only insofar as they support sustainable development by increasing local capacities and reducing local vulnerabilities.*

2. *The way that such resources are transferred must be held to the same test.*

3. *Programming must not be solely preoccupied with meeting urgent physical/material needs, but must integrate such needs into efforts that address the social/organizational and motivational/attitudinal elements of the situation as well.*

Policies

NGOs adopt policies which are based on their principles. However, it appears that few agencies systematically test each policy against its principles to ensure their consistency. For example, if an agency adopts the principles suggested above, it would have implications for policies regarding partnerships, staffing, decision-making among programmatic alternatives, sectoral priorities, the use of technical assistance, what goods to ship in an emergency, etc. In each policy realm (funding, hiring, programming), NGOs should explicitly adopt policies that link relief and development.

What would such a policy look like? Several examples were discussed in Chapters 2-7 above. One example would be a policy that stated:

> In hiring for any project, we shall rely less on expatriate than on local staff, even for positions of authority. If we hire expatriate staff, we shall hire a local counterpart who works alongside the expatriate, as a colleague/apprentice, who can move into the position, or others like it, as soon as s/he acquires the skills.

Another example would be:

> Whenever our agency undertakes work within a refugee camp, we will also undertake programming with people in the surrounding community.

Evaluation/monitoring policies are especially important for ensuring that principles are incorporated into practice. If every project were held accountable for its impact on capacities and vulnerabilities, then programming decisions would soon begin to reflect the criteria by which such impacts are assessed.

Practice

The most difficult gap to close is the gap between policies and practice. The literature of social science is full of studies about why policies are not implemented. What arrangements can agencies adopt that will help ensure that development principles and policies are applied on a day-to-day basis in field activities?

One mechanism that several agencies in the IRDP study used was that of orientation/training. Most Northern NGOs train expatriate staff before sending them to the field. However, in many cases, orientation sessions are focussed on an introduction to the bureaucratic and communications requirements of the job and less on the philosophical (principled) approaches of the agency, or their practical application.

Where agencies provide a strong orientation in their developmental philosophy, coupled with training in the application of principles in day-to-day field operations, the work of the agencies has been far more effective in development terms, in both development and emergency programs. Training need not, and never can, cover all aspects of field work. Much learning occurs in actual field experiences. Nonetheless, an agency can teach its staff to *think* in terms of the fundamental developmental principles and policies it has adopted, and provide ideas of how these apply in field circumstances.

In addition to training the staff, agencies can develop systems for entering a new field environment. Such systems can include specific steps in a) gathering information; b) making contact with participants and local government people; c) generating ideas on initial project activities and ways to work with local communities to identify these and initiate them; and d) gaining exposure to particular problems commonly encountered and practical suggestions, based in experience, on how to solve such problems. Each of these can reflect the policies the agency has adopted.

Finally, agencies are well aware of the important role they can play in development education. As they increasingly educate the general public and their own constituencies (including their donors and boards of directors), they can free themselves from some of the pressures and constraints that these groups impose on their programming which, in the past, have reduced developmental outcomes. IRDP findings suggest that such education should focus primarily on the competence of those we seek to help.

The fundamental message of this project effort is precisely that people in Africa, Asia and Latin America are competent, in "normal" times and in times of calamity. They have abilities and capacities that are critical to their efforts to develop. Whatever your political philosophy and however you think some of the world became poor while other parts became rich, we agree that poverty should not continue.

TAKING PRINCIPLES TO THE FIELD

The scene is an orientation for field workers being sent by an NGO to work during a major famine.

- *Staff Trainer:* Today we are going to deal with this principle we have about community participation. Where does this come from?
- *Alma:* We saw it mentioned as part of the organizational charter—the part that talks about "listen to the aspirations of the people."
- *Patrick:* Right, and the "Guidelines for Program Design" in the Field Manual call for community participation.
- *Staff Trainer:* OK. How do we implement community participation under conditions of urgency?
- *Alma:* In an emergency where people are dying every day, how do we slow the process down to include participation?
- *Mario (regional staff person):* You are right that it can be difficult. In fact, the forms of participation may be different from a traditional community development project, at least at first. But when I worked with earthquake-affected people in Guatemala, we found ways to work with local people within a few days after a big quake.
- *Patrick:* Great, but how? What kinds of decisions were people able to think about at that point?
- *Mario:* Well, I met with the mayor and the surviving town council members in the Town Hall which was only half standing. You could see the sky through the roof! We assigned local people of all types to coordinate damage assessment for each part of town. Some were young people, but one was an elderly grandmother who had lost all of her family and asked to be given something to do. These assessment coordinators worked with our staff people and developed a system for rating each house in the community.
- *Alma:* Did people get involved in decision-making too?
- *Mario:* Yes, they had to decide whether to rebuild the town in the same spot, or move it to a safer area close by. We helped the local people negotiate with regional authorities about that. The information from the assessments was crucial in that process.
- *Patrick:* All right, I'm beginning to see how it can be done. We're going out to deal with a famine, not an earthquake, but I can see that we could train people from the community to monitor nutrition in the severely affected areas.
- *Alma:* Sure, and local people will be able to help identify the families most at risk. At the same time, they will have a sense of the long-termconditions that led to the famine—agricultural factors that we can work on together over time.

But development cannot be imposed. "Imposing aid"[1] often undermines people's development. Aid can only be effectively given by people and agencies that give it in the spirit of trust—trust that the recipients are able to act and shape their own lives and futures. As one NGO leader said, "We can only act as allies in development, allies of the people whose lives are engaged in their own development."

"Allies" are people who join cause with others and work, alongside them or on their behalf, in achieving the goals they have set. Allies are not the principal managers of a campaign; in some sense, they are not even equals in a campaign. They interact with the primary group and may join them in developing a strategy, but they do not, in the final analysis, set the terms or make the decisions, because their lives and livelihoods are not at stake. Allies are accountable to the groups with whom they ally themselves. If that relationship breaks down, they cease to be allies.

A PERSONAL NOTE
FROM A DEVELOPMENT WORKER

One development professional told the following story.

"I am frequently challenged by other people from North America and Europe to explain how I can enjoy working in the Third World. They ask me repeatedly, 'Don't you find it depressing—all that poverty?'

"Over the years, I have found that my best answer is: 'No. It is not at all depressing. On the contrary, it is often inspiring. I find myself working, so often, with people of such high dedication and competence. They work under circumstances and hardships that you and I would never be able to face day after day. And they do so with a great deal of spirit and creativity. With so many people working so hard and so effectively to make theirs and others' lives better, I find it a privilege to work with them. They are very able people.'

"When I tell my friends this, they are at first surprised. They have never thought of Africans, Asians and Latin Americas as anything but poor and uneducated. It never occurred to them that these people are competent adults, solving problems and working hard. I think this is the basic development education message."

---

1. See Barbara E. Harrell-Bond, *Imposing Aid, Emergency Assistance to Refugees,* Oxford University Press, 1986.

This is merely a statement of conviction. It implies, however, an operational approach. It requires that "outsiders" constantly seek ways to join cause with those, across the world, who support the basic development undertaken by so many people in so many villages across the continents of the South.

IRDP
Case Histories

Introduction to Part II

Background and Development
of IRDP Case Histories

Range and Selection of Projects for Study

The IRDP visited thirty projects in Asia, Africa, and Latin America that successfully linked short-term emergency relief with longer-term social and economic development. Case histories of these projects describe their planning and implementation and examine their developmental impacts.

The projects included relief efforts following drought, flood, earthquake, volcanic eruption, tsunami, typhoon, and refugee emergencies. They were implemented by a diverse set of non-governmental organizations(NGOs), large agencies and small, technical and general, concentrating on relief and on development, and both in the North (North American or European) and in the South (African, Asian, Latin American). Of the thirty cases, eleven have been included here. A full annotated list of all thirty cases is provided in Appendix B.

By comparing the experience of numerous agencies in multiple projects, and across different disaster types, generalizable lessons for the future design of emergency programs emerged. Some of the lessons drawn from the cases appear in Part I of this book. The reader will find others in the cases that follow.

Case Writing Process

From the start, the IRDP intended to provide practical lessons for agencies engaged in disaster response. Therefore, the project was designed not as a rigorous academic study, but as a careful examination of NGO experiences from which a composite picture of the acquired wisdom in this field could be drawn.

The cases are not evaluations of the projects in the usual sense. We did not assess project outcomes against stated objectives and measure success in those terms. Rather, we were interested in the results of the project for *development*, an objective that was rarely enunciated in project proposals. Each case is, therefore, a description of the project process and an analysis of its impact on development, stated in terms of increases in capacities and reductions in vulnerabilities.

In order to write the case histories, case writers read project documents and conducted field interviews with agency staff, project participants, local and national officials, the staff of other agencies working in the area, and any other relevant persons with knowledge of the project and its effects. In some cases, agency headquarters staff or former field staff were also interviewed. A crucial part of the case-writing process was the application of Capacities and Vulnerabilities Analysis to the disaster areas and project interventions. A complete explanation of this analytical framework is found in Chapter One. *Readers are advised to read that chapter before reading the cases.*

Case Content

Although the cases vary in style and format, each includes a description of the project context and the conditions that led to the disaster, a summary of the planning and implementation of the project itself, and a final section which presents the implications of the experience for future planning. In some instances clear lessons are suggested. In others, important dilemmas illustrated by the project are offered.

The eleven case histories are presented in three categories: 1) straight relief operations; 2) development projects to which a relief component was added; and 3) refugee/resettlement projects. We have placed them in this order because we have found that more salient lessons are learned about developmental impacts through the differences represented by these circumstances than through other categorizations (such as by disaster type, region of the world, or NGO type).

Relief Projects

We look at three projects that could be characterized as "straight relief," except for the fact that, in each case, the methods of providing relief were innovative and developmental. In one situation, a joint project of the Ethiopian Red Cross and the League of Red Cross and Red Crescent Societies in Wollo, Ethiopia, the NGOs took the "opportunity" of the drought of 1983 to shift their focus from limited disaster response to disaster prevention. The case describes the two-pronged approach undertaken in that region of traditional feeding programs coupled with "the structural development of [the] community" to enable it to "withstand the shocks of drought" through "improved self-reliance...in food production, water harvesting, conservation of natural resources and basic health."

The other cases in this section provide two examples of an NGO (Save the Children Federation, USA) responding to severe crises with relief programs in areas where it had not worked previously. Though its partners in the Save the Children Alliance had been in Ethiopia for some years, Save the Children Federation (SCF) began its work in 1984 in the district of Yifat na Tamuga, Shoa Province, in response to the emergency famine conditions. Though it had programs in other parts of Colombia prior to the earthquake and mudslide at Armero, SCF's response to this disaster took it into an entirely new area of the country. In both instances, SCF based its relief programming on its basic developmental philosophy, and these cases tell the interesting story of how this approach shaped relief efforts and resulted in long-term positive, and sometimes quite surprising, outcomes.

Development Projects Interrupted by Disaster

The next grouping of case histories includes four examples where agencies were already working in a country in a long-term development program, and a disaster occurred, causing them to take on relief efforts (usually reluctantly). Two of these cases involve examples of basic developmental and environmental work which was interrupted by drought, forcing the NGOs to take up some aspect of emergency feeding. In Burkina Faso, three NGOs (FONADES, Six-S, and Foster Parents Plan International) had been developing local initiative and organizations through cereal banks when the drought of the early 1980s put such severe pressure on these banks that they very nearly failed. The three agencies responded somewhat differently, each with an eye to protecting and maintaining the gains made through their earlier developmental programming. The different outcomes of their different approaches are instructive for future work.

The other drought case, that of CARE working in Kordofan, Sudan, illustrates several stages in an agency's program evolution. CARE's ongoing development program in North Kordofan was interrupted by famine, causing the agency to undertake feeding and food distribution efforts simply to sustain the people with whom their staff had been working. This experience, in turn, caused CARE to refocus its long-term efforts to address basic vulnerabilities that underlay the drought in the area. Thus, CARE developed, even while the drought persisted, an agroforestry project that began the fundamental rebuilding of a resource needed to prevent future drought.

In Joyabaj, Guatemala, several volunteer agencies joined together to respond to the earthquake of 1976, and a new alliance (ALIANZA) continues to be involved in more effective development work that has grown out of its intense relief response. In Santo Domingo in the Bicol

Region of the Philippines, a village development project of the International Institute of Rural Reconstruction was pre-empted by a sudden volcano eruption in the area of the intended work. This case tells how the trained community development workers became a part of the emergency response effort and, while living in evacuation centers with disaster "victims," began the process of village organization which has continued since.

Refugee and Resettlement Projects

The final set of case histories involve circumstances in which war or natural disaster forced people to move across national boundaries as refugees or to resettle within their own countries under conditions starkly different from their former settings. These circumstances pose challenges to NGOs concerned with supporting development. Often refugees and settlers do not have sufficient land, or other resources, for self-sufficiency. They remain dependent on decisions made by governments and agencies beyond their influence. They live with high uncertainty about their futures. Still, as each of these cases demonstrates, NGO work in these situations can be developmental.

The first case chronicles the involvement of ACORD in working with Ethiopian refugees who were settled in Qala en Nahal in the Sudan. ACORD began its involvement in the settlement as only a funding partner, but was asked, in 1980, by the government of Sudan to take over certain agricultural management functions within the refugee villages. When the 1980s drought ensued, the focus of ACORD's involvement changed (as occurred in the cases discussed above), both as it undertook an emergency response and, subsequently, redirected its development work to address systemic issues that made the community vulnerable to drought.

In Mali, when the drought of the 1970s caused many nomads to seek government assistance, the American Friends Service Committee agreed to help a group of displaced nomads establish a village on the shores of Lake Faguibine. This settled village represented a basic shift in the way these individuals lived, turning away from sole reliance on their animal herds and learning other skills including farming. This case allows a longer-term assessment of the outcomes of the AFSC's project, because we can learn how the residents of the village coped with the second major drought that hit them, after the project, in the 1980s.

The final two cases come from Thailand, where much has been learned about work with refugees in closed refugee camps. The first, a case of Catholic Relief Services work with health care in a major and long-existent camp, illustrates options that NGOs face in refugee work and raises important issues about the various long-term outcomes of the different options. The second Thai case involves a situation where a Northern agency, CUSO, agreed to work with local NGOs to increase their capacities to work on refugee programming. From this activity, further work with refugee-affected villages was undertaken by the Thai NGOs, leading to the establishment of a new private voluntary development agency working entirely in the villages affected by the war and refugee influx.

As these quick sketches of the eleven cases indicate, reality is not so "neat" as the lessons learned in Part I might imply. Change is constantly occurring and NGOs, as well as project participants, must adjust, alter course and, when possible, take advantage of the new opportunities that it offers. The importance of the roles of individuals is highlighted when we read about actual project experiences. The issues of the context in which projects are planned and implemented, dealt with in Part I, are made clearer in the concrete examples of the cases. These eleven cases provide a sample of the substance of IRDP, the actual, on-the-ground experiences of people engaged in responding to crises and supporting development.

Chapter 9

WOLLO REHABILITATION AND DISASTER PREVENTION PROJECTS
Wollo, Ethiopia

Project Implementing Agencies:
Ethiopian Red Cross Society
League of Red Cross and Red Crescent Societies

Case Writer:
Ann K. Qualman

I. INTRODUCTION

This case history examines a series of relief, rehabilitation and disaster prevention programs of the Ethiopian Red Cross Society (ERCS) in two districts (the *awrajas* of Ambassel and Kalu) in Wollo province of northern Ethiopia.[1]

International and Ethiopian Red Cross organizations have been involved in relief activities in the area since the 1973 famine. When famine struck the area again in 1983-84, they once again provided major relief assistance. In 1985, as part of a rehabilitation strategy, the Ethiopian Red Cross and the League of Red Cross and Red Crescent Societies distributed

---

1. The English spelling of Ethiopian words varies. Wollo may be spelled Welo, Kalu is Qallu, etc.

ETHIOPIA

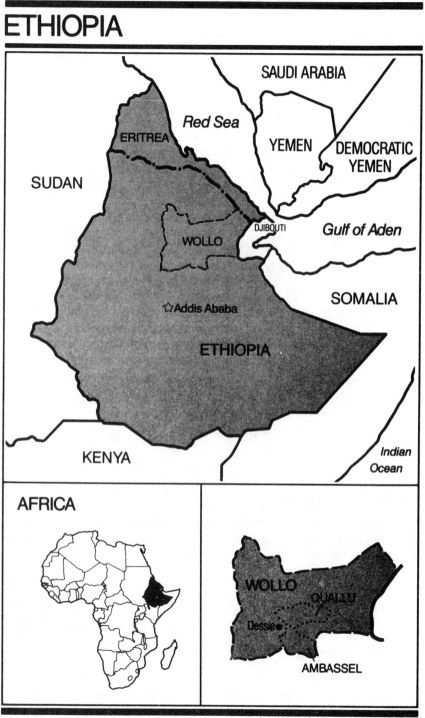

SAUDI ARABIA

Red Sea

ERITREA

YEMEN   DEMOCRATIC
         YEMEN

SUDAN

DJIBOUTI   Gulf of Aden

WOLLO

SOMALIA

☆Addis Ababa

ETHIOPIA

KENYA   Indian
                        Ocean

AFRICA

WOLLO
        QUALLU

Dessie●

AMBASSEL

Map By Jerry Alexander

agricultural inputs including seeds, tools, oxen, pesticides, and fertilizers, to 122,000 families. In 1986, the ERCS, in collaboration with the Red Cross Societies of the Nordic countries (represented by Sweden), and the Federal Republic of Germany and Japan, took over the remaining work of the agricultural inputs program and commenced a multi-sector "disaster prevention program" (DPP).

II. DESCRIPTION OF PROJECT CONTEXT

History of Drought in Ethiopia

With forty-two million people, Ethiopia is Africa's third most populous country. To feed this population, the country purchases food and receives a substantial amount of food aid every year. Even in the best of years, food rations are distributed to a million people. Although Ethiopia was never colonized, it was occupied by the Italians during World War II, it has been engaged in lengthy, costly conflicts with the northern provinces of Eritrea and Tigray and with neighboring Somalia. It must feed and support both the largest army of any African country and a large bureaucracy.

Ethiopia has experienced cycles of drought, famine, pestilence, and relative plenty for many centuries. The disastrous droughts of 1973-74 and of 1983-84 are but two of the most recent.[2] The regime of Emperor Haile Selassie refused to recognize the 1973 famine or to take any effective action against it. This refusal was a major factor leading to the revolutionary overthrow of the regime. Under the new regime, the feudal system of land tenure and the accompanying class structures (extremely rich landowners and poor peasant tenants) were dismantled in 1975. These changes in land tenure and rural policy continue to this day.

Land was assigned to newly created administrative units, called Peasant Associations, and in turn to peasant households. To promote greater equality, the land assigned often incorporated non-contiguous plots of land of different quality. Land is owned by the state and is periodically reallocated. As a result, there is little incentive for making improvements on holdings.

While the revolution has reduced social inequities, poverty has remained widespread. Few households can hold surplus grain in reserve against a poor harvest. A growing number lack the labor or traction power (oxen) to provide for family needs, but must depend on others in the community to farm their land.

2. The 1987-88 drought occurred after this case was written.

Wollo Province

Wollo had a population estimated at 3.4 million in 1984. It is densely populated and is one of the least developed of the seventeen provinces in one of the world's poorest countries. Transportation is difficult and two-thirds of the rural population cannot be reached by road. Dessie (69,000 people) is the provincial capital and largest town. Nearby Kombolcha has 16,000 people, while Haiq and Bati, two towns in the project area, have less than 10,000 each. Economic interaction between urban and rural areas is minimal, although some of the rural unemployed find their way to the towns. Rather than being mutually interdependent, the towns depend on the rural economy. Handicrafts are denigrated by the local population and the variety of manufactured goods available in rural markets is even less than before the revolution.

Wollo lies in the Northeast zone of Ethiopia, along with the provinces of Eritrea and Tigray. The topography is extremely rugged. The mountainsides are steep: 22 percent have at least a 60 percent grade, unsuitable for farming but often cultivated nonetheless. A great escarpment runs north to south, cutting the province in half. The Upper Mille and the Cheleka River catchment areas are the focus of the Ethiopian Red Cross Society disaster prevention program, an area covering at least 6000 square kilometers. The altitude of the project area varies from 2,700 meters in the Ambassel mountains to 550 meters in lower Cheleka.

There are two rainy seasons in the ERCS projects area and many farmers follow a bi-modal system. The *meher* season from mid-June to early September provides 75 percent of the annual harvest in a normal year. The shorter *belg* season from mid-February to the end of April provides critical support for families until the next main harvest.

Parts of Ambassel and Kalu districts are self-supporting in years of normal food production, but they suffer food deficits like the rest of the area in difficult years. Agricultural productivity has remained unchanged since 1974 due to land fragmentation and minuscule holdings, deterioration of soil and other resources, frequent changes in rural policy, agricultural policy disincentives such as high taxes, and the destabilizing effects of rural conflict, famine and drought.[3]

Famine conditions spread through Wollo unevenly. In the war-torn areas of northern Wollo, famine came as early as 1981. In some other areas

3. Dessalegn Rahmato, *Famine and Survival Strategies: A Case Study from Northeast Ethiopia*, Food and Famine Monograph Series No. 1, Institute of Development Research, Addis Ababa University, Addis Ababa, May 1987, pp. 67 and 197. This well-documented report is based on peasant interviews and written documents describing Ambassel and Kalu districts, the area which is the focus of this case history.

the food crisis came in 1982 when the rains failed. In most of the province, the crisis struck in 1983 when the fall season's rains were 26 to 60 percent below normal. In December 1984, the Ethiopian Relief and Rehabilitation Commission (RRC) reported that 75 percent of Wollo peasants were in danger of imminent death. Indeed, more than one-third of the estimated seven to ten million Ethiopians facing starvation were Wollo peasants.

Capacities/Vulnerabilities Analysis of Wollo Province

Motivational/Attitudinal Capacities and Vulnerabilities
  Coping with crisis is an important aspect of peasant life. Look closely at the routine activities of average peasants in any normal season and you will discover that some of what they do is aimed at insuring their families against death and hardship. The decision to grow a particular crop mix in a particular season, to acquire or dispense with this or that farm animal, to sell one kind of produce and buy another... each of these decisions will involve at least two important considerations: a purely economic one, i.e., whether or not they will obtain the best possible returns on their investments or labor; and a 'survival' consideration, i.e., whether or not the household will be exposed to privation should an unexpected situation arise shortly after the decision has been made. Crisis anticipation forms a central part of peasant agronomy, and rare are the rural communities that do not have elements of 'disaster preparedness' built into their farming systems and exchange relations.[4]
  Dessalegn Rahmato notes that peasants have *anticipatory* survival strategies, which they employ during normal years, and *crisis* survival strategies. The effectiveness of anticipatory strategies influences the outcome of crisis strategies. Anticipatory strategies include fairly elaborate methods for forecasting weather and agricultural production and for following price changes in local markets.
  In regard to crisis strategies, Dessalegn Rahmato notes:

  A peasant community does not just give up and wait for death when confronted with a food crisis. A crisis lasts from nine to fifteen months, or more, and the threat of imminent famine triggers a heightened awareness, and a spate of defensive activity within peasant communities. Everything is done to anticipate, prepare for, withstand, and finally withdraw from the ambit of, the crisis.[5]

  To withstand the crisis, peasants take initiatives to move out of their subsistence economy into the cash economy and exchange system, migrate (usually within the area) to seek employment or help, alter food choices,

4. Dessalegn Rahmato, p. 5.
5. Dessalegn Rahmato, p. 134.

mobilize the family, and take advantage of community support systems.

"The Wollo peasantry is diligent, frugal and highly skilled." Drought and famine are so much a part of their lives that they view such events without remorse and even with humor. Even when faced with memories of terrible suffering and loss, "this cheerful attitude, this refusal to brood over what had happened, [is] a reflection of the strength of character of the rural population and part of their survival strategies."[6]

Wollo peasants are highly motivated to deal with drought crises as they arise. Their psychological vulnerability resides in feeling helpless to change from production and survival strategies that they recognize as destructive to the environment and to their livelihood. In addition, when crisis becomes a disaster and they lose everything, they become dependent on others for survival. This dependency is, however, based on material deprivation, not on feelings of worthlessness or lack of motivation. The Red Cross found that if people were adequately assured of food and the means to re-establish their lives, they were usually willing to leave relief camps and return home.

Social/Organizational Capacities and Vulnerabilities

Peasant survival strategies are based on cooperation within the family and the community. An effort is made to maintain the integrity of these units, particularly the family, even in severe hardship. "Peasants believe the family has better chances of survival if it remains as a unit." Both men and women collect famine foods and the family is pushed into the cash economy; it sells what it can to buy food. The contribution of each adult to the family's survival becomes critical as famine sharpens divisions of labor. Men play the role of seeking wage employment, monitoring markets, and travelling to seek help from relatives. The role of women in the management and preparation of food becomes crucial. As the situation worsens, women may leave home to beg.[7]

Families were traditionally grouped in *mender*, clusters of homesteads resembling hamlets. One or more *mender* formed a *got*, the most important level of community organization until it was replaced, to some extent, by post-revolutionary Peasant Associations (*kebbelae*).[8]

Each community provides a basis for friendship, kinship ties, and economic cooperation. There are three common forms of community cooperation underlying survival strategies:

6. Dessalegn Rahmato, p. 4.
7. Dessalegn Rahmato, pp. 180-182.
8. Peasant Associations (*kebbelae*) are grouped into administrative structures called *woreda*. These, in turn, are grouped into *awrajas* (districts) such as Ambassel and Kalu. Several *awrajas* form a province, such as Wollo. Wollo, Tigray, and Eritrea make up the Northeast Zone.

1. Families share draft animals and work land in turns.
2. Families who do not have oxen and labor turn to those close by who do have them, to plow their fields in exchange for part of the crop, an arrangement which serves both. Social stratification is thus used to promote community survival.
3. The community as a whole provides labor and other resources to help needy peasants.[9]

There are other forms of cooperation peculiar to peasants in Wollo which occur as famine intensifies:

1. Families forced to sell their homes (selling the building material piece by piece) move in with friends or relatives, sharing the proceeds of the sale with the host family, until the impoverished family is able to rebuild its home.
2. An impoverished family may share the surplus grain stored by another family with the expectation that the former will replenish it as its fortunes improve. This form of cooperation becomes less and less common as the general levels of poverty increase.
3. When a family is forced to migrate in search of employment or assistance, another family may care for its belongings and tend its land until the family returns.[10]

Other forms of organization in Wollo are government bureaucratic structures and non-governmental organizations (NGOs). The governmental organizations include administrative units, ministries offering technical services, the Peasant Associations, and other mass organizations for women and youth.

There are seventeen non-governmental organizations (mostly foreign-based) and bilateral aid agencies operating in Wollo, mainly doing development work. The most notable indigenous NGOs are the Christian and Moslem organizations and, increasingly, the ERCS. The Ethiopian Red Cross is one of Ethiopia's few indigenous NGOs and the only one of major importance which is not based in a religious organization.

In most Ethiopian organizations, hierarchical relationships guide most activities. The social hierarchy that existed before the revolution has been replaced by political and administrative hierarchies. In terms of getting tasks done, Ethiopia is clearly well organized. Almost all of the population (in principle, everyone) is at least a member of a Peasant Association (or its urban equivalent), which itself is closely linked to ministries and other organizations. Participatory democracy has been taken over by the revolutionary government, although indigenous

9. Dessalegn Rahmato, pp. 25-26.
10. Dessalegn Rahmato, p. 26.

organizational structures do play a role in the development process.

In short, Wollo had an extensive organizational network of varying capability at the time of famine. The family and community proved most effective in coping with crisis. The government and NGOs helped by distributing foreign-supplied disaster relief rations. The Red Cross, the Ethiopian Orthodox Church and the American NGO, Catholic Relief Services, were those most involved in relief assistance. The church organizations and Peasant Associations were unable to play a disaster prevention role and the ministries (such as Agriculture and Health) which had development programs lacked the necessary resources to prevent a disaster.[11]

Physical/Material Capacities and Vulnerabilities

The population of Wollo is able to survive in years of normal rainfall through subsistence agriculture and trade of livestock for food from crop surplus areas. Some progress has been made, even during the famine years, in developing infrastructure and water supplies: a textile factory, an irrigation scheme, dams, electric power, and rural road construction.

In years of crisis, peasants implement survival strategies developed over centuries. At times these strategies fail because of the overall regional inadequacies in water supplies, food production, food storage, forage, household cash reserves, and health. The physical vulnerability of the region is increasing. Peasant practices of farming, animal husbandry, and wood gathering are destroying the environment while current agricultural policies discourage the production and storage of food surpluses.[12]

The Ministry of Agriculture has identified development needs in Wollo, but a Ministry of Planning official explained that less priority is given to agriculture in this region than in some others where the agricultural potential is greater. The Ministry of Agriculture lacks the financial resources to implement an integrated rural development program. The rural population has almost no knowledge of modern agricultural or other techniques needed to improve water conservation and farm productivity.

11. According to Dessalegn Rahmato, the Peasant Associations, in many cases, failed to withstand the famine and disbanded and disappeared. The PAs proved incapable of helping, so that PA officials suffered from famine like their kinsmen (p. 186.)
12. Dessalegn Rahmato, p. 167.

III. PROJECT HISTORY AND DEVELOPMENT

Program Initiation

The Ethiopian Red Cross celebrated its 50th anniversary in July 1985. At that time, its activities were largely confined to ambulance services and other local, small-scale emergency work traditional to the Red Cross until the 1973-74 famine. Since then, the recurrent drought and famine have engaged the Red Cross in relief operations year after year. The joint operations of the ERCS, the League of Red Cross Societies and the International Committee of the Red Cross (ICRC) served over a million Ethiopians in 1984-86.[13] The report corroborates much of the data presented here but has a different theoretical framework and objectives.

Given the strong likelihood that similar crises would recur, ERCS decided to adopt a strategy focussed on disaster prevention, rather than the usual Red Cross strategy of responding to disasters after they occur. The Swedish Red Cross influenced this decision by hosting a League symposium on disaster prevention in 1982. The Swedish Red Cross publication, *Prevention Better Than Cure* by Gunnar Hagman, also provided the rationale. By 1985, the ERCS had adopted disaster prevention policies, as have the national Red Cross Societies in Scandinavia, Germany, Japan, and Italy. The League as a whole has maintained its traditional relief approach. The divergence of views between the League and some of its members helps to explain why the Wollo recovery program has two components. The rehabilitation program, begun in the fall of 1985 by the League, is funded by USAID and the Canadian Red Cross. The disaster prevention program (DPP), on the other hand, is funded by the Nordic Societies, through the Swedish Red Cross, and by the Red Cross Societies of Japan and the Federal Republic of Germany.

During the 1984-85 famine, 60 to 70 percent of ERCS relief activities were in Wollo. The rehabilitation program and DPP grew out of these operations, particularly those at Bati in the eastern highland escarpment. The Bati shelter was opened in October 1984, when a small Red Cross assessment team found 4,000 people gathered there, picking up crumbs. Within two weeks, the numbers sheltered by the Red Cross at Bati grew to 28,440. Red Cross and Ministry of Health (MOH) medical teams provided emergency care, but many people arrived too weak to survive and up to one hundred died daily.

13. The objectives, results, and evolution of Ethiopian Red Cross programs for the country as a whole are detailed in a report by ERCS staff member, Elizabeth Kassaye, "From Disaster Relief to Development: The Experience of the Ethiopian Red Cross," Working Paper 12:87, Institut Henry-Dunant, Geneva, 1987.

The massive operation, which served 32,000 people at its peak, was largely operated by Ethiopians, including eighty-four youth volunteers. Approximately four volunteers plus one MOH health assistant cared for recipients grouped in units of 2,000 to 3,000. In addition, 700 people paid through food-for-work undertook a variety of tasks, including child care, splitting fuel wood, collecting the dead, and washing and burying them. In November 1985, the Red Cross ended "wet feedings" when it closed shelters in Bati, Mille, and Gewane and smaller ones in Ambassel, Kalu, and Awsa districts. It closed seven dry ration distribution centers in June 1986.

The Ethiopian Red Cross made use of opportunities provided by the 1984 crises in Wollo. Youth volunteers working at the shelters were given a one-week course in nutrition, general health, environmental hygiene, and Red Cross principles. The course improved their work in the relief camps and helped prepare those who later joined the rehabilitation program or who might be hired for future relief work.

The ERCS also used the famine situation to build the institutional base of the Red Cross in Wollo. The growth of the ERCS in the province has been dramatic. Before 1984, the ERCS in Wollo consisted only of an inactive committee at the provincial level. As the famine ended, rather than return to this previous situation, ERCS hired a few of the most effective volunteers to fill critical posts to develop the ERCS Wollo Branch. Active ERCS committees operated by volunteers (many of whom became acquainted with the ERCS through its relief activities) work in eleven out of twelve Wollo districts and in sixteen of the thirty-seven *woreda* (sub-districts). Before the famine there were 8-10,000 ERCS members in Wollo (all in Dessie). By 1987, the province had over 67,000 members who had paid the two birr (US $1.00) membership fee.

Program Design

The Red Cross has had two post-disaster projects in Wollo: a rehabilitation project completed in December 1986, and the Upper Mille and Cheleka Catchments Disaster Prevention Program (hereafter referred to as the DPP), which began in mid-1986 and is expected to last at least five years.[14]

The project areas overlap. The rehabilitation program reached 194 Peasant Associations (PAs) while the DPP covers approximately 60 PAs (all of Ambassel, part of Kalu, and a small part of Dessie Zuria district). The rehabilitation program was essentially a stop-gap measure, a way of

14. An evaluation during the fifth year will determine whether and how the project will continue.

carrying the poorest families to the next harvest. However, the DPP aims to change fundamental aspects of economic and social life for the thousands of families in the project area.

The project area was selected because it is a part of Wollo that is overcrowded, devastated by erosion and no longer suitable for farming, and chronically affected by drought and famine. Moreover, the Red Cross had experience in the area and was beginning to be known.

The goal of the rehabilitation program was to encourage shelter beneficiaries to return home and to enable them to resume subsistence farming. The idea of the program is said to have come from the shelter inhabitants themselves who saw that they could not return home if they had no animals, seeds, or tools with which to farm.

The immediate objectives of the rehabilitation program were to deliver agricultural inputs before the 1986 *Belg* rains to the neediest peasants in the two districts, to assist peasants with food-for-work rations until they had means of subsistence, and to monitor developments so that the rehabilitation program could lay the foundation for long-term disaster prevention projects.

According to the project proposal, the goal of the DPP is "the structural development of a community, which can withstand the shocks of drought." These include attitude change: "a return of confidence...to produce" and "an awareness of how the last disaster came about." The project aims at "improved self-reliance within a short period of time—a minimum of five years—in food production, water harvesting, conservation of natural resources and basic health."

The ERCS proposal for the Upper Mille and Cheleka Catchments Disaster Prevention Program refers to vulnerabilities which correspond closely to the physical vulnerabilities described earlier. It has identified four major problem areas:

- inadequate marketing and cash saving system,
- low agricultural (animal and crop) production,
- lack of water storage (natural or artificial), and
- human disease.

To reduce the vulnerabilities of people in the project area to future severe drought, the DPP has eleven components. These are summarized in the Appendix to this case and can be grouped as follows:

- human resources (training),
- soil and forestry resources,
- animal resources,
- agricultural (crop) resources, and
- fisheries resources.

The DPP contains the usual sectors found in an integrated rural development program but differs from the latter by emphasizing conservation more than production.

Program Development

Agricultural Rehabilitation Program

ERCS carried out a survey in April 1985 to determine the needs for rehabilitation of those at or near the Bati shelter and concluded that the most urgently needed items were seeds, tools, pesticides, and fertilizers. They then implemented a pilot project from April to July in cooperation with the Ministry of Agriculture under which the Red Cross distributed 490 metric tons of seeds, fifty tons of seed potatoes, 20,000 agricultural tools (spades, hoes, picks), and pesticides and fertilizers.

Based on that experience, an expanded rehabilitation project was carried out from December 1985 to December 1986. Preparations for the project began in September 1985, but the late organization of the project, delayed funds, and early *Belg* rains made it impossible to implement the project in time to affect the early 1986 *Belg* harvest. Instead, the project was completed in advance of the *Meher* rains.

The Ministry of Agriculture implemented the rehabilitation activities while the ERCS and League financed, supplied, and monitored the project. The experience was a first for the ERCS. As the Red Cross did not have sufficient supplies for all farmers, guidelines for selecting recipients were drafted by the Red Cross rehabilitation staff, and approved by MOA district and sub-district staff. Each Peasant Association submitted the names of needy peasants to the distribution committee, which included representatives of the Ministry of Agriculture, the Relief and Rehabilitation Commission, the ERCS, and the Peasant Associations. The program reached 122,000 families (approximately 70 percent of the population of the two districts).

Three thousand tons of seeds were purchased (wheat, corn, sorghum, teff, barley, chick peas, horse beans, field peas, lentils) from the Ethiopian Seed Corporation, supplemented by purchases in Addis Ababa and Wollo local markets and in Kenya. More than 100,000 tools (shovels, sickles, plow points) were distributed, as were fertilizers and pesticides, mostly supplied from Kenya. In allocating fertilizer, preference was given to producer cooperatives in order to monitor its effective use more easily while the MOA retained the pesticides for use as the need arose. Over 2,500 oxen were distributed to some of the most needy farmers.

The Red Cross staffed the rehabilitation project with an American project coordinator provided by the League, an Ethiopian project field manager, four youth coordinators, eleven youth volunteers (paid a stipend to cover their costs), and support staff. During their six-month assignments, youth volunteers received training in market surveying, reporting, registration of data, etc., in monthly sessions as the need arose. The rehabilitation project also presented a one-week training course to local farmers on a variety of agricultural topics.

The Disaster Prevention Program

Work began in some areas in December 1985, six months before the project was officially inaugurated. In its first year, the project used food-for-work to accomplish terracing (gullies and gabions) of 2-3,000 hectares, gravity flow irrigation of 130 ha (2,000 meters of canal work), construction of over fifty-five km of roads, the establishment of ten village nurseries and one larger nursery, and digging of 10,000 holes for reforestation.The MOA assigns a development agent (extension worker) to every three to five Peasant Associations. The DPP project has trained them to interpret land-use plans.

By the end of the project's first year, irrigation works such as diversion dams were delayed because funding was not yet available to acquire the necessary heavy machinery. Several training programs of farmers were completed during the first year:

• seventy-six farmers from one sub-district learned improved agricultural practices (2 weeks);

• twenty-five housewives from two sub-districts participated in a one-week refresher course in home economics (food preparation, fuel conservation, income generation, hygiene); and

• thirty-two farmers from one sub-district studied accounting and budgeting (ten days).

In order to implement the DPP, the ERCS created appropriate structures to plan, direct, and monitor the project. According to the Director General of the ERCS, "the aim [of the DPP] is to build efficiency into the government structure without taking it over, to build a proper decision-making structure within the Government." The project was conceived to support the MOA's development program for Wollo and the MOA is the implementing agency, except for the health component, which is under the Ministry of Health.

The project staff report to the MOA, MOH, and ERCS offices in Addis Ababa. However, the major direction is provided by a Technical Committee made up of representatives from the Wollo offices of these organizations. An important side benefit from the project is this structure which encourages cooperation between the two ministries. The project manager reports to this committee and has overall responsibility for the execution of the project. The head of MOA's Natural Resources Conservation Department for Wollo serves as the project manager.

A project coordinator handles the day-to-day operations, assisted by a management unit which includes the project manager, key project staff (including expatriates), and the Wollo heads of technical departments of the MOA and MOH.

A monitoring team is stationed in the field. It follows the progress of the project, keeps the management unit, the technical committee, and donors informed, and makes recommendations as appropriate. It is comprised of a chief monitor who represents the ERCS and a monitor from each of the three donor Red Cross Societies. The expatriate monitors prepare detailed monthly reports which assess the productivity, stability, sustainability, and equitability of the project according to indicators identified at the project's inception. In 1988, an experiment in participatory evaluation was also instituted.

Because the MOA did not assign a project coordinator during the first year of operations, the chief monitor (from ERCS) served as acting project coordinator. He was formerly the head of the MOA for the Northeastern Zone which may explain why the MOA has not chosen to appoint a member to the monitoring team.

In many development and relief projects with international funding, expatriates fill all the key project management positions or, at the other extreme, merely fund local initiatives. The DPP presents a innovative model for donor participation which differs from these more common models. The ministries provide all of the line management and nearly all of the technical staff for this very large project. The donor Red Cross Societies are linked to the project through the provision of facilities, supplies, and equipment, through three technical personnel (a German agronomist, a Swedish soil conservationist, and a Japanese nurse), and through their participation on the management unit and monitoring team.

IV. VULNERABILITY/CAPACITY ANALYSIS OF PROJECT IMPACTS

The relief, rehabilitation, and DPP programs all emphasized reducing *physical vulnerability*. The post-relief programs have given nearly equal importance, in stated objectives, to attitude change: increasing people's *psychological ability* to deal with drought crises. Interestingly, stated program objectives generally do not mention the need to strengthen the area's *organizational capacity*, although the greatest long-run impact of Red Cross assistance may be in this area.

Physical/Material Capacities and Vulnerabilities

The objective of the rehabilitation project was not to regain the status quo but to help farmers start agricultural production. An evaluation carried out between November 1986 and January 1987 showed that the *Meher* (principal) harvest achieved 77.2 percent of normal harvest production for Ambassel and 80.35 percent for Kalu, an improvement over the previous four or five years. However, it is too early to judge the long-term impacts of the DPP activities on the physical capacity of the project area.

The rehabilitation program corresponds to the recovery needs defined by the Wollo peasants: the major constraints to recovery after serious drought have been human illness and shortages of draft animals and seeds.[15]

No doubt, seeds, tools, oxen, fertilizers, and pesticides provided by the ERCS helped strengthen the area's immediate physical capacity. While increased food production generates seeds and income for future planting, the Red Cross recognized that in order to sustain the gains from the rehabilitation program an effective long-term disaster prevention program was required. Ironically, the League delegate who coordinated the rehabilitation project suggested that Peasant Associations set up seed banks. The MOA approved as long as the Red Cross would accept some responsibility. However, Red Cross policy forbids the sale of its supplies so the idea was never implemented.

Another issue affecting project impact is the role of women within the DPP. Under the rehabilitation program, women were treated as home rather than farm managers in the rehabilitation training course. The engagement of women in development efforts is difficult as long as men are selected almost exclusively for leadership roles and training. ERCS expects women to play leadership roles principally within their own homes. However, women head 20 percent of farm households, including many of the poorest. Dessalegn Rahmato and the ERCS staff have observed that women recover from famine better than men and therefore have skills to share.

Motivational/Attitudinal Capacities and Vulnerabilities

The rehabilitation project encouraged the attitude that farmers could once again provide their own food needs. There is no precise demographic data that indicates to what extent peasants, who were forced to migrate in search of food or earnings during the famine, returned home when the situation improved and the shelters were closed. It would be even more difficult to estimate the extent to which Red Cross rehabilitation assistance played a role in this and helped to inspire confidence. According to Dessalegn Rahmato's findings, the food relief and the rehabilitation assistance provided to the people of Ambassel and Kalu districts "were

15. Dessalegn Rahmato, p. 242.

supplementary support measures, and did not constitute the central element of indigenous survival or recovery strategies."[16]

The Red Cross views the psychological impact of its relief and rehabilitation programs particularly in terms of the relationships of trust they helped to establish between the Red Cross and the people (and authorities) of Wollo. The Red Cross is now a recognized and positive symbol. People now listen receptively to Red Cross suggestions for the region's development.

This approach supports the ERCS view of how development occurs. People are open to changing their attitudes in a period of crisis, because they are more likely to recognize that the old ways have not been adequate to meet their needs. By demonstration, the Red Cross can help teach people better methods of production, saving, and marketing. In their view it is futile to imagine that Peasant Associations will have "felt needs" for irrigation if they have never seen an irrigation system and the results it can produce. The ERCS can help MOA to demonstrate such solutions to peasant farmers.

The DPP seeks to promote more fundamental attitude change: attitudes favoring new and better ways of providing for the family and the community while protecting and improving the environment. On the whole, farmers are very responsive to the suggestions of the DPP project staff. In one case, an ERCS official proposed a gravity irrigation scheme to a local religious leader. The priest commented that the community had never thought of such a possibility. Volunteer work crews immediately began digging a long irrigation trench for which the Red Cross has provided pipes.

Within the first year of DPP operations, some participants already recognized the potential value of improved farm practices. One farmer has asked permission to set up his own nursery to grow trees for the community, and at least ten farmers who participated in terracing activities under the DPP have started terracing on their own. Some individual farmers have decided to use fertilizer on their gardens.

Social/Organizational Capacities and Vulnerabilities

Red Cross activities in Wollo sought to strengthen the organizational capacities of the Ministries of Agriculture and Health, the ERCS, and the Peasant Associations. Of these, the clearest impact has been on the ERCS.

An important element of the ERCS rehabilitation and DPP programs was to build its institutional presence in Wollo. By strengthening its organization (increasing membership, program activities, links with other

16. Dessalegn Rahmato, p. 255.

organizations, leadership within the province and communities), the ERCS increases its potential effectiveness in crisis intervention. The ERCS development work is an integral part of this process. As a result of its rehabilitation and DPP work, the ERCS operates the largest NGO development program in the area.

The DPP is integrated into the MOA and MOH development programs; the goods and services provided thereby strengthen those agencies. Besides material assistance, the DPP has promoted communication and cooperation between the MOA and MOH, with increasing success.

The ERCS hopes to promote the crisis and economic development capacities of Peasant Associations, but will have to proceed carefully in a domain where the government has interests (i.e., creating Red Cross youth corps could be seen as competing with political youth organizations).

The Ethiopian Red Cross, in contrast to most externally-based non-governmental organizations, relies heavily on Ethiopians to manage programs. A small number of International League and ICRC personnel did help plan and execute ERCS relief activities along with many Ethiopian staff. The rehabilitation program for Wollo engaged only one expatriate, as League counterpart to the Ethiopian project coordinator.

Ethiopians manage and implement the daily operations of the DPP. Three full-time monitors, each representing a donor (the Nordic, German, and Japanese Red Cross Societies), three technical staff, and short-term contractors who carry out planning studies are the only expatriates involved. The MOA (and MOH) can implement the DPP with minimal outside technical expertise but with significant external supply and capital inputs.

V. DILEMMAS AND LESSONS FOR FUTURE PROGRAM DESIGN

Phases for Long-Term Development

The ERCS recognized, from the beginning, that the problems in Wollo were long-term. This was not a drought with a short-term cause or short-term solutions. Many programs in Ethiopia in this period had the classical program phases of relief, rehabilitation, and, usually much later, a "return" to development efforts. The ERCS program was distinct, in that the relief, rehabilitation and disaster prevention projects were integrated. In certain respects, each project built on the previous one and the projects even overlapped for a time. The program offers a viable model for linking emergency relief with development.

Local Participation

NGOs widely accept the notion that local participation is essential to establish "ownership" of the projects in which they are involved and thereby increase the likelihood that project results will be sustainable. It is assumed that project decisions made democratically are in every case preferable to those made autocratically.

In the early stages, decisions in the ERCS projects were made top-down, with the rationale that the people of Ambassel and Kalu did not know how to solve their problems and could not envisage solutions they had not seen. This approach reflected the hierarchical traditions of Ethiopian society. The dilemma for NGOs is whether, in such circumstances, to push for more participatory approaches, or to embrace an autocratic approach which is culturally accepted. The top-down system may achieve greater popular support in the long run than an outsiders' model which calls for grass-roots participation at every stage of project planning and implementation.

While the ERCS did not engage in wide-scale consultation with project recipients and participants, it did take local realities into account for the DPP by means of land and socio-economic surveys, by consulting appropriate ministry and administration officials and by discussions with community leaders (heads of Peasant Associations, religious and other traditional leaders). Other community members were involved only as project recipients and as laborers. In later stages of the project, once project participants recovered from the dislocations of the famine, ERCS undertook a number of steps to engage community members more fully in project decisions. Starting in 1987, workshops with community members also involved them in participatory monitoring and evaluation.

Institution Building

The experience of the Red Cross was to establish different relationships with government agencies, depending on the nature of the assistance provided, from fairly minimal association in the relief project to complete integration into government services in the case of the DPP.

The Red Cross ran its relief operations with considerable autonomy. It set up the Bati shelter and closed it when the crisis had passed; the facilities built for the emergency remain with the Red Cross and are being used for development work by the DPP. Although the Red Cross initiated the operation, it obtained the cooperation of the Ministry of Health.

Rehabilitation activities were coordinated with the Ministry of Agriculture from the outset as some farm supplies were obtained through government sources. The need for cooperation was one reason for delays in project implementation.

The DPP represents a much greater degree of collaboration between the Red Cross and the ministries as ultimate responsibility for the project lies with the ministries rather than the Red Cross. The progression in the three projects toward ever greater cooperation with government agencies reflects the choice of the Red Cross as well as the possibilities for institution building of government services that the different situations presented.

During the crisis, the Red Cross already had enormous responsibilities without adding others. When the crisis had passed, it explored possibilities for improving its early-warning capacity and for integrating its access to information at Peasant Association and sub-district levels to the RRC's early-warning capability whereby information is gathered at district and higher administrative levels.

Building the NGO

The Red Cross experience in Ethiopia is an interesting example of institution building. The famine proved to be an opportunity for furthering the international Red Cross movement. Because of the large-scale emergency assistance in 1984-86, the Red Cross became a widely recognized symbol in Ethiopia.

Although the League and the International Committee of the Red Cross (ICRC) were instrumental in this period, the ERCS was the principal beneficiary. Relations between the Ethiopian Government and the ICRC, in particular, were sometimes strained, and the position of the League and of ICRC in Ethiopia has been difficult. By contrast, the ERCS benefitted from public recognition of the Red Cross. According to ERCS records, total membership of ERCS rose from fewer than 100,000 before 1985 to 300,000 at the end of that year, and reached 750,000 by 1987.[17]

As the most recent membership figures suggest, the strength of the ERCS is not dependent on relief activities. If outside assistance were entirely withdrawn, the ERCS program would suffer tremendously, but the organization would likely survive. Ethiopians provide organizational direction and human power. The pool of skills acquired in the relief and recovery activities is substantial.

The institutional development of the ERCS is all the more important because ERCS is an indigenous NGO in a country where there are few NGOs, particularly secular agencies. Moreover, by making the link between emergency assistance and long-term development, the Red Cross activities have generated Red Cross volunteers and members who can help meet the vast need for emergency assistance, whatever the crisis. They spread the message that disaster can be prevented, thereby promoting attitude change that will promote long-term development. The

17. Elizabeth Kassaye, p. 30.

organizational development of the ERCS increases Ethiopia's capacity to cope with future crises.

Training

Many NGOs report that they see few possibilities for training during relief activities, and "ag pack" rehabilitation projects (oxen, seeds, and tools) rarely have training objectives. Urgency, lack of time and resources, and the temporary nature of the assistance are among the reasons given.

The ERCS projects demonstrated the usefulness of training in all phases of activity. Training of Red Cross volunteers, in fact, served to link the emergency efforts to the later prevention projects, since the training material was developmental in its orientation. Volunteers who received the training were carried from one project phase to the next.

Relationship Between Donors and Implementing Agency

The ERCS programs in Kalu and Ambassel provide a creative model for the relationship between outside donor agencies and an implementing agency. The program clearly belonged to the Ethiopian Red Cross. However, it was also of great interest to the Red Cross Societies of Sweden, Germany, and Japan which provided the funds, partly because this was a new kind of program for the international Red Cross movement. The donor agencies provided monitors and some technical assistance, while the ERCS took responsibility for management and carried out the day-to-day implementation of the program. The monitors from the donor Societies freed Ethiopian staff from the burden of writing extensive reports to donors, while the interested Societies were able to participate in the evolution of the program.

APPENDIX : Upper Mille and Cheleka Catchments Disaster Prevention Program Activity Goals (summary)

1. Community Water Resources Development: increased water supplies through: a) providing spring protection in all Peasant Associations, 100 shallow wells; b) constructing fifteen earth dams, five subsurface dams, and fifteen ponds; and c) building five river diversion structures for irrigation, thirty irrigation systems, and eighteen rainfall stations;

2. *Agriculture*: improve crop production through distribution of improved seeds, pesticides, fertilizers, plow points, and hand tools along with intensive extension work (i.e., extension of rehabilitation program);

3. *Agriculture*: improve agricultural practices by training one percent of farmers who will spread the new techniques of improved tillage, strip cropping, contour cultivation, use of fertilizers and pesticides, small scale irrigation, etc.;

4. Home Economics: train about 240 housewives in better food use;

5. *Food Storage*: construct one store per development agent for food seed grain to initiate a seed bank and one per DA for storage of pesticides, fertilizers, and implements;

6. *Land-Use Management*: develop plan based on detailed data;

7. *Reforestation*: produce forty million seedlings, prepare sites and plant through food-for-work and cash-for-work, and manage planted areas;

8. *Cash Savings*: train two service cooperatives in planning, budgeting, and accounting;

9. *Marketing*: train two service cooperatives in marketing standards and road improvement;

10. *Community health*: train a community health agent and a traditional birth attendant in each PA, create clinics, provide materials for MCH and family planning and for clinics, and construct ten model latrines per PA and waste disposal pits, supervise and monitor community health activities;

11. *Animal Resources*: provide improved livestock, establishe two veterinary clinics, provide improved animal feed, construct cattle dips, and control grazing, undertake pilot poultry production, provide materials for improved fish production, and develop beekeeping.

Source: *Ethiopia Upper Mille and Cheleka Catchments Disaster Prevention Program: UMCC-DPP*, Volume 1, Project Plans and Budget, Ethiopian Red Cross Society, 1986.

REFERENCES

INTERVIEWS

Ethiopian Red Cross:

Abraham Assefa, Volunteer

Bekele Galeta, Director General

Costantinos Berhe, Head of Disaster Relief and Prevention Department

Getahun Tabege, Head, UMCC Disaster Prevention Program Monitoring Team

Getachew, Wollo Relief Administrator, Youth Coordinator

Mehary Maasho, Chairman, Wollo Board

Messele Ambaye, Wollo Branch Secretary

Marliese Rothweiler-Spohn, DPP Fodder Specialist

Teferra Shiawl, Former Director General

Yabowork Haile, Project Coordinator, Wollo Rehabilitation Project (Phase II)

League of Red Cross and Red Crescent Societies:

Harold Drivon, Wollo Rehabilitation Project Coordinator

Sven Lampell, Chief Delegate

Robert Schneider, Development Delegate

Red Cross Sister Societies:

Gunther Rusch, DPP Monitoring Team

Eiichi Sadamatsu, DPP Monitoring Team

Helmut Spohn, DPP Agronomist

Government of Ethiopia:

Birhane Gizaw, Head of Early Warning and Planning, Relief and Rehabilitation Commission

Hailu Meche, Director, Planning and Programming Department, Ministry of Health

Michael Miller, Head of Projects Center, Relief and Rehabilitation Commission

Dr. Solomon, Head of Planning Commission, Northeast Zone

Taye Gurmu, Deputy Commissioner, Relief and Rehabilitation Commission

Tegegne Desta, Head of Zonal Planning Office, Northeast Zone, Ministry of Agriculture

Tesfaye Neegusse, Head of Agricultural Development Department, Northeastern Zonal Office, Ministry of Agriculture

United Nations:

Wendy Bjoerk, UNICEF

Thomas Franklin, NGO Liaison, Office of the Assistant Secretary-General for Emergency Operations in Ethiopia

Dag Hareide, NGO Liaison, Emergency Planning Preparedness Group

Thomas F. Grannell, Project Officer, World Food Program

WRITTEN SOURCES

Almaz Tesgaye, "Report on Emergency Supply of Agricultural Inputs for the Rehabilitation of Disaster (Famine) Victims: ERCS/LLORCS Minimum Package Programme," October 1985.

Chambers, Robert *et al*, "An Independent Review and Evaluation of the Africa Drought Relief Operations 1984-86 of the League of Red Cross and Red Crescent Societies." IDS Report No. 1, Institute of Development Studies, University of Sussex, September 1986.

Dessalegn Rahmato, *Famine and Survival Strategies, A Case Study from Northeast Ethiopia*, Food and Famine Monograph Series No. 1, Institute of Development Research, Addis Ababa University, May 1987.

Drivon, Harold, "Wollo Rehabilitation Project." Reports, 1986.

Ethiopian Red Cross Society, *Upper Mille and Cheleka Catchment Disaster Prevention Program*, Vol. I, Project Plans and Budget, 1986.

Hagman, Gunnar, *Prevention Better Than Cure. Report on Human and Environmental Disasters in the Third World*, Swedish Red Cross, Geneva, 1984.

Kassaye, Elizabeth, *From Disaster Relief to Development, The Experience of the Ethiopian Red Cross*, Working Paper 12:87, Institut Henri-Dunant, Geneva, 1987.

DPP Monitoring Team, UMCC-DPP Monthly and annual reports, 1986-87.

Relief and Rehabilitation Commission. *The Challenges of Drought: Ethiopia's Decade of Struggle in Relief and Rehabilitation*, Addis Ababa, 1985.

"Wollo Rehabilitation Project, Program Implementation Plan," 1986.

ACKNOWLEDGMENTS

This case was written in January, 1988. In gathering information for this case, Ann Qualman held discussions at the Ethiopian and League of Red Cross offices in Addis Ababa in June 1986 and in February and May 1987, and visited project sites in Wollo. We are grateful to the Ethiopian Red Cross, in particular to Bekele Galeta, Costantinos Berhe, and Yabowork Haile for their interest in the IRDP, and for their information and logistical support, as well as to the many who provided interviews for this study. Information and encouragement from Gunnar Hagman of the Henry-Dunant Institute is also greatly appreciated.

Chapter 10

ETHIOPIA EMERGENCY PROGRAM
Yifat na Timuga, Ethiopia

Project Implementing Agency:
Save the Children Federation

Case Writer:
Peter J. Woodrow

I. INTRODUCTION

This case describes the experience of Save the Children Federation (USA) in the district of Yifat na Timuga in the Shoa Province of Ethiopia. In late 1984 in response to the drought and subsequent famine, SCF provided food and health services to the entire population of the district.

The project is of particular interest because its design was based on several assumptions that are quite different from those of many of the other agencies that undertook food distribution in Ethiopia during this period. Some of the interesting aspects of the program which will be described below include: 1) SCF's assumption that the human resources for dealing with the drought and implementing its program existed in Ethiopia; 2) an aggressive public health campaign closely tied to food distribution; 3) a commitment to deliver food directly to villages, or as close as possible, even in extremely rough terrain. Farmers, idled by the drought, were mobilized to build 450 kilometers of roads, providing vehicle access to villages which had been entirely isolated previously. These roads represent a permanent improvement in infrastructure. SCF also started the program with a commitment to work in the area over an extended period of time, and planned the emergency work with this commitment in mind.

ETHIOPIA

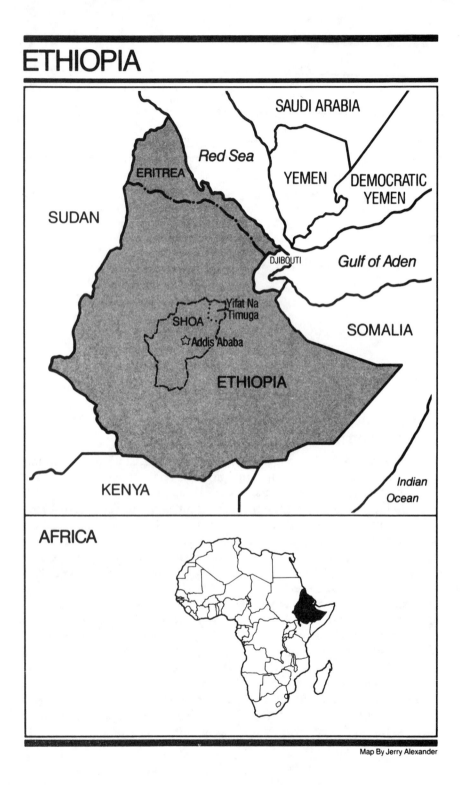

SAUDI ARABIA

Red Sea

ERITREA

YEMEN   DEMOCRATIC
         YEMEN

SUDAN

DJIBOUTI   Gulf of Aden

Yifat Na
Timuga
SHOA

Addis Ababa   SOMALIA

ETHIOPIA

Indian
Ocean

KENYA

AFRICA

Map By Jerry Alexander

II. DESCRIPTION OF PROJECT CONTEXT

Ethiopia is one of the largest, most densely populated, and poorest nations of Africa, with a population of forty-two million people and annual per capita income below $150 per year. Ethiopia has three major, and numerous smaller, ethnic and language groups. More than 85 percent of the population is engaged in agriculture. The country is extremely diverse geographically, ranging from tropical rain forest to high, rugged plateau and mountains rising to 10,000 feet, to flat arid semi-desert areas, and the Rift Valley which slices through the middle of the country. Since the early 1960s the nation has been fighting ethnic/nationalist insurgencies, principally with the Eritrean secession movement in the North, but also with military insurgencies among Somalis, Oromos, and Tigrayans.

Origins of the 1983-85 Drought

The whole Horn of Africa region, at the eastern extremity of the Sahel, is subject to periodic drought. Ethiopian history has recorded regular periods of drought and famine going back for centuries. A severe famine in 1972-74, in which the government response was highly criticized, finally precipitated the ousting of Emperor Haile Selassie and the establishment of a military regime adhering to Marxist-Leninist policies which rules Ethiopia today.

Controversy has surrounded the drought and attendant famine of the 1983-85 period, particularly its prediction. As early as mid-1983, Ethiopian government and NGO reports showed signs of a massive problem. The rains in 1983 were quite poor throughout the region, and crop yields suffered. In the spring of 1984, the Ethiopian government's Early Warning System, part of the responsibility of the Relief and Rehabilitation Commission (RRC), predicted that over six million Ethiopians were at risk of famine by that fall. RRC called a meeting of NGOs, embassy representatives, international agencies, and bilateral donors to alert them to this danger. By the fall of 1984 the situation in the countryside was as bad as predicted. Large-scale American efforts to meet the crisis were not undertaken until after a dramatic BBC film was shown on American television in late October, alerting the general public to the situation, and pushing private agencies and the U.S. government into action. The Canadian and European communities were also slow to respond.

Yifat na Timuga District, Shoa Province

The Shoa province of Ethiopia occupies the whole center of the country, surrounding Addis Ababa, the capital. Yifat na Timuga district is in the extreme northeast corner of the region, about 250 km from Addis Ababa, on the border of the region of Wollo. The area of about 8,000 square kilometers is the home of about 350,000 people, including 50 percent Amhara farmers living in the highlands and central valley, 35 percent semi-pastoral Oromo in the central valley area and to the east, and 15 percent nomadic Afar living in semi-arid pasture lands in the eastern portion of the district. One survey of vulnerability to famine in Ethiopia classifies Yifat na Timuga as both famine-prone and of poor environmental quality, though the soils in the farming areas are relatively fertile and erosion is not so severe as in other areas of Ethiopia. The people usually live at a moderate level of subsistence and development in the Ethiopian context.[1]

A major road runs north to south in the valley through the middle of the district. To the west of the road, the steep and rugged mountains rise to heights above 3,000 meters (about 10,000 feet). The people living in the remote areas of the mountains must walk several days to reach the road. Until recently there were few secondary roads connecting the countryside to the main road. The Afar to the east have had little government contact. They are an independent-minded people who defend their independence with the arms they carry everywhere. They have seen their isolation as an advantage, rather than a deprivation or vulnerability. The district is further divided into six sub-districts and 175 villages. Each village is organized into a Peasant Association (PA), the basic unit of the Ethiopian regime. This governmental structure was well established in Yifat na Timuga by 1984 and constituted a strong force for mobilizing peoples' energies. Unlike areas to the north, there is no insurgency in Yifat.

Analysis of Capacities and Vulnerabilities

Physical/Material

Without question, periodic drought poses the most serious threat to stable agricultural production for the vast majority of people in Yifat. This is true both for those who depend on farming for family livelihood and for pastoralists who depend on livestock. Semi-nomadic peoples who farm and keep animals also find their fortune linked to weather. In the 1983-85 drought, many herders lost almost all of their animals. For herders, recovery does not come with the return of the rains, as restocking herds can take years.

Even when there is no drought, there is a chronic shortage of water in some parts of the district, particularly in the semi-arid areas to the east. In these areas, there is a particular need for improved water sources for

1. Mesfin Wolde Mariam, *Rural Vulnerability to Famine in Ethiopia: 1958-77*, Vikas Publishing House, New Delhi, 1984, pp. 156-166.

livestock. And across the province, there is a need for clean water, free from water-borne diseases.

Compounding the problem of drought is the ongoing process of soil degradation and erosion. Much of the farmland in Ethiopia, including that of Yifat, has been farmed for centuries without fallowing or replenishing nutrients in the soil. Under previous feudal agricultural systems, landlords taxed the produce from the land without regard for its conservation. Farm land is depleted not only through intensive cropping, but also from water and wind erosion. Many farmers use land that is on steep unterraced slopes, where both rains and winds, unabated by trees or grasses, carry away fertile soil. Steadily increasing population pressure adds to the decreasing ability to feed families on the small plots held by most peasant farmers.

A further difficulty in the area of agriculture is the lack of crop diversity. Tree-based crops, vegetable crops, and more nutritious foods are not in widespread use. In addition, the prevalent varieties of staple crops are not always the most drought-resistant available.

Farmers in the district also face government marketing and pricing policies which do not provide strong incentives for growing anything beyond what they need to survive.

There is little basic infrastructure in many rural communities in Yifat. As mentioned above, large numbers of people are completely isolated, lacking roads, electricity, or any means of communicating with government or other potential sources of assistance or information. Many villages are on dirt tracks over which donkeys or other animals can carry goods and produce, but a trip to town takes several days. Frequently, facilities for grain storage, health services, and education are also lacking.

In famine most people do not actually starve to death; they succumb to diseases to which they become prone as they are weakened by hunger. There are only two full health clinics in the district, both located in larger towns on the main road. For most of the population, these are a two- to three-day journey away. Smaller health stations have been established under the Ministry of Health in each sub-district. These are staffed by a health assistant who usually has a high school diploma and a certificate degree in health care. The Ministry has plans to place, in each village, a community health aide (a literate person who is given three months training in identification and treatment of key illnesses plus preventive measures). By 1984 only a few villages had community health aides. The result was that there was little capacity in most rural communities for educating about, preventing, or treating the major health threats such as malaria, cholera, acute diarrhea, or childhood diseases.

Social/Organizational

The people of Yifat na Timuga have strong social organization. The Peasant Associations exist in all villages, and are the basic political and social unit for the socialist regime. These Peasant Associations are able to secure the participation of a large percentage of rural people in all kinds of activities, from discussions of the new constitution to work on community projects. If the leadership is convinced of the value of a particular activity, they can ensure that local people will participate in it. While the Peasant Associations are relatively new to rural Ethiopia, having been introduced only since the 1974 Revolution, this government/party structure has permeated the entire society, with the possible exception of Afar areas.

There are, however, potential areas of organizational and social vulnerability in Yifat. The same ethnic groups who are in open and violent conflict also live in Yifat na Timuga. While groups are not in serious conflict at present in Yifat, the difficulties in other areas could spill over.

The isolation of the rural areas was also seen to be a potential problem. While the isolation may have been merely physical, it had social consequences. The degree to which isolated groups felt committed to the national program or connected to local government administration had an effect on the unity of the district and on responses to crisis events such as drought. An aspect of government policy that was having a profound effect on local people was the controversial villagization program. Through it, people were moved from their ancient and isolated highland villages to new, planned communities that were more accessible to future government programs of health, literacy, electrification, etc. Villagization was welcomed by some people, particularly those in less sustainable locations. It has been questioned by others who do not want to leave their ancestral homes, regardless of the potential benefits. These people also recognized the hazards of moving, such as increased exposure to malaria in lowland areas. For certain farmers it also meant several hours of walking back to their fields.

Psychological/Motivational
Ethiopians are known to be proud. Despite the conflicts and problems of the past fifteen years and the extremities of drought and famine, this has not changed. There are examples (which will be described in greater detail below in the project section) of acts of initiative and responses on the part of rural peasants in Yifat that indicate strong motivation and spiritual reserves.

But, as in the area of social organization, there are factors which have potential for difficulties in the motivational realm. The villagization program has reduced cooperation among local people in some areas. Some villagers hesitate to participate in long-term projects, because they do not know how long they will be in their present location. Why plant a tree in your field if you may not be there in five years when it begins to bear fruit?

III. PROJECT HISTORY AND DEVELOPMENT

Program Initiation

Although its partners in the Save the Children Alliance, Redd Barna (Norwegian Save the Children) and Save the Children Fund (UK) had been working in Ethiopia for several years, Save the Children Federation (USA) had not worked in Ethiopia before 1984. In order to plan its response to the Ethiopia emergency, SCF sent a delegation to Addis Ababa in November 1984 to explore program options. Included in the delegation were SCF's vice president for program, the director of primary health care, and the director of their field office in Tunisia; the latter had experience in Ethiopia and spoke fluent Amharic.

The SCF delegation consulted with their Alliance partners and with other NGOs working in Ethiopia, but their primary contact was with the Relief and Rehabilitation Commission (RRC), the Ethiopian government agency charged with coordinating the response to the emergency. The RRC had been established in 1974 in the wake of the 1972-74 famine. In the years since, the RRC had developed its ability to predict crop failures and relief needs among the population. It was the RRC which had in the spring of 1984 predicted that by the fall there would be six million Ethiopians at risk of famine.

The RRC suggested several areas of the country where SCF might work and invited the delegation to visit these areas. After the visits, the SCF team chose to work in the Yifat na Timuga District. The following were the criteria used in making that choice:

1. The area was desperately in need, as documented by RRC, and as witnessed by the SCF delegation. More than 60 percent of the population was in immediate need of relief assistance, according to RRC surveys.

2. Few other agencies were operating there.

3. It was in a secure area, therefore allowing more opportunity for SCF's ultimate goal of community-based development and closer contact with the people in their own communities.

4. It was not completely depleted ecologically, and therefore there was hope that SCF could help rehabilitate the area (unlike some northern areas where soil degradation had rendered rehabilitation unlikely).[2]

The SCF report described the conditions in the area at the time of their decision to work there:

2. Ethiopia Field Office, SCF, Draft Proposal for Lessons Learned, 1986.

rains came. The survival of their families depended on their access to relief goods. Crews of 500 or more people were organized by the Peasant Associations (not SCF) to build roads, using hand tools and the plentiful rock of the area. SCF provided a technician with road building experience to advise village crews on grading and routing. By December 1985, approximately 450 kilometers of feeder roads had been constructed.

Even with these remarkable roads, there were villages that could not be reached. The villages solved this problem by organizing donkey trains to carry grain into these remote areas. Again, this ability was organized at the village level by the Peasant Association leaders. SCF estimates that at one time there were as many as 1,500 donkeys in service moving relief goods. (Unlike many other domestic animals, donkeys did not suffer as badly from the drought, and were not slaughtered for food). In contrast, other relief agencies were spending thousands of dollars an hour to deliver goods by helicopter in areas not far away.

In the second year of the program, most communities in the district were beginning to recover their independent ability to produce food. However, the pastoral Afar nomad communities still needed aid because their economic self-reliance depended on the longer-term process of restocking their herds. SCF was ready to continue to supply them with food. Previously, food distribution for the Afar had taken place in territory quite close to other ethnic groups who now no longer needed food rations. This posed a delicate problem—how to continue to supply the Afar with crucial food while their territory was still inaccessible and the drop-off points were in the areas of the Afar's traditional rival tribes.

The SCF Project Manager in Yifat took the bold step of calling together a group of Afar leaders and discussing the problem with them. After much heated discussion, the Afar decided that there was no reason that they could not build roads just as other communities had done. The result was that the nomadic Afar constructed seventy kilometers of roads reaching deep into their territory to reach the small villages where the old and infirm traditionally live. SCF trucks started delivering relief grain into areas where others, including government officials, had never been.

In addition to building roads and providing donkey trains, community members loaded and unloaded trucks, offered warehousing space in homes or schools, and provided guards and storekeepers at the village level. No one was paid for these activities. The importance of the close cooperation between SCF and local leaders, and the wisdom of SCF in relying on local capacity, were especially notable in these circumstances where many agencies were assuming that Ethiopian "victims" were destitute and unable to solve problems or help themselves.

Geographic Coverage: The SCF program started slowly, due to delays in the arrival of trucks and relief grain as explained above. However, by

Month 1985	Trucks Available	Villages Served	Food Delivered	RRAs	Crude Death Rate
Feb	1*	4	139 MT	67	98.5/1000
Mar	3*	11	299 MT	138	"
Apr	2*	13	208 MT	"	"
May	2**	46	877 MT	"	"
June	10	46	711 MT	"	"
July	16	88	2,247 MT	360	27.5/1000
Aug	20	118	3,047 MT	364	17.9/1000
Sept	20	158	3,341 MT	"	10.4/1000
Oct	20	155	5,217 MT	"	10.2/1000
Nov	20	158	2,535 MT	366	10.8/1000
Dec	20	168	5,225 MT	"	10.?/1000

* Borrowed trucks
** With assistance of 34 RRC trucks.

July 1985, all of the program components were in place and the numbers of people served increased swiftly. The following chart summarizes the number of villages served, the number of trucks available, the amount of food provided, the number of RRAs working on enrollment, and the crude death rate at intervals over the life of the program.

Primary Health Care

The SCF health program was designed to address the most frequent causes of death. Coupled with the provision of food, an aggressive health program could assist the recovery of the people of the district. According to the priorities set out by SCF in consultation with local health officials, the program aimed to reduce or eliminate death due to diarrhea, measles, and malaria. In addition, the program also dealt with vitamin A deficiency. The essential elements of the health program were:

1. Training of mothers in *Oral Rehydration Therapy* using methods that could be replicated in the typical rural household. SCF estimated that during 1985, 60,000 women were taught a simple ORT method using cereal and salt. In its early surveys, prior to its food distribution, SCF found that acute diarrhea was cited as

the cause of death in 43 percent of cases. Studies show that ORT can reduce deaths from diarrhea by fifty percent.

2. *Immunization* of young children and pregnant women. During 1985, 14,460 children and women were vaccinated against six of the most common childhood diseases, and an additional 6,062 were vaccinated in 1986. By 1986 measles had all but disappeared in Yifat na Timuga. SCF provided supplies, equipment for storage and transport of vaccines (cold chain), transportation, and per diem incentive pay for Ministry of Health staff who performed the immunizations at food distribution sites.

3. Distribution of *vitamin A*. While the fatal consequences of vitamin A deficiency have not been established, there is firm evidence that it can lead to blindness.

4. Provision of *chloroquine* to lower altitude areas and villages near swamps for malaria treatment. Even a single dose of chloroquine can prevent death from malaria. SCF helped to establish a rotating fund in vulnerable villages. Villagers paid a nominal fee for the drug and the village was able to replenish its supply from the MOH stores.

During the emergency famine period, SCF also began a program on sanitation, hygiene, and water protection. A special team (of former RRAs) was put together to provide health education in villages. They focussed on diarrhea disease vectors (hand-washing, use of latrines, water protection) and worked with villagers to protect springs, to dig wells and provide pumps, and to build ventilated improved pit (VIP) latrines.

Staffing
Throughout the emergency program, SCF operated with four expatriate staff, two of whom were stationed in Yifat na Timuga. The project manager, in charge of all aspects of the field operations and staffing, was an Ethiopian with considerable experience in development work with NGOs. The two expatriates served under this man, one as director of food and logistics and the other as primary health care director (a medical doctor). At its peak, SCF had 568 staff, including RRAs, storekeepers, drivers, mechanics, district supervisors, health trainers, and a special team working on water and sanitation. In addition to the field staff in Yifat na Timuga, there was a small staff in Addis Ababa which included a field office director and an assistant who were both expatriates.

Subsequent Program Directions
In the year after the worst of the emergency passed, SCF continued food distributions in areas of need. Staff were reduced to about 195, of whom eighty were drivers by January, 1987. At the same time, the program staff have developed a long-term development program in Yifat. Based on

these relationships with local officials and with the population at large, this program development follows the SCF "C-BIRD" process. Designated communities identify their most pressing problems and SCF works with the community to devise solutions based on the ideas, decisions, labor and material provided by the community. SCF, for its part, provides technical and/or material inputs as needed.

In Yifat, SCF worked with local officials to identify six "impact areas," villages targeted for intensive work by SCF. The programs to be developed in those areas included primary health care, agricultural development, water resource development, and the introduction of appropriate technology. In addition, in keeping with its traditional concern for children, SCF worked with several homes for orphans that they helped to establish in the district. This involved the usual child sponsorship program in the impact areas. Under this program, children from the community are "sponsored" by individuals or families in the United States. The donations of the sponsors are used to pay for development activities which benefit the entire community.

This follow-up program took on an integrated approach, but the key village link was through the health sector. This was partly because the only person with a particular development focus in each village was the community health aide (CHA). SCF assisted in the training of CHAs, 40 percent of whom were women, particularly emphasizing the practical aspects and setting up a system of monthly seminar/problem identification sessions in each sub-district, along with the health assistants who staff the district health stations. Thus, the CHAs could build stronger supportive relationships with each other and with the MOH staff. Regular in-service training programs for the health assistants and other Ministry of Health staff were also developed and aims to have 300 eventually spread through the 175 villages (with a ratio of 1:1,000 population).

The primary health care program was designed to include a number of facets: training of additional traditional birth attendants, organizing of community health/development committees, collaborating in building health posts in each village, supporting a rotating medical supply system, and establishing two primary health training centers.

In addition to working on health issues, SCF developed a program in agriculture and forestry. The main objectives of this program were to work with village farmers to introduce crop varieties better adapted to local conditions, and to introduce moisture conservation methods and crop diversification (especially vegetables, fruits, and pulses in order to improve nutrition as well). Specific activities that were planned included: supply of seeds and tools; operation of tree nurseries (three already established); experimentation with crops, fertilizers, seed varieties, and irrigation in demonstration fields; experimentation with ponds for water catchment;

work with Afar nomads on experiments with agriculture; and experimentation with small-scale horticulture in river beds and well sites. In addition, SCF continued well digging, pump installation, spring protection and latrine construction.

Capacities/Vulnerabilities Analysis of the SCF Program

Physical/Material

The greatest impact of the SCF program was in the area of reducing physical/material vulnerabilities.

1. The roads that were built (450 kilometers in 1985, another 240 in 1986), if maintained, can be a permanent improvement in infrastructure, providing access by rural communities to services and markets. In the event of future famine, the villages could be more accessible to relief efforts, and less likely to be ignored due to their relative isolation. The creation of infrastructure was particularly striking in the case of the Afar nomads.

2. Each village increased its capacity for storing grains in emergency periods, in some cases by converting buildings to other uses, in others through construction of new facilities.

3. About 60,000 women were trained in the crucial skill of treating their families for the number one killer, diarrhea. This capacity should last in the communities for years, especially if reinforced by follow-up health education and other health care improvements through the CHAs.

4. The immunization program has reached 70 percent of the children in the vulnerable age groups, permanently protecting them against the most common childhood killing diseases. In one year SCF, in cooperation with the local Ministry of Health, reached the 1990 goal for immunization for the entire district.

5. A few communities developed access to safe, clean well water. In other cases, latrines were built or springs protected.

6. Later project interventions in health and agriculture were expected to have an effect on the long-term capacity of the communities to cope with future drought, particularly as people learn strategies for safeguarding their health even when they are weakened by famine. The agricultural programs were also expected to help the people develop strategies to broaden their sources of income and food that are less prone to drought. SCF promotion of terracing and reforestation was intended to retard soil degradation and erosion in the long run.

Social/Organizational

The SCF program has had less impact on social/organizational vulnerabilities and capacities in Yifat na Timuga, partly because this was already an area of relative strength. Perhaps the greatest effect of the program was to reduce the isolation of the remote communities where few government services had been extended in the past.

At a more subtle level, the way the program was organized elicited a level of cooperation among people that had rarely been required in the past. The joint efforts needed to build roads in difficult conditions and to organize donkey trains to bring in food demanded extraordinary efforts on the part of local leaders in the Peasant Associations and positive responses on the part of people.

One result of the food distribution program, particularly its insistence on bringing food to the village level, was that families and communities were kept together and their social structure maintained. In other areas of Ethiopia, where people moved out of their villages to the large feeding camps or to towns, family and community structures were disrupted and, in some cases, destroyed. In these areas, children were abandoned as families were unable to feed them. In Yifat, this was a minor problem. SCF found only eighty orphans, twelve of whom were eventually reunited with their families. The remaining sixty-eight youngsters were living in groups of six in homes in the community run by women who received a small salary.

Psychological/Motivational

SCF staff reported that when they arrived in the district to begin work, many people were desperate and despondent. However, once they saw that they could work together to ensure that some material assistance was available, they responded quickly. Those who were able began, even before SCF arrived with food, to build roads and arrange for storage facilities. The program assumed that there were skills and abilities in the communities, and that the overall effort would benefit by making use of them.

In reference to the road-building activities, an SCF report states:

> Not only did this massive effort make it possible to bring the food closer to the people, it instilled pride and dignity in them. Rather than accepting food as a handout, they could claim it as their due, since they had worked to make it arrive.[5]

In more general terms, the SCF program constantly affirmed that the Ethiopian people and government were competent to deal with the crisis, even if material assistance was required from outside. During the early period of the food distribution program, SCF received assistance from RRC

5.   Ethiopia Field Office, SCF, Draft Proposal for Lessons Learned, p. 10.

to move its food. By maintaining an attitude of respect at every level, SCF reinforced pride and competence among Ethiopians who had contact with the program. SCF has been richly repaid in cooperation and strong relationships with people, both official and non-official. The longer-term prospects for effective development efforts in Yifat na Timuga are directly improved as a result.

IV. DILEMMAS AND LESSONS FOR FUTURE PROJECT DESIGN

The SCF program in Yifat na Timuga was successful in terms of saving lives, achieving some development goals, and setting processes for longer-term development in motion. Some people have suggested that the strong and inspired leadership of the SCF field office director and project manager explains this success. These two men did provide enormous energy, dedication, intelligent strategies and deft handling of delicate situations. But many of the successes of the program can be replicated.

The SCF experience in Yifat na Timuga suggests a number of lessons learned that should be considered in relation to future programming in emergencies.

Dispersed Distribution of Food is Better than Feeding Centers

A salient element of the SCF program in Yifat was the commitment to deliver food as close to each village as possible. Because this approach kept communities and families intact, it enabled people to resume productive work as soon as possible. It also avoided the diseases and the psychological debilitation of feeding centers. In addition, the community activities that were generated (road building, organization of donkey convoys, provision of storage facilities) resulted in long-term infrastructural improvements and a heightened sense of the efficiency of group problem solving and action.

Always Assume and Promote National/Community Capacities

SCF assumed that human resources to be mobilized for handling the famine existed both nationally and at the local level. SCF found ways to support and elicit these capacities by consulting communities, whereas most agencies assumed the people to be totally destitute. They also placed trust and major responsibility in the hands of Ethiopian staff.

Use Few Expatriate Staff

Many other western agencies in Ethiopia brought in large numbers of expatriates to run their programs. They relied on trained health workers such as doctors and nurses to staff feeding centers. Because SCF chose not to set up feeding centers and used a preventive approach to health care, western medical personnel were not needed. Of the 568 field workers in Yifat, only two were expatriates (and an additional two expatriates worked for SCF in Addis Ababa). SCF placed an Ethiopian as project manager in Yifat with the two expatriates working under him. The control of the project was clearly and visibly in Ethiopian hands. Expatriate involvement at a high level provided the project manager with some protection from the inevitable pressures that come with this kind of field position. SCF also hired people with extensive experience in Ethiopia and fluent Amharic as its field office directors (based in Addis Ababa). This improved SCF's ability to operate in the delicate logistical and political climate of Ethiopia during this period.

Health Care is as Important in Famine as Food

Food, while essential, is not the only need in famine programs; health care is crucial for saving lives. However, a curative approach that involves large amounts of imported medicines and medical personnel is not necessary. SCF worked on an aggressive preventive program that attacked the most common causes of death in a population weakened by famine. People were dying from acute diarrhea and malaria, and children were dying from measles and neonatal tetanus, etc. SCF combined community health education with systematic immunizations of vulnerable children to generate an environment more healthy in the long run. SCF staff report that local people, having seen the effects on children who have been immunized, have been "converted" to the wisdom of vaccinations. Mothers are beginning to come voluntarily to health stations, asking for vaccinations for their newborns.

The public health components of the SCF program resulted in follow-up activities in cooperation with the Ministry of Health. CHAs trained during the emergency became key players in long-term health efforts and primary communicators in their communities about sanitation and hygiene issues.

Show Respect for Government Efforts and Agencies

While SCF did not accept all Ethiopian government actions and policies uncritically, it maintained the firm practice of relating to government officials with respect and consulting them regularly. They did not promote separate or parallel organizations. Two government bodies with whom they worked particularly closely were the RRC and the Ministry of Health. At the local level, close cooperation with the leadership of the Peasant Associations was crucial to the success of the program. SCF's recruitment of Ethiopian staff for visible positions of responsibility and leadership within their own organization helped reinforce the reliance on Ethiopian competence.

In an international atmosphere in which the Ethiopian government, and the RRC in particular, were coming under constant criticism, it was tempting to join the chorus. To its credit, SCF instead built solid working relationships based on mutual respect. The cooperation they have enjoyed as a result has provided excellent opportunities for longer-term development work.

Use "Lag Time" in Getting a Program Started

SCF faced enormous logistical difficulties in getting its program in Yifat na Timuga started. It took time for trucks and food to arrive. They used this time well. They found ways to borrow transport and supply small amounts of food to develop their logistic capacity and to establish credibility. SCF had to be careful not to make commitments of food delivery that it could not meet; starting small was important. Local people used this time to build roads that were ready once the trucks and food arrived. The time was well used for developing community initiatives.

Develop Relations with Agencies Already on the Ground

Early in its involvement in Ethiopia, SCF considered using its Save the Children Alliance partners, Redd Barna and SCF/UK, as conduits for its assistance. Although they decided to set up an independent program, they relied heavily on the experience and facilities of those who were already there. Redd Barna, in particular, provided office facilities, staff time, import privileges, and immediate credibility with government officials that otherwise would have taken months to establish. The field office director for SCF was "borrowed" from Redd Barna as well.

The issue here is how agencies that are new to a country enter an emergency situation, always a matter of some difficulty and delicacy. Under conditions of urgency, "newcomer" agencies need information, background knowledge, and political sophistication in order to make appropriate program decisions. Unless they find a way to work closely with agencies or individuals who are already fully informed, their work is hampered and they may make unfortunate mistakes. Mechanisms for interagency coordination seldom exist. New ways for agencies to pool information and experience that will benefit the entire community, and the people they aim to serve, are needed.

REFERENCES

SCF Documents Used:

"Draft Proposal for Lessons Learned," Ethiopia Field Office, 1986

"Ethiopia Background Information" (briefing document for visitors), Ethiopia Field Office, February 1986.

"Funding Proposal: Primary Health Development Training, An Ethiopian Model District Project," Dennis Carlson, M.D., November 1986.

Otten, Mac W., Jr., M.D., Health Coordinator, "Nutritional and Mortality Aspects of the 1985 Famine in North Central Ethiopia," Draft, March 1986.

Other References:

Mesfin Wolde Mariam, *Rural Vulnerability to Famine in Ethiopia :1958-1977*, Vikas Publishing House, New Delhi, 1984.

Relief and Rehabilitation Commission, *The Challenges of Drought: Ethiopia's Decade of Struggle in Relief and Rehabilitation*, Addis Ababa, 1985.

ACKNOWLEDGMENTS

This case was written in March 1987. The author wishes to thank SCF staff who assisted the writing of this case history, either by answering many questions, or by making logistical arrangements: Willet Weeks and Ethan Atkin in Westport; Gerry Salole in Addis Ababa; and Mulatu Tafesse in Yifat na Timuga.

Chapter 11

PROYECTO NUEVA VIDA ARMERO
Armero, Colombia

Project Implementing Agency:
Save the Children Federation

Case Writer:
Ronald S. Parker

I. HISTORICAL AND POLITICAL BACKGROUND

The Armero disaster came at a critical time for the Colombian government. As will be seen below, the government was responding to circumstances outside the disaster zone when it defined policies that affected the agencies that worked within it. Events beginning very early in the history of Colombia could be considered part of the political context in which this disaster should be understood.

Colombia won its independence from Spain in the 1820s. From the very early days of the revolution, however, there was a tradition of violent sectarianism between the followers of Simon Bolivar and one of his generals, Santander. From the rift between these two leaders came the Liberal and Conservative parties. Differences between these two political groups led to seven civil wars before the beginning of the present century. The first thirty years of the 1900s were dominated by the Conservative Party, due to a long period of popularity and electoral triumph.

The Conservative hegemony ended in 1930, and the Liberals came to power, bringing with them major changes in the life of Colombia. The Liberals developed agricultural reform, supported the creation of labor unions, and promoted a modern transportation system and the

COLOMBIA

CARIBBEAN SEA

VENEZUELA

Guayabal
Armero
Nevada
del Ruiz
Lerida
Volcano
Bogata
PACIFIC OCEAN
Ibagué
TOLIMA

COLOMBIA

ECUADOR

BRAZIL

PERU

SOUTH AMERICA

development of heavy industry. These changes threatened the Conservatives who were landholders and based part of their power on the continuance of an agricultural economy (although they also held considerable industrial power). The competition for influence and control between the two parties led to a new period of violence in rural areas including the state of Tolima, where Armero is located.

Following the assassination of the Liberal leader Jorge Gaitan in 1948, an escalating wave of violence swept the entire country until a 1953 coup, when a military group (with the tacit approval of both political parties) seized the government. Over the next five years, the military was able to pacify and disarm the countryside. In 1958, the country returned to civilian control. The two political parties agreed to form a united national front (*Frente Nacional*) which lasted for sixteen years. In an effort to prevent a return to violence, they agreed to alternate control of the presidency over four presidential terms.

During the period of the Frente Nacional, the population became increasingly disenchanted with the prevailing party structure but no *apertura* (opening) was given for the formation of new parties. The influence of the Cuban Revolution in 1959, coupled with the unwillingness of the Conservatives and the Liberals to allow the formation of any other party, led to the emergence of various leftist guerilla groups. Over time, these groups gained increasing public acceptance. Today, guerilla groups control large areas of the country and maintain a strong economic base.

After unsuccessful military attempts to defeat the guerrillas, recent governments have offered other options to them in an attempt to reach peace. The government signed agreements with several of the key guerilla groups in 1984, but by 1985 they claimed the government continued to assassinate their leaders. Just before the Armero disaster, one of the groups, the M-19, occupied the Supreme Court. Some sources say that they wanted to destroy the records of drug-related offenders, others that they wanted to put the government on trial for their alleged betrayal of the agreements and to gain publicity. Whatever their reasoning, the army was brought in. Tanks fired on the court. The Court slowly burned, causing the death of many justices and court officials. The guerrillas also lost many of their leaders. Soon after the Supreme Court battle came the eruption and avalanche that destroyed Armero.

The government's handling of the Supreme Court situation came under strong criticism and created a serious political crisis. The government was just one year away from the next presidential and congressional elections. The government was also disturbed that an absolute majority of Colombians had abstained from voting in the last elections. The magnitude of the Armero catastrophe captured the attention of the nation, giving the government an important political opportunity during an election year.

The Armero eruption shunted the political crisis around the storming of the Supreme Court to the back pages of the newspapers. The Conservative party was keenly aware that the way in which it handled the Armero tragedy would have significant political repercussions. During his last year of power, President Betancourt took personal responsibility for the rehabilitation of the zone. His plan of action included the creation of a new national agency, RESURGIR, which, for the duration of the emergency, outranked the cabinet ministries and formed a part of the executive branch. The president became the chairman of the board of this institution and named the owner of a well-known construction company to manage the program.

Origins of the Disaster

Colombia has eight active volcanoes, three of which are snow-covered. This snow cover is a rare condition for tropical volcanoes. It makes major eruptions particularly hazardous due to the danger of landslides and flooding in addition to the normal risks of lava flow. Armero was totally destroyed twice before by volcano-caused mudslides: in 1595 and 1845. The most recent eruption of Nevado de Ruiz started with limited volcanic activity more than a year before the destruction of the town in 1985. Three months before the tragedy, a Colombian TV news special warned of impending disaster in the area and urged government action. Although the volcano erupts about every forty years, most eruptions cause no damage to the valley below. The fact that the 1845 destruction of Armero is well outside living memory contributed to the residents' unwillingness to consider emergency measures.

Volcanic activity prior to the disaster caused a landslide which blocked the natural flow of water from the snowcap by forming a dam. As the volcanic heat and lava from continuing eruptions melted the snowcap, massive quantities of water, ash, and mud began to accumulate behind the dam. On the night of November 13, a strong eruption increased the volume of mud held back so much that the pressure broke the dam.

Although Civil Defense forces had been placed on the mountain to warn of additional eruptions, no contingency plan had ever been established for the evacuation of Armero. That night, Civil Defense forces blew sirens to warn the inhabitants of the new eruption, but all official sources and radio stations advised the population to remain calm. The public address system of the Catholic Church broadcast the same message. A few people who were either cautious or had somewhere to go left town, but it was a rainy night and most people decided to stay put.

The breaking of the earthen dam made so much noise that villages fifteen miles away heard it snap. The avalanche took well over an hour to reach the town. If the landslide had distributed itself over the hillside, much of the damage would not have occurred. Instead the entire slide went into a narrow canyon which opened up right above Armero. Though the noise was deafening, it was dark and impossible to see what was happening in the canyon. When the immense wall of mud reached Armero, it slowly swept away all objects in its path including virtually every building in the town. The avalanche finally deposited the shreds of the town miles from the former city center. The mudslide killed 23,000 people and left several thousand wounded.

In view of the destruction of Armero by Nevado de Ruiz twice previously, why was the town rebuilt on the same dangerous site three times? The explanation seems to be economic expediency. The fertility of the soil provides a livelihood which cannot be obtained elsewhere. After agricultural soil is covered with a thick layer of volcanic ash, it takes several years before it will produce a crop, but when organic material returns to the soil it becomes extremely fertile and capable of producing greater yields than before.

This leads to the unpleasant thought that the world may yet see another Armero disaster. At present, none of the survivors are considering returning to Armero to live, but already a few farmers are cultivating usable land at the edges of the avalanche and the construction of new homes and a town will probably follow in time. The Colombian government has proposed creating a memorial park to the victims of Armero for the purpose of reminding posterity of the vulnerability of the valley. Unfortunately, no progress has been made on this front, and the passage of time increases the likelihood that the government will spend its resources on new priorities. Many survivors still own legal title to land in Armero. As it increases in value, they will want to make some use of this asset.

Description of the Project Area

The city of Armero was located in the northern end of the state (*departamento*) of Tolima. Geographically, it is in the center of Colombia. It can be reached by car in five hours from Bogota, and it is an hour and a half drive from the state capital, Ubaque. Formerly, Armero was the county seat (*cabecera municipal*), but following its disappearance, Guayabal has been designated to serve this administrative function.

Armero was located at the bottom of the Nevado de Ruiz volcano at the source of the Lagunilla River. Armero was the center of an immensely rich agricultural area, one of several breadbaskets which supplied the rest of the country. A number of large haciendas in the valley employed day laborers from Armero. Many small farmers in the *cordillera* above the valley produced coffee and traditional foods (yucca, plantain, other vegetables) for the weekly market. As a consequence of vast agricultural production emanating from the area, many large agribusinesses had their offices, warehouses, and silos located in the town or on the roads leading to it. These enterprises provided employment for thousands of people in the region. In addition, there was a large migrant population which worked half the year in the fields of Armero, and the other half on the farms of the north coast.

The city was a market center for many of the surrounding villages, and about seventeen of these towns could only be reached by roads that passed through Armero. Farmers living in the rural areas surrounding Armero brought their produce to sell there. Many more rural villagers came to Armero to purchase groceries and other supplies to carry back home again. A train service to Armero, which enabled the area to export its products to Bogota and Medellin, always an uncertain service, had yet to be restored a year and a half after the disaster. Many other agricultural services were only available in Armero, such as four crop-dusting enterprises and several airfields.

Because fertile fields surrounding the town were planted in cotton, the town gained the nickname of the "White City." Aside from cotton, the area was a major producer of rice, sorghum, soy beans, and other cereal grains. Coffee grown in the mountains around Armero was processed in the town. Several national federations of producers of these products had main offices or administrative centers in the area. Agriculturally, the Armero region produced the highest per-hectare yields in the country in sorghum and peanuts. It was the center for the economic infrastructure of the region. A branch of the University of Tolima and high schools which served many surrounding towns were located there. Eight banks that made agricultural and business loans to the region, telecommunications facilities, and the offices of the civil service and courts were all found in Armero. It was also a recreational center; there was even a country club for the local elite.

Capacities and Vulnerabilities of Project Area

Armero was a prosperous town located in a relatively developed country. Until the November 13, 1985 mudslide swept it away, an outside observer might have been impressed with the capacities of the town without noticing its principal vulnerability. Physically, the population was well-housed and had ample food and clothing. Medical care was generally available and there was no shortage of paid work.

For its more prosperous citizens, Armero had well-developed social organizations. The larger businesses and trade groups had strong associations, including credit unions and cooperatives for marketing and agricultural services. However, Armero was noted for having only weak church organizations and no active neighborhood-based groups, although political parties were quite active. The organizations that did exist in the town did not, however, touch the poor or the marginalized population—the very people who later survived the mudslide.

In terms of attitudes, the *Armeritas* (citizens of Armero) tended to consider themselves somewhat superior to those in neighboring areas. The town took pride in its prosperity and cosmopolitan attractions. The dominant philosophy was that economic success was the natural outcome of combining hard work with a sound idea. This attitude seems to prevail among the survivors. The area had a strong tradition of individualism and reluctance to work cooperatively.

Effects of the Eruption/Landslide

In 1987, an observer looking down into the valley of Armero would not see one building. The only impact from the passing of the two years since the mudslide was the presence of hundreds of tiny white crosses placed where survivors estimated their family members died.

The missing buildings are not buried under the mud. Instead, it appears as though heavy machinery came and bulldozed away the town, and then spread two feet of sandy grey soil very evenly over the valley floor. You can stand in the former village site and find tile and brick floors exposed here and there. From the mountains it appears as though thirty percent of the land visible in an enormous semicircle is covered with grey, and not a weed or blade of grass is growing yet, with the exception of the very few trees which survived and are in leaf.

The disaster introduced a devastating complex of new vulnerabilities. In a sense, the townspeople had gained control of their basic necessities only to find that the mudslide swept it all away. The disaster took with it many of Armero's capacities. Materially, the people lost all their possessions as well as the possibilities for work and income in the short term. They lacked homes and had no clothing other than what they wore on their backs when they fled their homes. They had no immediate access to medical care and many were seriously wounded. There was no food and the only available water was dangerously contaminated. They were frightened most by the uncertainty of whether the mud would come again and how far it might rise. After seeing their town swept away by the avalanche, the survivors asked themselves: where was a person truly safe?

The survivors dispersed to the highest available ground in a completely unorganized manner. Families were separated and neighbors went off in different directions. In the days following the disaster, none of Armero's indigenous organizations, either public or private, were operating.

Perhaps the greatest vulnerability of the survivors was psychological. In the tent camps where the victims stayed during the nights following the disaster, the darkness was filled with moans and crying. When it rained, panic broke out because the survivors feared that the rising mud would overflow the camps (it had rained the night of the avalanche).

An additional trauma which beset the survivors was that some had been forced to make difficult choices about which family member to save. Others had saved no one and felt remorse thinking that they could have. Family units had dissolved, leaving individuals without parents, spouses, and/or children. An additional element of agony was the uncertainty as to whether loved ones were living or dead. Culturally-accepted ways of grieving were denied to them: there were no wakes, no burials, no tombstones, and no masses for the dead.

This situation was exacerbated by the initial rescue operation. Most of the seriously wounded were airlifted out of Armero on helicopters, taken to medical processing centers, and then shipped off to hospitals with the space and capacity to handle their problems in major cities all over the country. There was no administrative control of the movements because of the enormity of the operation. As a result, survivors did not know whether their families were living or dead, and where they might be. Hundreds of "wanted" posters appeared, noting the description of a missing loved one with perhaps a picture, an address, and an offer of reward for information. There were still a few of these visible a year and a half later.

Many of the survivors suffered a loss of identity. The various bases for social status and power were gone: money, possessions and jobs. Staff who worked in the tent camps reported that survivors would start sentences with the words, "Now that I am nobody..." With the advantage of hindsight, staff members of several agencies involved in the relief of Armero commented that some coordinating agency should have regrouped the victims by block, or neighborhood. An opportunity was lost to build on surviving social structures and to reduce some of the psychological trauma of victims.

An additional series of disaster-related vulnerabilities became apparent as relief agencies began to work with survivors. The survivors of Armero were of the lowest educational, economic, and social class of all the people who had lived in Armero before the tragedy. The more prosperous and educated people had lived in the center of town and very few survived. The poorest people, primarily agricultural day laborers, lived in the hills outside of the town center. That small difference in altitude gave them time to climb to safety. The area where the brothels were located also had a high survival rate.

There are several implications of the social composition of the surviving population which affected the activities undertaken during the emergency relief phase:

1. There were no traditional leaders left among the survivors. Political leaders, teachers, clergy, and businessmen were almost all eliminated, and the few who survived removed themselves from the area immediately, using their own resources.

2. Tent camps were hastily thrown together by numerous relief agencies and the Colombian government. While these camps did help to house the homeless, there was no privacy and many families slept for months in these undivided shelters. Many of the survivors were from the poorest and most marginalized sectors of the Armero society. Rape, violence, child abuse, and alcoholism were frequently reported in the camps. Prostitutes were housed along with other survivors, which contributed to sexual promiscuity and the breakdown of family units.

3. Poor families from outside the Armero area rushed to Armero to take advantage of relief goods and services. This contributed to an atmosphere of disorder and breakdown of community.

4. Those survivors who had actually lived in Armero quickly divided themselves into two groups: those who lived in the camps and those who "floated." The relief agencies used the term "floating" to describe people who refused to occupy the tent camps and managed to house themselves through a series of temporary measures including renting quarters in Lerida or Guayabal; staying with friends or relatives; out-migration to Bogota or Ubaque; and (most frequently) a combination of the above. The floaters tended to be the easiest groups to work with (since they showed more initiative and had somewhat greater resources), but they were not the neediest sector of the surviving population.

Initial Response to the Disaster

When the citizens of Armero were evacuated to the two nearest towns, Lerida and Guayabal, they were very well received by the people in the neighboring villages. When the government and the agencies decided to resettle them there permanently, the attitude of local people changed drastically. Demand for rental units pushed the price beyond the levels that the original inhabitants of those towns could pay. Competition for scarce jobs became acute.

In many ways the people of Armero received preferential treatment: they received a monthly stipend from the government; they were given new homes; they received free food, medicine, and other relief supplies; they were hired for work with the relief agencies; and they were eligible for special loans. The local people saw the *Armeritas* receiving more and better things than they had ever had themselves, and this provoked jealousy and resentment.

There was an ongoing, though low-level, conflict between the floaters, the camp dwellers, and the original residents of the two villages. Perhaps the greatest impediment to social peace between the Armero people and their neighbors was that there was simply no economic infrastructure in either town. The relief agency staff, who were living in close quarters with the victims, quickly realized that the success of the long-term rehabilitation process would be contingent on finding employment for the relocated *Armeritas*. Because of its political situation, the Colombian government wanted to demonstrate its concern for the survivors for the rest of the nation to see. That interest, coupled with the fact that the director of RESURGIR was a builder, resulted in government pressure on the agencies to construct houses.

Meanwhile, the donor nations were acutely aware of the Colombian avalanche. Although it followed soon after the Mexico City earthquake, the Armero disaster attracted worldwide attention. For many people, Armero was symbolized by an unsuccessful effort to save one little girl named Omayra. Omayra had her foot trapped under the rising mud, and though rescuers spent days trying to save her, she succumbed to a heart attack before she could be extricated. During the last days of her life, she made the news broadcasts on an hourly basis, moving donors everywhere to contribute to the relief of Armero.

World reaction to the tragedy in Armero had a direct impact on the attempts to rehabilitate the zone. Within days of the tragedy, newspapers in Colombia announced massive donations from countries and agencies around the world in almost every edition. All the agency personnel visited by the IRDP team agreed unanimously that the Colombian media exaggerated quantities of relief goods and dollar amounts of "donations for the victims." This led thousands of "victims" to migrate from other states to take advantage of the donations meant for the people who had survived the mudslide.

Several agencies managed to get relief supplies to the victims within a day or two of the disaster. Their first impression was that there were not many survivors from Armero itself. However, the citizens of neighboring towns considered themselves to be victims and entitled to participate as beneficiaries of the relief effort. Many of these local people were later officially classified as *damnificados indirectos*, or "indirect victims" and were eligible for certain benefits. An identity card was issued by RESURGIR to the head of each family in the area that claimed to be a disaster victim, which entitled the families to participate in many of the NGO projects as well. Possession of the card would eventually entitle the bearer to a new home, multiple loans, free food, and even a monthly cash subsidy that in many cases exceeded what the victim family had earned before the disaster.

According to the official figures of RESURGIR, 9,235 family identity cards were issued, covering 28,317 people throughout the country.

Perhaps the whole area should have been considered a disaster area for economic reasons. The valley of Armero had been settled very early in the history of Colombia. The citizens of Armero formed a local elite relative to the neighboring towns, because of the economic prosperity. Over the years, new inhabitants from many other states, mainly from the higher social classes, came there to live to take advantage of an economic boom. Neighboring villages which were economically dependent on the more prosperous Armero suffered an almost total economic collapse with its disappearance. Volcanic ash, boulders, and mud covered agricultural land, destroyed an irrigation system, and buried agricultural machinery which had previously served an entire region. Thousands of farm animals were also lost. Thus the economic impact of the mudslide was felt far beyond the immediate Armero area.

II. THE RESPONSE OF SAVE THE CHILDREN

Emergency Efforts

On November 13, SCF/Colombia in Bogota had an acting director in charge of operations. When he heard about the disaster, he was in a quandary about what to do. The Armero disaster hit an area that was outside of SCF's area of operations. As a Colombian, the acting director felt that he should do something to help, yet he was unsure if the home office would support his decision. He created an emergency committee within the Colombia office, and sent six people from his staff out to the disaster zone to report on conditions. He also called the home office in Westport, Connecticut for instructions.

On the day of the tragedy, the regional director of Save the Children for Latin America (also a Colombian) was working in the home office in Connecticut. When the office in Westport heard about what had occurred in Armero, an emergency fund was created and an ad hoc committee was formed to coordinate the operation between the field office and headquarters. The regional director was familiar with the area, especially the zones affected by the volcanic eruption. He called SCF/Colombia for more accurate news on the magnitude of the disaster, and, to keep well-informed, he requested hourly updates on news from the region.

On November 15, there was a meeting of the SCF staff in Westport, and they decided that the regional director should travel to Colombia immediately, taking with him an emergency fund of US $10,000 and a media specialist to provide information for fundraising at home and to assist with media relations in Colombia. Simultaneously, SCF began a mailing to its donors requesting special contributions for the Colombian disaster.

Before his departure for Colombia, the regional director instructed SCF/Colombia to purchase emergency supplies including tents, lanterns, food, and medicine on the local market. He earmarked US $10,000 for these initial purchases. He also gave orders that the three field offices in Colombia (referred to by SCF as "impact areas") should each send personnel to Armero on a rotating schedule.

Three days after the disaster, the regional director arrived in Bogota. He rented an airplane to fly over the disaster zone so that he would have a better understanding of the magnitude and location of the disaster and its impact on the surrounding communities. Later the same day, in the company of the acting director, he attempted to travel to the disaster area by car. He was stopped in Mariquita by the army which had instructions to keep all extraneous personnel out of Armero to prevent looting and ensure an orderly rescue operation.

The next day, by using a series of pretexts and promises, he managed to obtain official permission to enter the zone, and traveled to Guayabal where he found that the SCF team from Ubaque had arrived with a rented dump truck filled with relief supplies. The SCF team had brought along an eight-person team from the civil defense force of their project area. Among the supplies they brought were a portable generator, picks and shovels, and clothing. The SCF team decided to begin their work in direct coordination with the military authorities. In a meeting with the military governor assigned to the area, SCF staff explained the objectives of the organization and the possibilities of relief aid they could contribute to the area. In spite of the official refusal of aid at the beginning, the military governor was finally persuaded to allow the participation of SCF in the relief operations. SCF considers the initial decision to cooperate with the military to have been very important in providing the basis for ongoing successful relations. The military governor sent them to work with the Local Action Committee of Guayabal, the only political organization in operation at that time in the village. The committee, impressed with the offer of help, and overwhelmed by the magnitude of the task before them, invited SCF to use the committee offices as their base.

The SCF team next tried to locate concentrations of survivors in the hills. As they walked around, they found individuals in a state of hysteria or shock. Some were walking around with photos of loved ones in their hands, asking everyone they met whether they had seen them. When the SCF found groups of survivors, they tried to convince them to come down to Guayabal where there were supplies and shelter from the rain. The survivors explained that they were staying on the high ground for fear that the rain would cause more mudflows that would endanger any low ground they occupied in the valley. SCF recognized that, for the moment, safety was of higher priority to the disaster victims than food, shelter or clothing. On the day the regional director arrived, there was already a temporary camp established up in the hills where the survivors wanted to stay.

The second priority of survivors was to find friends and relatives. In response to these needs, SCF/Colombia began to adapt a software program to register family names and locations. When they were about to put it into use, they were informed that the Instituto Colombiano de Bienestar Familiar (a government family welfare organization) had been assigned the task of reuniting families. The SCF software was never used by that agency, and the problem of reuniting families was never adequately handled.

One of the larger groups that the SCF team found had occupied land that belonged to the El Balso farm. This farm was located about five kilometers from Guayabal, and included one of the higher hills in the Armero valley. SCF requested and received permission from the farm administrator to install tents on the property. Later, the army identified the site as an evacuation point, which led to an increasing number of survivors coming to the camp. Some of them moved on to stay with families and friends elsewhere, and the camp stabilized at thirty tents. Families that had enough money found their own lodging.

At first, the Red Cross established camps for survivors. Later, several other agencies opened tent camps of their own, but little coordination existed between them. Some of the organizations found that running the camps exceeded their administrative and logistical capabilities. One organization offered to turn over their camp to SCF. After considering the problems involved, SCF declined the offer, reasoning that it was better to run one camp well than two camps badly. The other camp had also started with too many people and the situation was out of control. Severe conflicts between the camp administrators and the victims would have been difficult to overcome. In the volatile camp situation, SCF decided to start small and build on success as a strategy for relief efforts in their own camp.

SCF accepted overall responsibility for administering the camp on the El Balso farm, playing a facilitative and coordinating role. They tried, as much as possible, to encourage camp residents to take responsibility for decisions regarding camp life. A *junta directiva* (steering committee) was established among residents, and received training, but suffered from constant shifts in membership.

SCF provided material assistance to camp dwellers and channelled assistance from other agencies. SCF provided tents, some bought and others donated from elsewhere, and built the communal kitchen and latrines. The Red Cross donated clothing, blankets, hygiene kits, food, and medicines, while SCF provided additional meat, eggs, milk and vegetables on a weekly basis. SCF also set up and supplied a health post in the camp run by three women trained through a government training program. During the whole emergency period, all registered "victims" also received a cash subsidy and a weekly market basket of food from RESURGIR.

When the tent camp was first established, the SCF staff decided to move into the camp and live with the survivors in order to know the community, its experiences and its problems better. SCF continued to rotate camp duties among their three in-country teams. The staff designed camp activities such as celebrations for holidays, and a children's art show on Mothers' Day, to foster togetherness between families and promote adaptation to the new complex of circumstances presented by the disaster.

During the first weeks of the camp, the people were happy with the help they got from SCF. Compared to other groups, they felt themselves to be well cared for. They began to refer to their hill as "Save the Children Hill."

One camp resident was an unemployed truck driver who stepped into the power vacuum created by the lack of continuity among the SCF staff. This man became a leader by organizing the camp youth while SCF staff concentrated their attention on parents and children. In the beginning, he attended staff meetings and worked with the rotating teams. As his power continued to grow, however, he became unreasonable in his demands which led to a conflict culminating in his departure. Local staff attributes this problem to the absence of full-time emergency program staff. An additional cause of the problem was that the *junta directiva*, the committee established among camp residents to ensure active participation, was not functioning well. Although more permanent staff were hired in January to provide continuity, the conflict of loyalties which the residents felt between SCF and their "leader" almost closed the project.

The Nueva Vida Project

Beginning of the Development Project

In a series of meetings with the survivors at the hill camp during the emergency phase, SCF staff elaborated tentative plans for a long-term development project. SCF offered the survivors participation in establishing a new community which would culminate in housing and employment for those who agreed to work together and hold communal property. SCF/Colombia hoped to have a financial commitment to the long-term project from the home office by January 1986, and they tried not to make promises to the survivors until they were sure of the funds necessary to complete the project. Despite these efforts, some false expectations were raised and came back to haunt project staff months later.

The key point of transition from the emergency work to the development project was the purchase of land for the new community. Once funding was assured in April, 1986, SCF bought the El Balso farm where the camp was located. A nearby river ensured a continuous supply of water and there was enough fertile land to provide farming possibilities. Of the approximately thirty-five families who benefitted at one time or another in the camp, nine families agreed to stay on and work in the self-help housing project. These were joined in April 1986 by forty-eight other families. SCF agreed to help the people establish themselves in small businesses and agricultural production.

SCF originally decided to limit the participation in the project to families from the camp. According to the SCF social work coordinator, this plan had to be modified because the *Armeritas* who were living in the camp were of the lowest educational, economic, and social class and showed little initiative.

The fact that most camp dwellers were poor, illiterate, marginalized, and lacking organizational experience was reinforced by the entire relief program in the area. RESURGIR provided a regular cash and commodity subsidy. All basic needs were satisfied in the camps, including the SCF camp. People came to expect such services as their right, creating a situation of acute dependency. This led to serious problems in participation and initiative as the SCF project tried to wean people from hand-outs and promote self-reliant strategies, problems that persisted for well over a year after the Nueva Vida Project began.

SCF staff recognized that the people occupying the camp were extremely difficult to work with, and that another group of survivors, the "floaters," were fending for themselves outside of the camps. They recruited thirty-four floater families to participate in the project. When the floaters started to work in the construction of the new village, the camp dwellers also started to work. SCF staff attributed this change in attitude to the camp dwellers' respect for the floater families' judgment. If the floaters, who were more prosperous and socially prominent families, thought that it was worth working in the project, then it must be. They were also motivated by the fear that they might be excluded from the benefits.

Program Principles

The Nueva Vida Project was based on SCF's development philosophy of community-based integrated rural development (C-BIRD) which emphasizes participatory strategies towards community self-reliance. The long-term work in the Armero area included a principle of no giveaways: people were required to provide a contribution of some sort (work, materials, funds) in order to receive program benefits. The active participation of the community in project design and execution was required while SCF played the role of advisors. The Nueva Vida Project also expanded beneficiaries of SCF work beyond survivors from Armero as strictly defined. The new SCF "impact area" was to include a number of nearby towns and villages that had also been adversely affected, especially economically, by the Armero tragedy.

As the Nueva Vida Project progressed, SCF placed a high priority on coordination with government agencies and with other NGOs. SCF worked with local Colombian government departments to reinforce their efforts in specific sectors (health, education, training, etc.). Later in the project, once relations with government agencies were fairly secure, the project director asked RESURGIR to compensate SCF for the purchase of the El Balso farm. RESURGIR agreed to co-finance the project by buying the land and paying for basic infrastructure in the new town of *Nueva Horizonte,* as it had for other reconstruction projects in the area.

Project Design, Goals, and Objectives

> The overarching goal of the Project Nueva Vida is to reduce the community's vulnerability to future disasters through the reduction of their vulnerability to physical, social, economic, and political factors that affect their lives.[1]

The project was designed to provide long-term development assistance to a new SCF "impact area" (there had been three such impact areas in Colombia before the Armero disaster). The new impact area was to include two levels: 1) the new town of *Nuevo Horizonte* situated on the El Balso farm, benefitting up to sixty families, and 2) the entire area of Guayabal-Armero (surrounding *Nuevo Horizonte*) with an estimated population of 12,000 who continued to suffer the effects of the volcanic eruption. Work in *Nuevo Horizonte* was to concentrate on production and employment and housing, while work in the wider community would emphasize health, education, and social integration, the latter aimed at reducing tensions between Armero survivors and the long-term residents of the Guayabal area.

The program was called Proyecto Vida Nueva, or New Life Project because, as envisaged by SCF, it represented a significant departure from the way of life to which the survivors were accustomed. Many of them had never owned land before. Also, they were accustomed to competing with each other in commercial activities and in the search for work. By encouraging cooperative structures in the new village of Nuevo Horizonte, SCF hoped to avoid a situation where a few families would prosper at the expense of the rest of the community.

The Nueva Vida Project was designed to provide production work for the whole community. This included income from agriculture on the farm and from small businesses and industries. The mix of agriculture and

---

1   Caroline Guarnizo Clarke and Luis Eduardo Guarnizo, "Project Nueva Vida, Armero, Colombia," project proposal, SCF-Colombia, July 1986.

other income activities was necessary because there was insufficient land to provide each family with a plot large enough to live solely from agriculture. Also, not all of the families were familiar with agriculture; some had held menial jobs in the agribusiness sector, or worked in small commercial enterprises.

SCF set criteria which determined who could participate in the program. Participants had to be able to work—either in good health or with their health problems under treatment. They agreed to work in the self-help construction of the homes, and participated in approved income-generating projects. They also joined the project as complete family units. SCF gave preference to families who had resided in the camp.

Description of Project Components

Proyecto Nueva Vida consisted of five components: production/employment, housing, education, health, and social integration.

Production/Employment

SCF planned to generate employment for the fifty-seven survivor families living in the new village, with the participation of the future entrepreneurs. The goal was for the program beneficiaries to own or operate some commercial activity. In a first phase, credit was given without interest. A second phase called for business loans at ten percent interest. By the third phase, businesses were to be well enough established to be eligible for commercial credit through normal banking structures. In addition to credit, the program provided vocational training and technical assistance.

Residents could engage in agricultural production on the 100-hectare El Balso farm by making a credit proposal to SCF. Not all of the land was used for crops, however. About 7.5 hectares was used for the construction of the village of Nueva Horizonte. An additional thirty hectares was hilly, and used for fruit trees and the construction of workshops. About thirty-five hectares of fertile bottom land was planted in basic grains by one group of ten families. As each crop cycle passed, the other available and cultivable land was divided into as many small parcels as there were families who wanted to use it. The more families who wanted to participate, the smaller the amount of land per family. Those families that used the land paid rent which went into a common fund for the benefit of all community members. An SCF agronomist worked with the farming families. Other national organizations collaborated with the project by providing technical assistance.

Housing

The housing program was supposed to create housing units for the fifty-seven participating families by means of self-help housing construction. This group activity was designed to strengthen the organization of the community and instill a cooperative spirit. Groups of ten families worked together in the construction of each other's homes. SCF provided the materials and paid the families a daily wage. The wage was provided because it would have been difficult for some people to participate in the housing construction and hold an outside job as well.

The houses themselves were designed through a participatory process. Those community members who wanted to influence housing design were invited to a series of meetings to give ideas and critique plans. Even streets and parks were laid out according to community preferences. The SCF project director, an architect-builder, added technical information about soil type and anti-seismic design features and drew up final plans. A Colombian training organization, SENA, provided ongoing training and supervision for the auto-construction process. RESURGIR provided funds for streets, drainage, and sidewalks.

The families agreed to pay back half the cost of the construction materials donated by SCF in monthly payments over the next fifteen years. This money was to go into a community-administered fund which would be loaned to individuals for housing improvements or spent on improvements to benefit the whole community.

Education

SCF believed that literacy would reduce the community's vulnerability to political and social exploitation. To achieve this, the Nuevo Horizonte community participated in a national adult literacy campaign called CAMINA. The village primary school used another program called *Escuela Nueva* which provided educational materials that allowed each child to progress and change grade levels at his or her own speed. The program was operated by an SCF social worker and technicians from the national Ministry of Education. Both organizations contributed funds to its operating costs.

Health

The SCF health program included training in preventive medicine and curative components. The health project coordinator was a doctor who coordinated SCF's primary health care program in surrounding rural villages. He also provided curative health services to the Nuevo Horizonte community. SCF's health program ran in collaboration with a local government hospital. Training activities were run jointly with SENA and ICBF, the government training and family welfare organizations.

In the rural villages, the primary health program trained community members as health promoters and supported the development of local health committees. The committees worked on sanitation to reduce the villagers' exposure to disease. They built latrines, sewage-disposing dry wells, and safe garbage collection sites. Attention was given to water use and kitchen sanitation, and to changing unhealthy practices in the traditional rural home. During the emergency period, the community was one of a few that participated in a primary mental health study, directed by a physician from Johns Hopkins University with a local group of psychologists. They worked weekly with groups of adults and children in the camps. It is interesting to note that their study found that three-quarters of those interviewed from the SCF camp said that they were happy with their life, while only one-quarter of respondents from other camps said they were happy.

Social Integration

There were serious divisions between those survivors who provided their own food and shelter (the floaters/*flotantes*), and those who lived in the camps (*albergados*). Both of these groups were resented by the villagers where they relocated. The villagers were hostile to the preferential treatment given to the victims, and competition for housing and jobs was severe. To reduce these conflicts, SCF created a range of cultural and recreational opportunities that all three sectors of the population could plan together, participate in, and enjoy. In a joint project with the Colombian Red Cross, a cultural center was built in Guayabal. This center was used for conferences, theater and dance groups, concerts, and other cultural activities.

There was also a plan to build a museum in the area to commemorate the destruction of Armero, and keep the need for disaster prevention in the minds of the local residents. Several national organizations were also planning to participate in this endeavor.

III. SCF PROJECT IMPACTS ON CAPACITIES AND VULNERABILITIES

It is always difficult to trace the precise cause and effect relation between program interventions and changes in people's conditions. However, the people most directly affected by the SCF program in Armero were a defined group with quite specific needs up until the time of this case history. Some conclusions can be drawn.

The SCF effort had two modes of operation: an emergency program for the first three to five months and then a more carefully planned long-term development effort. It is possible to identify key transition points from one program to the other (purchase of the farm, acceptance of families into the longer-term program), but there was some overlap and interplay between the two. Although it is difficult to sort out the impacts of one from the other, we will explore them separately below.

Emergency Program

The SCF emergency program took place in the broader context of relief to the survivors of a major disaster. Scores of agencies, both Colombian and international, descended on the area to help. Massive amounts of assistance arrived to benefit a relatively small number of people. In this context, the classic patterns of dependency that result from well-intentioned giveaway or handout programs were sure to arise, and did. Although SCF's own organizational philosophy and implementation strategies oppose the giveaway approach, they did not have control over the broader context. For instance, residents in the SCF camp continued to receive direct cash and food subsidies from RESURGIR quite independent of any SCF actions.

Despite these difficult circumstances, the SCF program in the emergency period was able to take developmental actions that have longer-term benefits for camp residents.

Physical/Material

The main thrust of the emergency program was to meet the immediate needs of the survivors, people who had lost everything they owned. The program provided short-term shelter, food, clothing, and even cash. Even during the emergency period, however, SCF began the process of discussing prospects for long-term solutions with survivors. Although these discussions risked raising expectations (and did raise them), they engaged people in thinking about their own futures.

Social/Organizational

The long term social/organizational vulnerabilities of the people who survived the Nevada del Ruiz eruption were acute. The case has already described the position most of these people held in the former Armero society. Few individuals had any experience with cooperative or group efforts. Working with this population was a challenge, one that SCF took on immediately. As soon as the camp was established, SCF organized a *junta directiva* (Steering Committee) among camp residents to work with SCF on decision-making for the camp. Although the membership on the committee shifted often, they received training through SENA. SCF also set up other committees to deal with health care and a day-care center. These committees also had a rocky history, exactly what one would expect considering the inexperience of the members and the important learning process that was underway.

Motivational/Attitudinal

Because of the handout atmosphere that prevailed in the region, short-term efforts by many agencies were increasing the long-term motivational vulnerability of the population. While SCF could not reverse this process, at least as long as the direct subsidies and food supplies continued, they did try to move towards positive attitudes of self-reliance during the emergency period. In doing so, they met resistance among camp residents. Some of the concrete projects aimed at self-sufficiency (such as the grain crop on the farm) were even sabotaged. Ironically, these reactions, on the part of people who had come to expect handouts as a right, show that SCF was making effective headway against the dependency pattern with some residents. The difficulty and pain of the transition period are not evidence of failure in this area, but are testimony to the depth of the dependency relationship and the short time it takes to be established.

The SCF program also addressed psychological factors among the survivors through facilitating the mental health project, and by initiating a series of sports, cultural, and celebration activities. These began building a sense of community among the survivors and reinforced the feeling that "normal" life was going on.

Nueva Vida Project

Physical/Material

The Nueva Vida Project began to address the longer-term vulnerabilities of the community in more fundamental ways, working with the project participants on housing, employment, and health care. Since many of the families in the new village of Nuevo Horizonte were the marginalized poor, the new setting provided a marked improvement in job security and living conditions over their lives in Armero before the disaster. The houses were built according to anti-seismic designs, another long-term reduction in vulnerability. Through the housing program, people also gained marketable construction skills, broadening their employment options.

The grant and credit programs supported agricultural production and creation of small businesses and other enterprises, improving local capacities in the economic realm.

Social/Organizational

The challenge of working with the particular social group that the survivors represented has already been discussed. In the longer-term program, SCF staff continued to encourage self-sustaining organization among the residents of Nuevo Horizonte, building on the modest successes of the emergency program. Although progress was slow, and particularly difficult in the transition period, there was good participation in the planning of family housing units and of common facilities such as the school, health post, etc.

The strategy of organizing residents into groups of ten families for construction work had more success than efforts with the larger group of residents. Within these functional groups, focussed on a specific task in which each family had an interest, it was possible to gain cooperation and mutual accountability. In the course of the self-help housing project, new leadership slowly began to emerge.

The SCF project recognized that conflicts between the different groups of survivors (floaters and camp residents) and between survivors and people from the neighboring towns in which survivors now lived represented an important vulnerability. (In fact, the conflict between *Armeritas* and the people of Guayabal went back many years). By expanding their program to benefit the whole area and promoting common cultural events, the project began to address the hostilities and reduce social vulnerability.

Motivational/Attitudinal

The people of Nuevo Horizonte had an important experience of successful cooperation through the self-help housing project. As their lives, housing, income, and social context stabilized, they began to show a change in attitude and motivation, shifting away from dependency patterns towards independent initiative. While this process was frustratingly slow for SCF staff (and in stark contrast to the vigor and speed of response in neighboring villages in the wider program), progress was made.

IV. DILEMMAS AND LESSONS FOR FUTURE PROGRAM DESIGN

General Lessons

Making and Breaking Dependency Patterns

The SCF project illustrates the ease with which dependency patterns can be established among disaster survivors, despite the firm commitments of relief agency staff. The case also shows that there is a relationship between dependency patterns and the *preexisting* conditions in the country. Colombia was a country where solutions to essential social problems came from the government or from nowhere. The benefits meted out by the government were also controlled by the complex systems of political patronage. The grassroots organizations that existed in Armero before the disaster were for the purpose of maintaining and exercising political influence, not for identifying and solving problems at the local level. The general population therefore had little experience with initiating efforts to solve their common difficulties.

In the wake of the disaster, the government, eager to demonstrate its competence and caring for the survivors, established a system of benefits that was almost guaranteed to lead to dependency. The NGO community was enlisted to augment, and in some cases implement, these schemes. The government dole to Armero survivors undermined efforts to encourage self-sufficiency.

The SCF project tried to wean people from dependence on government handouts and to promote various schemes for greater self-reliance. During the several months of transition, SCF staff came under repeated pressure to continue dependent patterns, including threats of violence and incidents of property destruction. Through tough determination over several months, SCF staff were able to withstand the pressure while people made the transition.

Several lessons emerge. First, if there is a strong dependency pattern in place already, efforts to break them down will meet with resistance, anger and resentment, and, at times, with the threat of violence. Ironically, the more effective the measures against dependency, the stronger the likely resistance: project staff can almost use the degree of resistance to measure the effectiveness of the effort. If people react, the moves towards self-reliance are probably in the right direction. Unfortunately, people sometimes have legitimate complaints that must be sorted out from resistance to anti-dependency initiatives.

Delayed Response to Disaster

Some agencies may decide, correctly, not to respond immediately to a disaster. The Armero situation is a good illustration of a "relief invasion." The disaster received massive publicity, including several days of moving coverage of the little girl, Omayra, who was caught in the mud and finally died. The result was an outpouring of donations from the public in North America and Europe. Relief and development agencies descended on the region, looking for ways to assist the survivors. Within a few weeks, agencies began to compete for "victims" to participate in their programs.

In retrospect, some agency staff have questioned whether they should have intervened—especially during the emergency phase. Emergency activities were being handled adequately by the Red Cross and government departments. NGO resources do not go very far in such circumstances and might be better reserved for longer-term efforts, when they become possible.

Some SCF staff suggested that a reasonable strategy might be to wait six months or a year, until the situation stabilized, before starting a program. Some agencies did exactly that with some success. By waiting that long, they were not connected at all with the massive handout programs which operated in the immediate aftermath of the tragedy. They were able to work with populations that were not in so much flux, with groups of people who had already decided to live and work together, rather than shifting groups of people with no long-term commitment to each other.

SCF staff also pointed out that there were things not being done during the emergency period that could have been picked up through creative programming. An agency could avoid involvement in the handout schemes while gaining a position from which to consider options for longer-term efforts. Such potential activities included providing information centers, assisting coordination of NGO activities, organizing the participation of program beneficiaries in decision-making, and development of a tracking/tracing system for survivors.

An important lesson is that development NGOs should move carefully in response to disasters. They should avoid reinforcement of dependency patterns, at the very least staying out of direct agency participation in handout schemes. If there are legitimate pressures to become involved, the agency can find creative ways to be active, visible and pro-development in the situation.

Education of the Donor Public

Education of the donor public is needed—along with new notions of accountability. The approach suggested in the section above means that an agency could find itself implementing a program that does not match the expectations of its donors, particularly private individuals who give in response to media coverage of a tragedy. The primary desire of donors from the general public is that aid be delivered speedily and to people in urgent need. In Europe and Canada the public is somewhat better informed about and supportive of development; in the United States the public responds to emergency needs in the wake of a disaster, and expects that its donations will be used for that.

In order for an NGO to take a different approach, one which places more emphasis on developmental efforts, some education of donors is needed. Part of this education must include changed perceptions of accountability. Many donors now consider that the NGO should be accountable to them. The alternative view is that the agency must be accountable, at least in part, to the population it seeks to benefit.

Working with Displaced Persons

The Armero disaster caused the internal displacement of several thousand survivors, people who lost everything. In addition, since the survivors were mostly from marginalized groups in the former town, and because former neighbors were split up, no community organizations remained. These conditions mimic those of many refugee groups whose social systems are completely disrupted by their move. In these situations, efforts at building either physical capacity or social capacity are slow. Even though the surrounding society may be intact, relief or development workers cannot assume that the social systems of disaster survivors are in operation.

Choice of Project Participants

The possibilities for implementing programs with long-term development effects were deeply affected by the social status, skills, and organization of the survivors in Armero. Over time, several overlapping and confused groups emerged: both camp dwellers and "floaters," among *direct* victims; indirect victims of the economic losses from Armero; and "professional victims" who came from elsewhere in Colombia to take advantage of the benefits offered. The definition of "victims" became a political issue.

Careful social analysis of the people with whom agencies had to work was complicated by the constant shifts in population as people looked for relatives and sought out the best set of benefits for their families. Nevertheless, it was clear that most survivors were landless, less educated, poor people with few skills. This had a profound effect on programming choices, including pacing and participation strategies. SCF found that the project began to move more quickly once people with slightly more resources (the "floaters") joined the project—whereas working only with the poorest groups had proven extremely difficult.

Specific Programming Issues

Living with Survivors

SCF staff in Armero found that, while it was helpful, at first, for staff (or full-time volunteers) to live in the camps with survivors, after a month or so, survivors began to look to them as all-purpose problem solvers (and at any time of day or night). Living and working closely with project participants is a useful way to get to know them better, but more distance is required if the people are to take responsiblity for their own development.

Staff Continuity

Staff continuity is important during emergency activities. SCF found that, while rotating regular staff in and out of Armero was a useful strategy for ensuring coverage by experienced people, it was difficult, under this system, to provide continuity. There was also no institutional memory. Staff did not know the agreements reached during the tenures of previous colleagues.

Loans and Gifts

Management of loans, gifts, and grants is crucial. The management of loans has been a problem for many of the agencies working in Armero. Loans for housing construction and for small enterprise development were offered at the same time as many free services and/or grants for similar uses. Survivors were also able to shop around among different agencies to see who would give them the best deal.

It is also evident that many people who accepted loans did not really believe they would be asked to repay them. This becomes a knotty problem when the loans are to be repaid into a community fund or a revolving loan fund under the control of the community. If the community is divided over whether and how to demand repayment and over the potential uses of the funds, mechanisms for actual collection fall apart or are never implemented.

After two years, SCF staff were themselves divided about whether or not to pressure the Nuevo Horizonte community to begin repayment. They felt that the community should decide the issue on its own. The president of the community organization noted that people were getting used to not paying and hoped that SCF would order him to begin a collection process.

It has been suggested that in such situations, organizations with experience administering loan programs, even commercial or semi-public institutions, should be given responsibility for implementing loan programs. This is a matter of judgment. If a community has sufficient leadership, organizational skills, and common will they should control a loan fund program themselves. If not, alternatives should be sought.

Former Associations

In planning for resettlement, consideration should be given to grouping people according to former associations. In Armero, the chaotic situation that followed the disaster resulted in groups of families living in camps and, later, starting new housing developments without consideration of any previous association. Grouping families with former neighbors would have provided more basis for community organization. Some agencies waited several months before selecting groups to work with, which allowed natural associations to build before the agency tried to work with them.

Self-Help Programs

Self-help programs must be approached flexibly. SCF discovered, through its housing construction program, that the self-help aspects had to be adapted to circumstances. The process of teams of ten families building homes together is credited with finally beginning to knit Nuevo Horizonte into a community. However, some families found that it was difficult to pursue jobs or other economic efforts while constructing their homes. In the end, SCF hired contractors to build some of the houses.

Among the agencies working in the Armero area, there was a wide range of approaches and uses of self-help methods. Some agencies rejected self-help for a variety of reasons (need for speed, difficulty of organizing this population, need to support efforts to find work). Others used a mixed system with some work by the participants and some by contractors. On balance, the SCF staff felt that the use of self-help, while costly in terms of time and organizing effort, was worth the gains in community solidarity.

REFERENCES

Departamento de Planeacion, Sistema de las Naciones Unidas, "Informe Sobre el Desastre Natural del Volcan Nevado del Ruiz en Colombia," Bogota, Diciembre de 1985.

Guarnizo, Luis Eduardo and Guarnizo Clarke, Caroline, "Project Nueva Vida, Armero, Colombia," Project Proposal SCF-Colombia, July 1986.

Guarnizo, Luis and Guarnizo Clarke, Caroline, "Save the Children Armero, Colombia: Our First Months," SCF/Guayabal.

Guarnizo Clarke, Caroline, "Proyecto de Majoramiento Integral de Vivienda Rural," SCF/Guayabal.

Proyecto Armero, "Proyecto Nueva Vida Armero," Descripcion Resumida, Encuentro Nacional Septiembre, 1986; Guayabal, Armero, Tolima.

Rivera, Humberto, "Informe de Comision del 24 de Diciembre de 1985 al 15 de Enero de 1986, en la zona de emergencia de Armero," SCF/Bogota.

Save the Children, "Del Desastre Al Desarollo," Bogota, Colombia, 1987.

ACKNOWLEDGMENTS

This case was written in 1987. Julio Castro and Carlos Salazar of CORDES (*Coporacion para el Desarollo Empresarial y Social*) assisted with field information gathering. SCF staff in Colombia spent hours taking the author to field sites and answering questions. Particular thanks are due to Jairo Arboleda, Norma Amador, Luz Angela Castro, and Oscar Medina. We are grateful to Caroline Guarnizo Clarke, former SCF field staff, for patiently reading drafts of the case and making helpful corrections.

Chapter 12

CEREAL BANKS IN BURKINA FASO
Food Security, Drought, and Development

Project Implementing Agencies:
Foster Parents Plan International
Fondation Nationale pour le Développement
et la Solidarité
Six S/Groupements Naam

Case Writer:
Peter J. Woodrow

I. INTRODUCTION

This case history includes an analysis of the cereal bank work of three NGOs: 1) FONADES, a Burkinabé NGO which receives most of its financial support from European donors; 2) SIX-S, a Sahelian regional NGO with international offices in Geneva and administrative offices in Ouahigouya, Burkina Faso; and 3) Foster Parents Plan International, an international NGO with headquarters in East Greenwich, Rhode Island, USA. These three NGOs are responsible for starting 49 percent of the cereal banks initiated by NGOs in Burkina Faso, or about a quarter of the total number of cereal banks including government projects. This case history examines the role and function of cereal banks in Burkina Faso 1) as mechanisms for distributing emergency relief goods, and 2) as contributors to longer-term development and in particular, food security. Several studies have evaluated the effectiveness of cereal bank programs and their developmental contribution. Most of those studies have only mentioned

BURKINA FASO

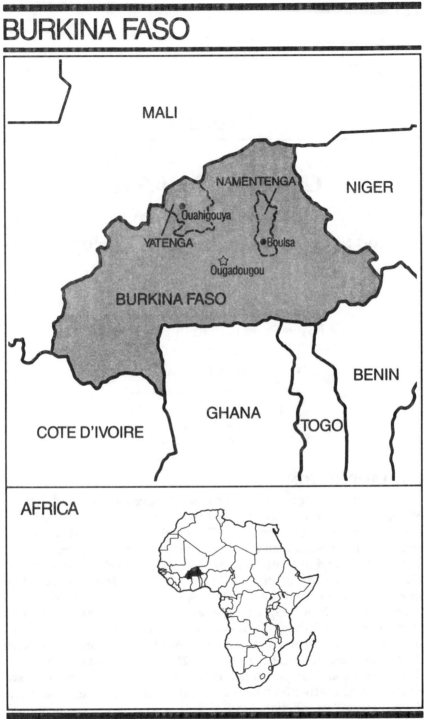

MALI

NIGER

NAMENTENGA

●Ouahigouya

YATENGA

●Boulsa

☆
Ougadougou

BURKINA FASO

BENIN

GHANA

TOGO

COTE D'IVOIRE

AFRICA

the crisis role of cereal banks in passing. Cereal banks interest IRDP because food security is important both in development work and in emergency relief. We have approached this case history asking whether cereal banks are effective elements of a food security strategy and whether, in times of crisis, they can be appropriate channels for relief assistance.

II. PROJECT CONTEXT AND CONDITIONS

Burkina Faso is a landlocked country in the Sahel region of West Africa, bordering desert areas to the north and areas of tropical rainforest to the south. In good years, annual rainfall in Burkina Faso varies from 1400 mm in the south to about 400 mm in the north. However, rainfall in the Sahel has been below normal since the late 1960s, including two periods of severe drought: 1968-73 and 1983-84. In the northern areas of the country, not only is rain scarce but even that small amount of rain is often poorly distributed over time and geography.

Burkina Faso has about seven million people, with an annual per capita GNP of $180. It is one of the poorest countries in the world. Ninety-one percent of the population remains illiterate and only 28 percent of school-age children are in school. One in three babies dies before the age of five.[1] The basic realities of rural life in Burkina Faso are problematic.

> Apart from these socioeconomic factors, the condition of the natural resource base in the region is equally disturbing and problematic. Soils are generally leached, erodible, and relatively infertile, and the vegetative cover is continuing to decline from the combined effects of agricultural clearing, fuelwood harvesting, overgrazing, uncontrolled bush fires, and drought. Population densities have increased beyond the theoretical carrying capacity for sustained production of fuelwood in many areas. Soil erosion, by both water and wind, has accelerated in recent years as soils are cleared and depleted of organic matter. As a result of degradation of the vegetative cover, erosion, loss of topsoil, and exposure of impermeable clay or laterite subsoil, more rainfall is now lost as runoff and less infiltrates to recharge the ground water reserves. And, of course, rainfall is still low and erratic over much of the region.[2]

Farmers are caught in a vicious economic cycle. Few are able to grow enough grain to meet their families' needs for the entire year. They store grain in traditional granaries, but many run short in the late spring or early summer. The pre-harvest months during the growing season when grain

1. Robert Winterbottom, quoting OTA statistics, in his report on Burkina Faso, part of the "Report on the African Emergency Relief Operation 1984-1986," International Institute for Environment and Development, 1986.
2. Winterbottom, p. 167.

is in shortest supply are called the *soudure*—the shortfall or gap. (The *soudure* comes at the crucial period when the rains begin and people need energy to prepare the fields and plant.)

Even if farmers grow enough grain for the full year, many are forced to sell some of it to merchants in order to obtain cash for other necessities. Farmers sell at harvest time when the prices are lowest, and purchase grain at high prices during the *soudure* in order to feed their families. It is not unusual for a farmer to sell grain at 60 CFA[3] per kilogram in November, and buy grain back in July at 120 CFA per kilogram. Farmers who do not have cash to purchase grain in July must get credit and the merchants (called *banabanas*) often charge very high interest rates. For instance, a *banabana* might require a farmer to pay for the loan of one sack of grain with two sacks—or 100 percent interest.

Burkina Faso, like the other countries of the Sahel, experienced severe drought from 1968 through 1972. During the later years of that drought, an estimated 150,000 people died from famine in the six affected countries of West Africa. Eventually, a massive relief effort was mounted, but it was too late to save many people. In the years following the crisis, many development efforts were undertaken by governments and non-governmental organizations. These were often oriented toward mitigating the effects of future droughts that were sure to come.

These development efforts were put to the test in the early 1980s. In some areas of the Sahel, poor rain caused poor or failed crops in 1983. The 1984 rains were even worse, with disastrous results. In Burkina Faso, an estimated 500,000 people were at risk in the northern arid provinces where the drought was most severe. The government revealed its estimates of the problem in October 1984, but the international community was slow to respond. Bilateral donors committed funds and grain by December 1984 or early 1985, but much of the material did not arrive in the country until the middle of 1985. NGOs reacted more quickly by purchasing smaller amounts of grain locally or in neighboring countries and using local organizations to distribute it.

Approximately 215,000 MT of food aid was provided to Burkina Faso in 1984 and 1985, more than 66 percent of it for emergency relief. The United States Agency for International Development (USAID) provided 38 percent of this total; other major sources included the World Food Program and the European Economic Community. Of the USAID contribution, 4,000 MT was provided to NGOs to be used to start or replenish the stocks of village cereal banks.[4] Some Food for Work projects also supported cereal bank construction.

3. Currency of the *Communauté Financière Africaine*. US $1.00 = about 300 CFA.
4. Winterbottom, p. 170."

Burkinabé society is in transition from traditional values and structures to the forms encouraged by the modern state. Since the resources of the government are few, the penetration of the new forms in rural life has been slow. In most villages, however, there is at least a village committee and a chapter of the *Comité Démocratique Révolutionnaire* (CDR), the Marxist government party. Their effectiveness varies considerably. With a 91 percent illiteracy rate, few villages have even one member who can read or perform basic mathematical calculations. This contributes to the organizational vulnerability of the village, especially as it interacts with the national government and with merchants.

III. HISTORY AND DEVELOPMENT OF CEREAL BANK PROJECTS

Cereal banks were originally initiated in Burkina Faso in 1974 by FOVODES (now FONADES), one of the three organizations whose work is examined in this case history. The idea has been taken up by numerous other groups, both non-governmental and governmental. By 1986 there were fifteen NGOs and about thirteen government entities working with cereal banks.[5] At the end of 1986, there were an estimated 1,177 cereal banks in Burkina Faso. The number of cereal banks had grown from only a few in 1975, to 153 in 1980, to 679 in 1983. The idea also spread to other Sahelian countries, with active programs of cereal bank creation in Mali, Senegal, and Niger.

Between 1974 and 1979, cereal banks in Burkina Faso were created exclusively by NGOs. Since 1979, the government has taken an active interest, and with assistance from UNDP and bilateral donors, by 1985 governmental bodies were responsible for financing half of the cereal banks. However, government programs have concentrated in the areas of surplus cereal production to the west and south of the country, while NGO efforts have focussed on deficit areas in the north and east. This reflects an emphasis on food security in the NGO programs, and commercialization in the government programs.

One of the essential purposes of the cereal banks is food security for rural communities, especially during the annual *soudure* after grain stocks have run out and before the harvest is in. Cereal banks also store grain better and reduce grain losses to pests. Some banks purchase the grain produced by their members, often at prices slightly above the low market price in the post-harvest period. The farmer can then buy his/her own grain back later, usually at a lower price than that prevailing during the *soudure*.

5. Guy Ledoux, *"Inventaire et Evaluation des Banques de Céréales au Burkina Faso,"* FAO, Rome, November 1986, pp. 26-30.

Fondation Nationale pour le Développement et la Solidarité

The National Foundation for Development and Solidarity, or FONADES by its French acronym (originally the Voltaic Foundation for Development and Solidarity or FOVODES) was established in 1973. Mostly government functionaries who were former members of youth movements, the initiators of FONADES were concerned with economic development in the rural villages from which many of them had come. It operated as a volunteer association for its first years, but in the 1980s began to hire a small number of paid staff. FONADES established the first cereal banks in Burkina Faso in 1974 and has concentrated ever since on the creation and support of cereal banks. It relies mainly on expatriate donors for funds to support its work.

FONADES considers cereal banks an important and basic village institution.

> A cereal bank can be defined as a village organization of stocking and commercialization of cereals, self-managed by the villagers who group themselves under the leadership of a managing committee.
> A cereal bank permits peasants to overcome, at the village level, problems of storage and commercialization of their food production.
> By avoiding the circuit of merchants, the villagers save the profit margin of the intermediaries, as in any producers' cooperative.
> By stocking cereals in the village, peasants guard against the relative lack of cereals which prevails during certain periods.
> Finally, in teaching villagers to manage the stock of cereals in a communitarian manner, FONADES follows an educational objective, without counting that the profits realized are reinvested in new village activities.[7]

A model set of internal regulations for FONADES cereal banks offers the following as a brief statement of the objectives of cereal banks:

> The objectives of a cereal bank are to guarantee the food security of the village, to promote the self-organization of the village community, and to combat speculation on the price of cereals.[8]

After the early 1980s, although some new banks were being created, FONADES placed priority on follow-up with existing banks. They have provided training in management, mathematics, literacy, and a range of other topics relevant to self-directed village development. Members of the managing committees of cereal banks (especially presidents and treasurer/accountants) were expected to attend annual three-day meetings of a "committee of reflection" where they exchanged experiences with

7. Denis Dolidon, *"Evaluation du Programme des Banques de Céréales,"* FOVODES, 1980.
8. FONADES, *"Règlements Intérieurs de la Banque de Céréales,"* undated.

members of other banks. These meetings allowed people to identify common problems and to work together on solutions on a regional basis.

FONADES also conducted forty-eight-day training seminars (four meetings of twelve days each) in which trainees, chosen from participating villages, received instruction in literacy, numeracy, hygiene, animal husbandry, erosion control and soil conservation, gardening, and forestry. Those who went through this training program were to become literacy trainers in their home communities.

In the FONADES system, each new cereal bank was granted thirty metric tons of stock. The village then sold the stock to its members for cash or credit and was to be reimbursed in cash or in kind with a small increment (e.g., one sack of grain repaid by one sack plus one tin).

FONADES found that a number of banks ran into difficulties with reimbursement, and that their stock and/or rotating funds were becoming depleted. Since 1980, FONADES has developed a set of internal regulations to ensure smooth management, maintenance of capital and high reimbursement rates. Some attempts were made to resuscitate banks that were in difficulty by providing better management training and small loans to recapitalize the rotating funds.

Bazaido

The cereal bank in Bazaido was started in 1981 during a period of famine. The village applied to FONADES for help. The grain store was built with funds and materials from FONADES and labor from the village. FONADES supplied 300 sacks of millet as the first stock. People were to repay a loaned sack with one sack plus a tin plus 100 francs that would go into a community "solidarity fund." The experience with reimbursement was fairly good except during famine years. During our visit, the granary was empty since, at the beginning of the *soudure*, they had sold all the stock and were in the process of looking for more. This bank had purchased grain from surplus regions in the south of Burkina Faso, rather than at local high prices.

Two of their members went through the FONADES training program and others attended the yearly "committee of reflection." People from the village saw the cereal bank as aiding overall community welfare, since it provided funds for other projects such as a community pharmacy (not yet built as of 1987). They also noted that the bank provided a measure of food security even during famine times. On the other hand, they saw the large amount of time required of the cereal bank manager as a problem. He is a villager selected by the other villagers, who is unpaid, although his neighbors provide compensation by helping in his fields. This bank also found it difficult to maintain high rates of reimbursement.

During the 1984-85 drought they found that the bank was able to provide grain at a reasonable price not only to their own members, but to people from surrounding villages as well (from as far as 60 kilometers away!). During the drought, they purchased 200 sacks of grain from OFNACER (the National Cereals Office) which they sold at cost plus 100 francs to cover transport. They also received 200 sacks from Catholic Relief Services (through SIX-S) which they distributed free.

The villagers remarked that the cereal bank had helped stem emigration from the area. Based on the experience of cooperating on the bank, people were mobilized to improve the road to the next town.

Warma

The cereal bank in Warma began in 1980, after the village proposed the project to FONADES. As in other cases, the materials and a mason were provided for construction of the granary. They received the standard 300 sacks the first year, but subsequently travelled to surplus areas to purchase their own grain. In this village, the people were wary of extending credit and fearful that people would not pay. But later they learned they could accept payment in-kind with a stated due date for repayment.

Several members of the management committee went through the FONADES training program and two became literacy trainers. They received visits from the FONADES follow-up team once or twice a year.

The village members saw the bank as providing food security, particularly in times of famine. They also appreciated that the cereal bank helped to avoid time lost in travelling to markets. They have also managed to build a classroom and a well with funds generated by the bank. They expressed appreciation for the training received, as it provided members with literacy, basic mathematics, and management skills. The bank meetings also provided a forum for discussion of other village problems.

This bank has experienced difficulties with reimbursement, especially in drought years. In addition, they lost grain due to deterioration in early 1987, as it had stayed in the store too long. The community felt that they had extended too much credit during the drought and found it was difficult to collect afterwards. They also were forced to buy grain at high prices, which depleted their capital.

They found it difficult to turn people away who were unable to repay, but who came to them in great need. At the time of this visit, they were still working on ways to deal with this problem. Another problem they encountered was the need for government permission to travel to other provinces to purchase grain at good prices. They were struggling with how to compensate the cereal bank manager for his time and have discussed giving him a percentage of the proceeds taken in each year.

They suggested that during drought years, food aid could be used to help replenish the capital of cereal banks so that they could better assist their members and others in the surrounding communities and not deplete the rotating fund. Food aid was received in the village during the drought, but not through the cereal bank (rather from SIX-S). They knew of other cereal banks in the area that did receive food aid.

Tebin

This village built a cement storehouse with FONADES' help in 1980, after a local priest promoted the project with FONADES. Their arrangements were similar to those of other FONADES cereal banks. They have had some unpaid loans since their first year. During 1987, OFNACER used their grain store to stock some grain which the bank sold on their behalf. However, the grain was red sorghum which is not very popular and some of it remained unsold. They saw the advantages of the cereal banks similarly to other villagers, mentioning that it helped stem emigration, that it provided credit, and removed the need for some travel. They bought grain for the bank primarily from merchants, although one year they asked for assistance from OFNACER since their stock was low. This was when they got the red sorghum. They noted a constant need to educate people about how credit works, as opposed to gifts, because otherwise they found they would not repay.

During the most recent drought they had trouble finding cereal to purchase. They did buy from OFNACER in Ougadougou several times and they received a tiny amount of food aid (ten sacks of corn meal).

Se Servir de la Saison Seche en Savane et au Sahel (SIX-S)[9]

SIX-S is an international organization with programs in several Sahelian countries, including Mali, Senegal and Burkina Faso. Its administrative headquarters are in Ouahigouya, the provincial capital of Yatenga, Burkina Faso. It also maintains an international office in Geneva. It was founded in the mid-1970s by Bernard Ledea Ouedraogo, a Burkinabé scholar who became impressed with the fact that the institutions of modern society were not rooted in rural Burkina Faso. He noted that rural workers, particularly males, were only active for the five or six months of the growing season and were essentially idle during the long dry season. One of his initial concerns was to find ways to develop productive work during the dry months. Hence the name of the organization.

After studying village structures, he became convinced that traditional forms could be revitalized to mobilize people for self-directed development. The particular traditional structure he chose was the "kombi-naam," an association of young people active each year during the rainy season and undertaking various projects to benefit the community. While this structure was specific to the Mossi peoples of Burkina Faso, similar traditions have existed in other West African societies. Bernard

9. In English: "To make use of the dry season in the savanna and Sahel."

However, those banks that dealt only in-kind (providing credit in grain only and receiving payment in grain only) were in real trouble, and in some cases, devastated, in the drought. Farmers withdrew all the grain in the store and then were unable to pay it back when the crop failed. Even the following year, farmers were deeply in debt to the merchants who extended them credit (once the cereal bank was empty), and had to repay those debts first. During the drought, even those farmers who sold off animals and other belongings to obtain cash to purchase grain had to buy at high prices. Those who obtained credit not only paid high prices for the grain, but paid high interest rates.

When the cereal banks were monetized, it was possible to purchase grain in common either locally or in surplus areas, so that farmers incurred less debt.

Even when banks are not so severely affected, many reported depletion of their rotating funds due to poor reimbursement rates following droughts. Clearly, the cereal banks are playing a useful role in blunting the effects of drought and mitigating or even preventing famine on a local basis. However, they do so only by risking their long-term financial stability, unless they receive special donations of grain or funds to use during the crisis period to supply people, or afterwards, to replenish their stocks and/or rotating funds.

The effects of cereal banks on the psychological well-being of rural villages are less obvious, and difficult to separate from the broader development programs in which they are often embedded.

V. DILEMMAS AND LESSONS FOR FUTURE PROGRAM DESIGN

Larger Strategy for Food Security

Cereal banks must be seen as part of a larger strategy for food security and agricultural development. While some benefits may be derived from a cereal bank in isolation, it cannot address the range of issues in rural production. As mentioned above, elements such as soil conservation and erosion, reforestation, small scale irrigation, market gardening, animal husbandry and development of marketable artisan products are among the elements of a broader strategy. Most agencies are aware of this and see cereal banks as only one part of their effort to support village-based initiatives for development.

Cereal Banks for Annual Shortfall vs. Periodic Drought

The effectiveness of cereal banks for dealing with drought and/or famine is not as clear as their usefulness for coping with the annual pre-harvest shortfall. Banks that use their collective assets to purchase grain, particularly in surplus regions, or rotate their funds to purchase grain repeatedly, do make a contribution to coping with famine. Even banks which were not able to provide grain on their own have proven, in some cases, to be effective distribution mechanisms for grain supplied through government or NGO relief efforts.

Drought Role for Cereal Banks

In the light of these experiences, it appears that cereal banks might serve several roles in case of drought and/or famine:

1. Relief grain can be used to help establish new cereal banks which will have the effect of providing an immediate injection of much-needed food assistance (for sale at a price below the market prices inflated by the drought) and establish a useful community institution with longer-term benefits as described above.

2. Relief grain can be simply distributed through existing cereal banks, either for free, for subsidized prices well below the market rates, or at reasonable rates, with some portion of the sale price going to the bank, and the balance to be used to purchase additional grain for sale, especially if connections can be made between surplus and deficit regions, preferably from one community cereal bank to another, or from a group of banks to another group.

3. Relief assistance can be used to assist cereal banks that are in difficulty to relaunch them by replenishing their grain stocks or rotating fund.

4. With any of the above activities, it is extremely important to include training programs, particularly when assisting banks in difficulty so that they will not fall into the same difficulties again. To do this effectively, it is necessary to analyze why the banks are in trouble and take corrective measures. This approach is necessary if the problems have to do with management skills, for which people can be (re)trained.

In-Kind vs. Monetized Cereal Banks

Among the small number of banks visited, it appeared that those banks that were not monetized, but dealt only in-kind, were more vulnerable in drought situations. Because their assets were only in grain, they could serve their members only by loaning them grain. Each season, then, all of their assets were extended as credit. In contrast, other banks could sell the largest portion of their stocks, extending credit to a smaller portion of their members. As a result, they tied up less of their assets in credit, and they were able to use the cash from sales to purchase additional stocks, if needed. Such a bank can rotate its funds (purchasing, selling, purchasing more, selling again) several times in a season. With careful management, a monetized bank can actually build up reserves in this manner. A bank that deals only in-kind has one single stock and no way to respond to added demand in case of drought or even mild shortages in a "normal" year. (In some of the in-kind banks, the small additional fee taken upon the loan of a sack of grain is paid into a community fund for other village projects, not for building up the cereal bank reserves).

Credit vs. Charity/Solidarity

Villagers have a lot of information about each other. It is usually clear to all whether someone is a good credit risk or not. Banks which are more strict and refuse credit to those unlikely to be able to repay, but also set up a system for providing relief to those in need (e.g., a "solidarity fund"), seem to be more successful. The management committee may have to make many more decisions about credit, but the bank will be a stronger village institution for it.

Further Study of Cereal Banks

Cereal banks can be viewed as experiments in decentralized, village-controlled institutions of credit, storage, management, and market activity—often in populations with low rates of literacy/numeracy. Additional careful assessment of cereal bank programs is needed. It is still unclear why some cereal banks succeed and others fail. Among the small number of villages visited by IRDP, it would appear, provisionally, that organizational skill coupled with motivation is a key factor.

REFERENCES

Dolidon, Denis, *Evaluation du Programme des Banques de Céréales*, FOVODES, 1980.

FONADES, *"Réglements Intérieurs de la Banques de Céréales,"* undated.

International Institute for Environment and Development, *Report on the African Emergency Relief Operation 1984-1986, on behalf of the UN Office for Emergency Operations in Africa*, 1986 (article on Burkina Faso researched and written by Robert T. Winterbottom).

Ledoux, Guy, *"Rapport de Mission: Assistance aux Banques de Céréales des ORD du Yatenga et du Sahel, Inventaire et Evaluation,"* FAO, 1986.

Ouedraogo, Bernard Ledea, *"De l'Association Traditionelle Kombi-Naam a l'Association Internationale SIX-S,"* SIX-S, undated.

Sherman, Jacqueline R., Shapiro, Kenneth H, and Gilbert, Elon, *The Dynamics of Grain Marketing in Burkina Faso, Volume I: An Economic Analysis of Grain Marketing*, Center for Research on Economic Development, University of Michigan and International Agricultural Programs, University of Wisconsin, 1987.

SIX-S, *Rapport du Secretariat Exécutif au Conseil d'Administration*, October 1986.

ACKNOWLEDGMENTS

This case was written in 1987. During the IRDP visit to Burkina Faso, in addition to contacts with the agencies directly involved, conversations were held with officials at OFNACER, the government cereals office; at the World Food Program; at CILSS, the Intergovernmental Committee for the Struggle Against Drought in the Sahel; and at other NGOs working in Burkina Faso (ACORD, World Council of Churches, GTZ and the coordinating group, SPONG). Visits to cereal bank sites were made in the area of Boulsa, in Namentenga Province (Foster Parents Plan projects) and around Ouahigouya, Yatenga Province (FONADES and SIX-S projects). Thanks are due to Harouna Ouedraogo who assisted the author as a consultant and as culture and language interpreter throughout the process. Thanks are also extended to others who helped facilitate the visits to field projects: Oswald Ouedraogo of FONADES; to Justin Savadogo, Ousman Ouedraogo, Adaman Kabré, and Pierre Forrat of SIX-S; to Raymond Chevalier and Abdullah Sawego of Foster Parents Plan International; and to Knud Jensen and M. Gilles of the World Council of Churches.

Chapter 13

KORDOFAN AGROFORESTRY EXTENSION PROJECT
Northern Kordofan, Sudan

Project Implementing Agency:
CARE-Sudan

Case Writer:
Peter J. Woodrow

I. INTRODUCTION

This case describes the experience of CARE in implementing the Kordofan Agroforestry Extension Project in the Kordofan Region of Sudan. The project was undertaken at the same time that CARE was operating the emergency food distribution system for most of Kordofan. The agroforestry program addressed the long-term effects of environmental degradation and desertification in the region, problems which underlay the drought and famine of 1983-85. The Kordofan Agroforestry Extension Project (KAEP) is of particular interest to the IRDP because it illustrates how an agency can devote major energies to meeting the urgent needs of people and, at the same time, attack some of the essential long-term development difficulties that contributed to the crisis.

The Kordofan Agroforestry Extension Project was funded by CARE Canada as a joint effort by CARE and the Forestry Department of the Sudan Ministry of Agriculture and Natural Resources. CARE's role was to provide technical assistance, special material inputs (cement, vehicles, etc.), and budgetary assistance, while the Forestry Department seconded members of its regular staff to work with the project. The Department's considerable network and years of experience were crucial elements in the project.

SUDAN

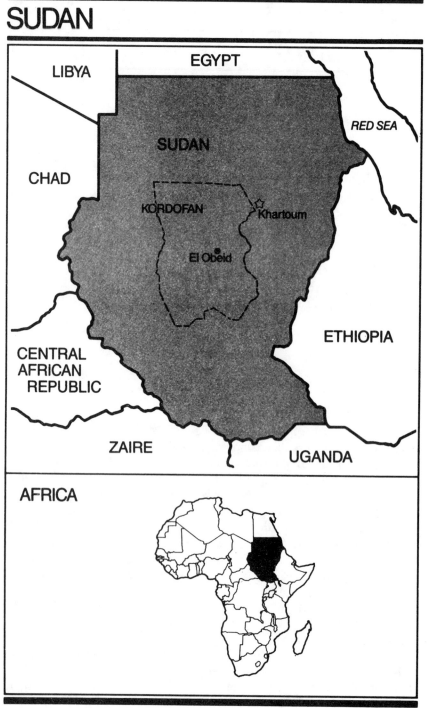

LIBYA

EGYPT

RED SEA

SUDAN

CHAD

KORDOFAN

☆ Khartoum

El Obeid

ETHIOPIA

CENTRAL
AFRICAN
REPUBLIC

ZAIRE

UGANDA

AFRICA

Map By Jerry Alexander

In addition to the KAEP and food distribution programs, CARE operated other projects in Kordofan including: supplementary feeding, water supply management, renewable resources conservation, household garden re-establishment, seed distribution, women's development, and child health. Thus CARE had developed a multi-sectoral approach in the region. This case history does not treat each of these sectors but focuses only on the agroforestry project.

II. DESCRIPTION OF PROJECT CONTEXT AND CONDITIONS

Sudan is the largest country of Africa and is home to twenty-five million people. The dominant ethnic group is Arabic speaking, although there are an estimated one hundred other language groups in the country. In many ways, Sudan is the meeting point of black Africa and the Arab Middle East. The long-standing conflict between populations of the North and other groups in the South has posed political and economic problems since independence in 1956.

Climatically the country is diverse, ranging from extensive desert in the north, to arid and semi-arid rangelands in central regions, to tropical forest in the far south. The economy is largely agricultural, and development efforts have concentrated in that sector.

Since independence from the British/Egyptian condominium in 1956, Sudan has had successive periods of democratic and military rule, culminating in the long military-dominated rule of President Jaafar al Nimeiri from 1969-85. Nimeiri was deposed in 1985 in a military *coup d'etat*. However, the conflict with the South has continued since the restoration of civilian government. Sudan has also experienced economic pressure (and internal dissension) due to the presence of about one million refugees, coming from Chad to the west, Uganda to the south, and Ethiopia to the east. In addition, diplomatic relations between Sudan and Ethiopia have been strained as each country has been seen to support insurgencies against the other, with Ethiopia supporting the movement in Sudan's South, and Sudan providing sanctuary for Eritreans and Tigrayans. These conflicts claimed resources that Sudan might otherwise have had available for development efforts.

Background to the 1983-85 Drought

At the time of the 1983-85 drought, there were approximately seventeen million *feddans* (1 feddan = 1.04 acres or 0.42 hectares) under cultivation in Sudan. Of these, only four million *feddans* were irrigated. Therefore, a large portion of Sudanese agriculture was dependent on rainfall, and consequently has been subjected to the periodic droughts that affect the Sahel. In both 1982 and 1983 the rains were poor in many areas of Sudan. In 1984 they failed altogether. The scant stored grain reserves had already been used to cope with earlier shortages; by late 1984 the situation was desperate. In addition to crop losses, much of the livestock died, destroying the means of livelihood for many nomadic people and those sedentary populations who also relied on animals.

Prior to 1984, the government did not have a functioning early warning system. Full recognition of the size and extent of the problem came very late. The migration of large numbers of people to urban areas signalled the crisis to the government. An appeal was issued to the international community for assistance, and by late 1984 relief efforts had been initiated by donors in Europe and North America.

Northern Kordofan

The Kordofan Region of Sudan occupies a huge square in the center of the country, although it is usually considered part of the "West" (which also includes the Darfur Region). It is one of the largest of the regions of Sudan, with 381,000 square kilometers, stretching 750 km by 525 km. The 1983 census indicated that the region held 3.24 million people. Of these, 63 percent were settled farmers, 24 percent were nomadic or semi-nomadic herders, and 13 percent were urban dwellers. The capital of the region is El Obeid, located in the southern part of Northern Kordofan.

The region includes rich savannah in the far south, semi-arid clay plains in the center, arid bush further to the north, and, finally, true desert to the north and west. The agricultural activities in these climatic zones include livestock herding in the bush and desert regions, traditional and mechanized grain farming in the clay plains, and other farming and cattle raising in the far south.

Of particular interest to this case is the "gum belt" which is in Northern Kordofan, south of the desert. Here rains have averaged 300-600 mm per year, and farmers planted mostly millet and sorghum with some sesame and peanuts. Following traditional practice, these crops were grown for about five years, followed by fifteen to twenty years when *Acacia senegal* or *Acacia seyal*, the source of gum arabic, was planted. This traditional rotation system allowed regeneration of the soil (the acacia is a fairly good nitrogen fixer), provided a secure dry season crop, retained soil and provided fodder. Also, gum arabic was one of Sudan's major export crops. In the years before the drought, due to factors that will be explained below, this rotation/fallow system had broken down, contributing to soil degradation and desertification.

Northern Kordofan was ecologically fragile and under increasing pressure from population growth, drought, changing agricultural practices, and demands for wood for charcoal.

Vulnerabilities of Northern Kordofan[1]

Physical/Material Vulnerabilities

CARE's proposal for the Kordofan Agroforestry Extension Project summarized the agricultural vulnerabilities of the area:

> Kordofan is currently beset by a number of severe economic problems, the most obvious of which are drought and famine. The agricultural economy of the region is floundering and family incomes have fallen. In recent years, desertification has been occurring at an alarming rate. Some of the main indications of economic destabilization are as follows:
>
> 1. Crop yields per unit area have declined dramatically over the past twenty years in the traditional rain-fed sector. Yields of sesame, millet and groundnuts have fallen by up to 80 percent and sorghum by 50-70 percent.
>
> 2. Sedentary cultivation has expanded far to the north of the traditional agronomic dry limit (250 mm isohyet[2]), thus severely reducing the nomadic rangelands.
>
> 3. The gum arabic land rotation has all but disappeared in most areas of Northern Kordofan as farmers attempt to cultivate their land for up to eight to ten years, exhausting soil fertility and creating further dehabilitation through wind erosion.
>
> 4. Widespread deforestation has occurred as a result of expanding agriculture, decreasing forage supplies, increasing prices for charcoal, decreasing production of gum arabic, and an increasing urban demand for cooking fuel. Large tracts of natural *Acacia senegal* stands have died because of drought. Gum arabic production in 1984/85 for Kordofan was 25 percent of the 1983/84 figure and only 15 percent of the average annual production of the 1970s.
>
> 5. Previously stable dunes have been rendered active through deforestation and overgrazing, in some cases threatening a number of communities practicing small-scale irrigated agriculture in wadis and depressions.
>
> 6. Livestock numbers expanded to a pre-drought level of 75 percent above the rangeland's carrying capacity, severely depleting the grazing resource and preventing natural regeneration of shrubs and trees.

1. This was one of the earliest cases written by IRDP and, as such, did not include a pre-project capacities analysis. The importance of the early assessment of capacities was a lesson learned through successive project visits. The impact of the project on capacities is discussed later in the case.

2. Isohyets are rainfall regions. For instance the 250 mm isohyet receives an average of 250 mm of rainfall per year.

7. Unfavorable pricing policies and marketing structures have reduced the real returns of gum arabic producers to levels of questionable economic viability. A farmer may earn up to 200 percent more from charcoal production than from gum arabic per unit land area in any one year, which acts as a disincentive to maintaining natural and planted stands of *Acacia senegal*.[3]

In addition, water, or the lack of it, was a matter of constant concern for Northern Kordofan. Water yards, with powered pumps, were constructed in the area. These have become gathering points for settlements which have led, in turn, to deforestation and overgrazing. An added problem has been maintenance of the pumping equipment. The government water department has been responsible for maintenance but often it has not had the resources to fulfill this responsibility. Many of the traditional catchment methods have deteriorated, due to poor maintenance and overuse. These problems have especially affected the nomads and their livestock who depend on a complex network of water sources. They have put further pressure on the mechanical borehole water yards, leading to conflicts with settled people.

Health is poor and health care scarce in Kordofan. Rural people are especially vulnerable to water-borne diseases and to the diseases of childhood that could be prevented through immunization programs. Health problems are compounded in times of drought when people become more susceptible to killing diseases.

Basic infrastructure is lacking in most of rural Kordofan. There are no permanent paved roads. In the rainy season many areas become completely inaccessible by vehicle, making marketing problematic. Most rural communities also lack electricity, storage facilities, or adequate school buildings. These factors are both symptoms and causes of the poverty of rural Sudan, leaving communities with limited capacity to cope with crises such as drought.

Pests have been a major problem for farmers, particularly in the period following droughts when many natural predators have died or migrated. Unfortunately, the pest population always springs back more quickly than that of the control animals. Locusts, grasshoppers and rodents have caused major crop losses over the years.

Social/Organizational Vulnerabilities

Villagers in rural Kordofan have remained isolated from each other and from any central authority. There have been no regular means for communicating and, as noted, roads have often been impassable. Reports about conditions and needs in outlying areas, therefore, often have not

---

3. CARE, "Kordofan Agroforestry Extension Project: Concept Paper," August, 1985, and "Kordofan Development Strategy Statement II," March, 1986.

reached the towns. While in "normal" times this has not posed a problem, in times of crisis isolation of this kind can mean that government or private agency assistance is slow in coming.

In terms of local leadership and government administration, rural Sudan has seen several changes since independence. Prior to the Nimeiri years, local government operated through what was called "Native Administration," a hierarchical system of traditional leaders. At the top of this system, for each tribe, there was a *nazir* who worked with several *umdas*, each of whom was responsible for several villages. There was a sheikh in each village. Conflicts between tribes over grazing or water rights were handled by the *nazirs* of the tribes in question. The Nimeiri regime abolished this system, replacing it with officers appointed by the central government and with a local party-based organization (the Sudan Socialist Union). As a result, many conflicts had to be contained by military or police action, and mobilization of people often failed. This system also proved, in the event, to be ineffective for organizing the delivery of relief goods to the local level.

After the *coup d'etat* of 1985 which removed the Nimeiri regime, the Native Administration system was reinstated. However, after 15 years of disuse, it has taken time to return to its former effectiveness, and resources for government programs have often been sorely lacking.

Partly as a result of these changes in rural administration, many villages in Kordofan have lacked an effective means for discussing village problems, generating solutions and implementing development.

As a consequence, villages have generally not been able to demand services from various government bodies. In some cases a powerful sheikh has exercised personal leadership and political clout to press for water yards, schools, etc. Because the Sudanese government departments lack resources to meet all the needs at the village level, those villages which tend to be closer to the towns, get what is available.

We have already noted that there is increased conflict between nomadic and sedentary groups in Kordofan. Sedentary agriculture has expanded into areas formerly reserved as rangelands for nomads. There have been increasing disputes over available water. The regulation of land use among farmers and nomads has been a major planning and implementation challenge for the government. The unresolved land and water conflicts increase organizational, as well as physical, vulnerability for the region.

Motivational/Attitudinal Vulnerabilities

Lack of resources and isolation have weakened initiative for generating ideas and solving problems in Kordofan. People in Northern Kordofan have learned to wait for government or some other agency to come to solve their problems. On the other hand, field workers have found that people are not hopeless, but are quite responsive. Once some initiative has been taken and skepticism has been overcome, village people have shown that they are interested and innovative. As we shall see below, after the CARE-supported project began to show some success, new ideas and plans began to spring up among villagers.

III. PROJECT HISTORY AND DEVELOPMENT

Program Initiation

CARE has been involved in Kordofan since 1982, working on water resource management and energy conservation (especially fuel-efficient stoves). In late 1984, CARE was chosen to distribute food to famine-stricken people, first in Northern Kordofan and later in Southern Kordofan as well. An initial 41,000 MT of sorghum (and an eventual total of 250,000 MT) were donated through USAID. CARE also operated a supplementary feeding program in the region for pregnant and lactating women and children under age five. They also distributed seed for the re-establishment of grain crops and household gardens.

Despite this intensive emergency program with its typical preoccupation with logistical problems and the reality of human death and desperation, CARE began to think about the long-term environmental trends in the region—the origins and effects of the drought and the other dynamics of environmental degradation and desertification. In August 1985, at the height of the drought relief program, CARE staff in Sudan drew up a long-term development strategy for CARE's work in Kordofan, and a detailed plan for work in forestry. Staff, who included several foresters or geographers, saw forestry as crucial for halting desertification and restoring the viability of agricultural activities in Northern Kordofan. The new forestry program began activities in November, 1985.

Project Design

The Kordofan Agroforestry Extension Project (KAEP) was designed to build the agroforestry skills of local people. It also combatted the destruction of natural and planted stands of *Acacia senegal* which had been ravaged by drought and its secondary effects such as the cutting and selling of trees for income. The program aimed to re-establish rural income from gum arabic in Northern Kordofan. The project helped establish community nurseries controlled and operated by local villagers. It also created and supported a network of forestry extension workers to provide technical assistance at the village level in key areas of the region. CARE worked closely with the government Forestry Department and supported the increase in institutional capacity of that key government agency. Apart from two expatriate technical workers, the staff of KAEP were all seconded from the Forestry Department and were to remain with the Department when CARE's involvement ended. Project planning documents which describe the goals of KAEP are described below.

Project Goals

Final Goal

The final goal of the Kordofan Agroforestry Extension Project is to increase the sustainable agricultural productivity and income-generating capacity of 50,000 rural inhabitants in at least sixty villages in the Kordofan region through the planting and long-term maintenance of 1.8 million trees.

Intermediate Goals

1. Sustainable, self-financing operation of 60 village nurseries by 1990 (i.e., total annual revenue exceeds total annual costs).
2. A self-help tree-planting effort, whereby villagers purchase, plant, and tend seedlings produced by village and demonstration nurseries:
   - 100,000 seedlings planted in FY '86
   - 200,000 seedlings planted in FY '87
   - 350,000 seedlings planted in FY '88
   - 500,000 seedlings planted in FY '89
   - 650,000 seedlings planted in FY '90
3. Establishment of an effective, region-wide agroforestry extension system, as part of regional operations of the Forestry Department, reaching all sectors of the rural population, and increasing their awareness of the benefits of specific agroforestry techniques.[4]

Not mentioned explicitly, but an integral part of the project, was a program of agroforestry and environmental awareness and practical skills training for young people through the school system.

Project Development

Village Nurseries

In its first year, KAEP established six village nurseries, five of them in Um Ruwaba district to the east of El Obeid and one operated by a local secondary school outside of El Obeid town next to KAEP's own demonstration nursery. The five Um Ruwaba nurseries were chosen because they each had a reliable source of water from a water yard that had

4. CARE, "Kordofan Agroforestry Extension Project: Project Proposal: FY 1987-1990"

previously been rehabilitated by the CARE water program. The nurseries used runoff water from the water yards. CARE provided materials and technical assistance for building a sunken tank to collect the runoff water. The Forestry Department provided seeds and plastic bags for seedlings. The villages provided labor for building the tank and seed beds and materials for fencing and shade.

As the first step for setting up the village nurseries, KAEP staff initiated a village meeting in each prospective nursery site to present a proposal for the project and to hear the reactions of local people. If the response of villagers was positive, the village elected a nursery committee, usually including the local sheikh and other important people. This committee was to mobilize people to work on the nursery, select a paid nurseryman and determine policies for the sale of seedlings and vegetables produced in the nursery. They would also help determine the needs for seedlings in terms of both quantity and variety. These committees included both men and women, although the participation of women in the program was lower than that of men. In some villages, women set up their own committee and suggested new activities and additional tree varieties to support their traditional work roles. An example was their suggestion to grow henna plants used for making dyes.

The main species planted included *Acacia senegal* for gum arabic, *Acacia mellifera* for live fencing, and other varieties for fruit or household shade. After the poor germination of Forestry Department seeds the first year, villagers were trained to collect seeds from healthy specimens in their local areas.

The costs of operating the nurseries were lower than expected. In most cases, the villages have been able to pay the nurseryman out of proceeds from the sale of seedlings and vegetables. In the dry season, when tree seedlings were not being grown, the nursery areas were used to grow vegetables, and income from their sale was split with the nurseryman. Thus, for the first time, the villages had funds that were completely in their control and held in common. Villagers have generated ideas for use of the funds and for expansion of the vegetable gardens/tree nurseries. Village people became more excited and committed to the effort once there was real income (however small) from the project.

Although the nurseries were successful in growing seedlings, the quantities produced were below targets because of difficulties getting started and low germination of Forestry Department seeds. In addition, a large percentage of the planted seedlings were destroyed by gerbils which pulled them up and ate the leaves. Remarkably, despite these setbacks, the village committees remained enthusiastic about the coming years and continued to change and expand the program.

After the first rainy season, CARE commissioned a village survey, using non-KAEP people drawn from other CARE projects, and staff from the Forestry Department and the government Statistics Department. They talked with village people at each of the nursery sites. They reported wide acceptance and enthusiasm for the project. The survey also showed that people wanted increased numbers of seedlings, despite the losses from rodents the first year. In a few cases, people thought the nursery belonged to CARE (or to the CARE staff person who had come to help build the tank and set up the nursery). Those misconceptions were addressed through village meetings and close work with the village nursery committees.

In 1987, the ongoing support of the Um Ruwaba village nurseries and regular contact with the field extensionist assigned to this area was turned over to Save the Children (USA) which worked in the district while CARE/KAEP moved on to setting up nurseries in En Nahud district to the west.

Agroforestry Extensionists

The emphasis of the extension program was to establish a sustainable corps of foresters trained to work at the village level to support and mobilize people to work with trees, to re-establish gum gardens and to plant fuelwood lots. CARE was determined not to become involved in paying for efforts or materials that could not be sustained by the Forestry Department (FD) after CARE's role was finished. All of the staff of KAEP were seconded from and paid by the FD, with the exception of two expatriates who were counterparts to FD staff in management roles and worked as project coordinator and extension coordinator. Thus, CARE focussed on building the capacity of the existing government structure, rather than establishing a parallel and competing organization.

A key element of this aspect of the program was the training of field workers in extension skills. All FD staff knew a good deal about trees and their care, but few knew how to work with village people to pass those skills along. CARE/KAEP set up a training program that will be utilized by several other forestry programs in the region (UNDP, UNICEF, etc.). The FD people chosen as field extensionists were forest overseers, FD workers who were secondary school graduates and who worked in their home areas. These overseers seldom advanced in the department since they lacked the required paper qualifications and could not find opportunities to take the few available courses. By working with people who were committed to their local area and unlikely to move away through advancement, CARE was able to support the development of a fairly stable cadre of extensionists. Part of the training of the field extensionists involved teaching them how to work with women. KAEP hired a woman with experience in village organizing to help male extensionists understand how to reach women with their extension program.

The KAEP program placed extensionists in the countryside with responsibility for working with a designated set of villages where nurseries had been established. In the past, FD workers did not have direct contact with rural people, except to enforce laws regarding tree cutting (when possible). To encourage work at the village level, the field extensionists were given an incentive allowance, a donkey or camel for transport, and a house to live in. In each district in the region, an assistant conservation forester supervised five field extensionists. Eventually, the program hoped to place an extensionist in each rural council (of which there are forty-seven in the nine districts of Kordofan region).

The duties of the field extensionists, as described in CARE/KAEP program documents, were as follows:

> He/she travels by donkey, camel or horse and conducts continuous extension to all (men, women, children, settled and nomad) at village gatherings, in individual houses, in schools, and through committees and other groups regarding the following:
> a) agroforestry awareness;
> b) ideas for agroforestry initiatives in the rural areas;
> c) techniques required to initiate and sustain agroforestry initiatives; and
> d) follow-up information and assistance to all conducting agroforestry activities.[5]

In 1986, the establishment of this network had just begun. The first training session for field extensionists was scheduled for February 1987. In the course of its work with the Forestry Department, CARE was also to provide funds for the construction of an office building to house the central office for the Agroforestry Extension unit in the FD compound in El Obeid. Housing the unit with the rest of the FD was intended to help integrate its activities with the ongoing activities of the department.

Education and Awareness

The education portion of KAEP was part of the extension effort, but it concentrated on schools and used teachers as agents, rather than the FD field extensionists. The school curriculum for Sudan includes units on "practical science" for rural areas. However, few teachers have been trained to teach such units and curriculum materials and/or budget supports have rarely been available. KAEP worked with the School Gardens and Nutrition Program under the Ministry of Education to promote the practical science curriculum and garden plots in school yards where actual horticulture and agroforestry skills were learned. The schools got fruit and shade trees for their compounds and grew vegetables to improve the

5. CARE, "Kordofan Agroforestry Extension Project: Extension Component," 1986.

nutrition of children. KAEP had two staff people devoted entirely to working with schools and teachers, one of whom, a woman, had been a teacher of practical science and was in a good position to assist other teachers with practical suggestions.

Another aspect of the program was the production of educational materials for use in schools, such as a comic-book-style environmental magazine for children, modelled after successful examples developed elsewhere in Africa. Film strips and posters were also planned. KAEP also produced T-shirts printed with a tree and slogan which were widely distributed and quite popular.

IV. CAPACITIES AND VULNERABILITIES ANALYSIS OF KAEP

The main thrust of the KAEP/CARE program was organizing village-based activities, disseminating skills for agroforestry, training field extensionists, and raising awareness regarding environmental issues. The orientation of the program was *not* on the provision of large amounts of material goods or funds, but on mobilizing and training human resources for working on the serious ecological and economic issues of the region. The immediate physical payoff from this approach would be relatively modest, but was expected to blossom as the project matured.

Physical/Material Capacities and Vulnerabilities

If successful, one of the main effects of the KAEP would be to slow the pace of desertification and soil degradation in Northern Kordofan, through re-establishment of gum arabic production and fallow rotation for rain-fed grain crops. By promoting local village action, the program was to mobilize large numbers of people in this campaign, with potential for a great physical impact on the environment. Previous efforts based solely on understaffed and under-budgeted government agencies could not hope to generate the kind of mass human effort necessary for combatting the serious ecological challenges of the region.

The project concentrated on developing a sustainable model for village agroforestry activities that could be perpetuated with no ongoing outside inputs, apart from the technical assistance and moral support from the FD field extensionist. By 1986, the nurseries in the five Um Ruwaba villages had already proved to be self-sustaining in financial terms, meeting some of the demand for seedlings, paying for the services of a nurseryman, and even providing a small surplus which the village nursery committees applied to improvements in the nursery or other village projects.

An expected physical benefit of the program was an increase in income from gum arabic for rural farmers. The combination of pressures from fuelwood demands, population increases, and the poor pricing and marketing incentives for gum arabic had devastated the industry in Sudan. With new pricing policies in place, plus these new efforts at the village level, there was hope that gum arabic production could again become a stable and significant source of income for rural communities. The diversification in income sources for farmers would also help make them less vulnerable to the consequences of drought.

The village nursery program created the additional by-product of vegetable growing. This provided additional income for some individuals and for the village fund plus additional nutritious food. In coming years, fruit trees produced in the nursery should also provide food and income for villagers.

Social/Organizational Capacities and Vulnerabilities

The impact of the KAEP program in the social/organizational realm was in two areas: 1) the development of a network of field extensionists under the Forestry Department; and 2) development of village-level organizations to take responsibility for agroforestry initiatives.

The KAEP program had a strong commitment to institution-building in the Forestry Department. The program aimed to develop a group of forestry officials to work directly with people in rural communities on issues relevant to their economic well-being and the long-term ecological viability of the area. This differed from past patterns of FD work. By training staff in the skills for working at the village level and by providing them with the means (transport, housing) and incentives for doing the work, the FD was establishing a system for penetrating rural culture and affecting the way local people interacted with their environment. The Forestry Department could become more closely integrated into rural life, rather than being a remote government agency. As an agency, they gained allies in the effort to combat desertification and promote reforestation—an impossible task for them alone. In general, the scheme had low costs with high potential returns.

At the village level, KAEP promoted new social units in the form of the village nursery committees. Although KAEP only provided minimal material inputs to set these committees in motion (tools, cement, technical information, seeds, bags), in the villages that established nurseries, the committees became an effective force. In most cases, the main village leaders, including the sheikh and other members of village councils, were involved. The mechanisms of the nursery program demonstrated what could be done. The committees will continue to generate small amounts of money for village projects, adding to their sense that they can get things done.

While the longer-term impact of the village committee structure is unknown, some committees began to generate ideas beyond the limits of the nursery program. CARE staff found on several occasions that when they called village meetings to talk about the establishment of village nurseries, people were eager to talk about other issues that were on their minds. Villagers commented that they had rarely come together to discuss problems. In several cases where CARE helped set up a village committee to deal with the tree nursery, the village took up other efforts that would affect village life or development. In addition, meetings about the nursery became forums for discussion of other village issues.

The KAEP program also provided a mechanism for gaining interagency cooperation among government departments, linking forestry with water management and with schools. The program could begin to break down the isolation of the villages and increase their contact with government departments that could assist them. At the same time, they were engaged in an effort that they could sustain on their own without dependence on outside help.

The KAEP program may not directly affect the conflicts among tribal groups within villages or between sedentary farmers and nomadic groups. It did plan some initiatives with nomads which could affect their relationships to trees, ground cover and fodder, and to the agricultural communities they move through annually.

Attitudinal/Motivational Capacities and Vulnerabilities

The main effect of the KAEP program was naturally on the people in the villages which had village nurseries. KAEP staff remarked on the transformation of village nursery committees once they saw actual income from the sale of seedlings. The cash in hand had a profound effect on their sense of what was possible with a little help and encouragement, and with organized effort on the part of people working together for common benefit. While the experience in each village was different (due to different leadership, different local conditions, different understandings of the project, different levels of involvement by women), each of the six villages was consistently enthusiastic about its nursery and its potential to benefit the community. This was significantly different from villages where there was a sense of waiting for someone else to intervene to help them. In the short term, KAEP seemed to have broken through a sense of inertia.

KAEP staff noted that villagers expressed a commitment to continuing the nursery project, despite widespread loss of seedlings to rodents in the first year. Another significant indicator of new capacity was the willingness of villagers to undertake activities that would not bear fruit for several years. They were willing to take risks, and to act for long-term future results.

A Note About Training and Education

As already noted, the main focus of the KAEP effort was in organizing people, passing along crucial skills and information, and raising awareness of critical environmental issues. Each element of the project concentrated on spreading knowledge and practical methods for addressing vulnerabilities through working with the Forestry Department, training field extensionists, establishing village nurseries and committees, training teachers, providing curriculum materials on the environment, and supporting school gardens.

V. LESSONS AND DILEMMAS FOR FUTURE PROJECT DESIGN

The CARE/KAEP project raises several issues that are useful to consider in terms of future programs in similar settings.

Education and Training Focus vs. Material Goods

KAEP focussed much of its effort on training specific groups of people (extensionists, teachers, village nursery workers) and on education in communities about environmental issues. The project provided remarkably few material inputs, recognizing that where the essential elements of a forestry campaign were present (seed, soil, water), the main constraints were knowledge and the mobilization of human energies. Many programs, particularly those in emergency settings (conditions under which KAEP began), assume that material needs are the most important. Under that assumption, there is a danger of providing too many goods, and thereby overwhelming potential community initiative. KAEP provided just enough material and personal support to make the program attractive, while clearly expecting full engagement and contributions from the communities. Thus, the organization of people and transmission of skills were as important as the actual trees planted and gum arabic production. In fact, the two are interrelated and CARE's programming approach relied on this.

Work on a Long-Term Issue in an Emergency Context

The Kordofan region had not recovered from the 1983-85 drought and famine when CARE proposed KAEP in mid-1985. Yet the effects of the reforestation program would not be felt in material terms for several years in terms of tree and gum production. By the time the program started, in November 1985, farmers were just seeing the results of their first good harvest in three years, but food distribution continued through most of 1986 while famine conditions persisted in some areas. Despite these conditions, farmers proved to be risk takers, and, with a little encouragement and modest success, initiators and innovators. The common assumption that drought/famine victims will not act for the long term or that they do not have community resources for doing so was proved false, at least in this case.

Focus on Institution Building

NGOs are often faced with the choice of setting up new organizations or working with existing institutions, however imperfect. In this case, KAEP chose to build the Forestry Department's capacity rather than establish a network of village forestry efforts outside of the FD's involvement. In this situation, the prospect for sustained follow-up to village-level efforts was greatly enhanced by working with and through the FD.

Sustainable Program Model

CARE consciously chose a strategy that was sustainable. The village nurseries could be financially viable. The Field Extensionist Program relied on existing FD staff. The other material inputs from CARE were very modest. When poverty and suffering are severe, agencies often feel they should provide significant material and technical resources to gain solutions. Such goods, funds, or technical assistance are usually welcomed by local people. But reliance on significant amounts of external inputs may, in fact, cause the ultimate failure of a program. The NGO must find the proper balance between giving enough and giving too much.

One concern is how the KAEP program will be evaluated. In the early stages, quantitative measures of numbers of seedlings produced and planted, and numbers of nurseries established, were low. More important were the strength of village level organizations, the understanding and commitment on the part of field extensionists, and the effective dispersal of knowledge in the community. However, these factors are difficult to measure, and therefore, to evaluate. They are the foundation on which later, measurable production must be based. Setting evaluation criteria that capture both measurable and non-measurable gains is difficult, but necessary, if programs such as KAEP are to be accurately assessed.

Dilemmas Regarding Participation

CARE/KAEP brought a pre-packaged program idea to the villages. They did not come in with an open agenda asking what people wanted, prepared to negotiate a different program with each village. This approach had the strength of being specific and practical. Villagers were not required, on fairly brief acquaintance, to negotiate a long-term relationship with the project for an ambiguous set of objectives. Nor were they asked to assess their own needs. The short-term success of the nursery initiative did, however, provide an opening for further and more open-ended program exploration. Once the nursery operation was running well, and village people sensed their own ability to accomplish something, they were in a stronger position to identify needs and generate possible solutions than they would have been before the nursery effort. In effect, they developed the ability to be an equal party to program negotiations.

The issue this raises is how to encourage participation in project design and implementation that fits the context, engaging local people at a point where they see the gains from being involved and move into positions to shape and control project activities. In a situation where needs are apparent to everybody, needs assessment by participants wastes time and is redundant. Beginning with the creation of local organization through which capacities are recognized and increased makes more sense.

REFERENCES : CARE Documents

"Concept Paper," a Kordofan Agroforestry Extension Project Document, August 1985.
"Project Activity Targets FY 1987," Kordofan Agroforestry Extension Project Document.
"Project Proposal: FY 1987-1990," Kordofan Agroforestry Extension Project Document.
"Extension Component," (annex to above documents).
"Kordofan Development Strategy II," March 1986.
"Kordofan Emergency Feeding/Drought Relief Program 1984-1986: Final Report," January 1987.

ACKNOWLEDGMENTS

This case was written in March 1987. The author wishes to acknowledge the contribution of Idris El Tahir El Nayal, a Sudanese geographer, who helped gather the field information and made important conceptual contributions. Thanks are also due to Rudy Ramp, Rick Embry, Charles Tapp, and Andy Pugh, CARE staff in New York; Earl Goodyear, Tom Alcedo, M. A. Khan, John Miskell, and Steve Wallace in Khartoum; and Patta Scott-Villiers, Ben Messer, B. B. Saha, and the other KAEP staff in El Obeid who gave enormous amounts of time patiently answering questions and making arrangements.

Chapter 14

EARTHQUAKE HOUSING RECONSTRUCTION AND RURAL DEVELOPMENT
Joyabaj, Quiché, Guatemala

Project Implementing Agencies:
ALIANZA
Redd Barna and the Save the Children Alliance

Case Writers:
Roberto Muj Miculax
and Don Schramm

I. INTRODUCTION

This case history studies the reconstruction work of a non-governmental organization known as the *Alianza para el Desarrollo Integral de la Juventud*, commonly known in Guatemala as ALIANZA.[1] The relief/development project began following an earthquake which shook much of Guatemala in 1976. The earthquake rehabilitation project has continued in various forms since, in the Quiché region of northern Guatemala. The project was successful both at the level of institution-building and at the level of community satisfaction. This case history covers a period of more than ten years, from 1976 to 1987.

1. ALIANZA receives active support from Redd Barna (Norway), and funding from Save the Children Alliance members: Rettet Das Kind (Austria), Canadian Save the Children, Red Barnet (Denmark), Radda Barnen (Sweden), Save the Children Fund (United Kingdom), and Save the Children Federation (US).

GUATEMALA

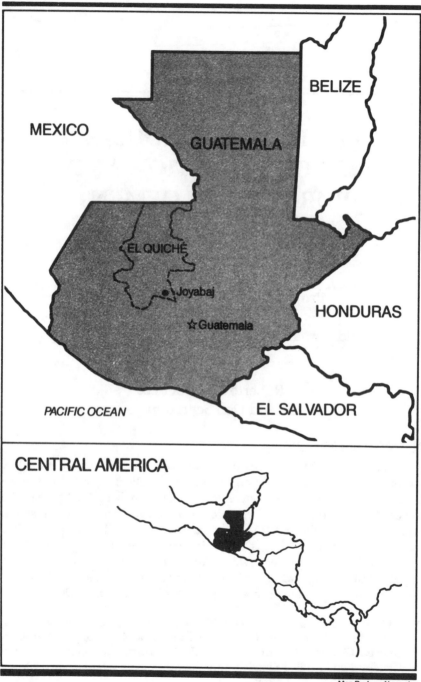

MEXICO

BELIZE

GUATEMALA

EL QUICHÉ

● Joyabaj

☆ Guatemala

HONDURAS

PACIFIC OCEAN

EL SALVADOR

CENTRAL AMERICA

II. DESCRIPTION OF PROJECT CONTEXT

The 1976 Earthquake

The story of this disaster began on 4 February 1976, at 3:33 a.m., when a tremendous earthquake struck Guatemala. Almost instantaneously, 23,000 people were killed and many thousands were injured. Throughout the country, from the capital city to the most forgotten and marginal rural *departmento*, there was widespread devastation. In some settlements, only 50 percent of the houses were destroyed; in others 100 percent of the homes were laid to ruin. Almost 4,000,000 Guatemalans were affected, with over 1,000,000 left homeless, more than 250,000 houses destroyed and $1 billion worth of damage to buildings and infrastructure.

The earthquake of 1976 was felt in more than 60,000 square kilometers out of the 130,000 that make up Guatemala and neighboring Belize. In Guatemala City, 1,200 people were killed and 45 percent of the city was destroyed. Thousands of landslides (secondary effects of the shock) blocked roads and cut surface communications throughout central Guatemala.

Guatemala has recorded seismic disturbances for centuries. Guatemala City and the old capital of Antigua have been severely damaged by earthquakes at least fifteen times since the sixteenth century. Before 1976, the most recent major earthquake had occurred in conjunction with a volcanic eruption of Santa Maria, near Quezaltenango, when some 1,000 people were reported killed in April 1908.

In 1976, Joyabaj, in Quiché, northern Guatemala, was struck by an intense seismic disturbance that registered 7.5 on the Richter scale and 9 on the modified Mercali scale. During the catastrophe, 600 *joyabatecos* (residents of Joyabaj) died and another 5,500 were seriously injured. Over 95 percent of the adobe construction (predominantly homes) was decimated, leaving an ambience of desolation, uncertainty and fear. In a few seconds, family and community economies were destroyed. During the post-disaster debris clean-up, much individual and community property was either lost or broken.

Background on Joyabaj

Located in the highlands, Joyabaj, or Xolabaj (meaning "place among rocks," or "jewels of rocks" in the local language, Quiché) is one of the *municipios* (a municipal unit of government, both urban and rural, something like a township in the central United States) of the *departmento* (department, or state) of El Quiché. This is part of the northwestern part of the country, situated 218 kilometers from the capital, Guatemala City. The *municipio* is located over the Motagua Fault, near the headwaters of the Rio

Grande, a river that runs to the Atlantic and separates Quiché from the neighboring *departmento* of Chimaltenango.

Joyabaj lies only 60 kilometers northwest of Guatemala City, but access is not easy. From the capital it can be reached either by the San Pedro-San Juan-San Raimundo-Paxchulum route, the Chimaltenango-San Martin route, or the Chichicastenango-Quiché-Zacualpa route. The last, covering more than 200 kilometers, is the longest but most certain in the rainy season.

The *municipio* has two distinct topographical/climatic regions: the Chuacus mountain range in the north/northeast and the mountainous but lower southern area, which is bordered by the Motagua River gorge on the south. The northern area has more precipitation and more temperature extremes, getting particularly cold at night. The southern region is more arid. Crops vary accordingly, with semi-tropical crops grown in the south while corn dominates the highest parts of the mountain range.

The climate of the *municipio* is temperate, with an annual rainfall of 900 mm The rainy season starts in May and ends in October. There is little irrigation, so most agriculture corresponds with the rainy season.

In 1976, the population of the *municipio* was more than 32,000 (up from 21,000 in 1950). That population included Guatemala's two major ethnic groups: 24 percent Ladinos and 76 percent Indians. There are two urban clusters in the *municipio*: Joyabaj, the main one with almost 2,000 inhabitants in 1976; and Pachulum, a town of about 1,000 located in the southeast corner of the *municipio*. The remaining population was scattered in rural settlements with Chuaquenum being the only rural community where houses were clustered.

Some Early History

The Quiché region was one of the more powerful indigenous kingdoms of the Mayan area at the time of the Spanish conquest. Tecun Uman, one of the Quiché leaders, who resisted to death the onslaught of the Spanish, is still a national hero.

Once the Spanish conquest took hold, the area followed the same pattern as the rest of the country. The Quiché population was taken into slavery at the beginning of the colonial period and later formed into a *pueblo de indios* (an Indian town), wherein the Indian population was forced into town settlement so as to be controlled more easily by the colonial authorities. The region of Joyabaj was then converted into an *encomienda*, and put under the control of an *encomendero*, to whom the Indians were to pay tribute in return for his responsibility to Christianize them. At the close of the colonial period, the *encomiendas* were broken up and the land became private property. The Indian population lost its communal land holdings, since they had no legal claim (by Spanish standards) to the land.

Economy of Joyabaj

The economy of Joyabaj is based in agriculture and livestock. Historically, the area was known for its production of corn, raw sugar (in the form of *panela*) and black beans. The *panela* was exported, but corn and beans were grown principally for consumption or local sale.

The main livestock production was pigs. Each family kept several pigs, with production decreasing as corn supply decreased toward the end of the growing season. Pigs were sold to buyers who took them to be butchered in Chimaltenango. Other animals, such as horses, cows, oxen, goats, and sheep were sold among neighbors.

Three forestry products were harvested from the wooded mountain areas: pom, turpentine and lumber. Pom is an incense made from pine pitch and sawdust, used for ceremonial purposes. Lumber was hand cut for local use. Turpentine, although production was outlawed by the national government, was still one of the main products of Pachulum. All these products contributed to widespread deforestation in the *municipio*.

Handicraft production was limited, with women weaving *huipiles* (colorful blouses) and belts, and the men crocheting bags. These were not sold outside Joyabaj.

Politics and Organization

Joyabaj was the administrative head of the *municipio*. The mayor of Joyabaj also functioned as the political head of the *municipio*. He normally was from the town, thus contributing to the geographic concentration of political power in the urban center. As in other parts of Guatemala, eighty auxiliary mayors were responsible for local administrative activities throughout the *municipio*.

Operating in semi-autonomous fashion alongside this administration was an Indian "mayorship," a traditional juridical institution carried over from colonial times. Its main function was to deal with domestic disputes among the Indian population and legal disputes concerning Quiché communal landholdings.

Political divisions of the *municipio* reflected national divisions. Every community was categorized according to the density of settlement and type of public services. The categories included: *villa, pueblo, aldea, caserio* (historically also known as *cantones* in the largest mountain *caserios*), *paraje, finca* and *hacienda*. The first three of these have some urban amenities and populations from 1,000 to 5,000. A *caserio* is simply a rural cluster of homes and a *paraje* is anything smaller than the first five categories. *Fincas* are big farms under one owner and *haciendas* are extensive landholdings.

The Physical Environment

In 1976, the 32,000 inhabitants of Joyabaj were distributed among the *cabacera municipal*, six *aldeas* (really only widely dispersed farms) and sixteen *caserios* (the smallest rural unit of settlement).

The nearest paved road to Joyabaj was at Santa Cruz del Quiché, 52 km and six hours distant from the town. A packed earth road led to Joyabaj through several other *municipios*—Chiche, Chinique, Zacualpa. Within the town, only the central plaza and several principal streets were of cobblestone. The remaining streets were dirt. Communications between Joyabaj and the outside world were handled through a local Post and Telegraph office. Telegrams normally took 2 to 3 days to arrive, so the *municipio* had no direct immediate communication with the rest of the country.

The Social Environment

The majority of the inhabitants of Joyabaj were of Maya-Quiché origin. Due to the distance from the capital, they were a "marginal" group within Guatemala. Families were organized into the traditional neighborhood organizations, the *cofradias*, for the celebration of Mayan rituals, sharing customs and folklore. At the time of the 1976 earthquake, the peasants of Joyabaj were unable to protect their rights or needs, simply because they could not speak Spanish. The majority of people spoke the native language, Quiché. Women lived a marginal life, with no power to express opinions or make decisions. They were responsible only for housework—cleaning, keeping the cooking fire, cooking, and caring for children.

Most inhabitants of the *municipio* were peasants with varying amounts of land. Most held small subsistence plots. Some owners of medium-sized plots occasionally hired workers, and a very small number of peasants had so much land that they hired others on a permanent basis. There was also a group of landless peasants who were sharecroppers. Finally, there were those whose main occupation was not agriculture or who had sufficient resources to live from simply owning, not working the land. This last group was typically Ladino. In addition, many of these rural families supplied labor to the coastal plantations. Annually, from eight to ten thousand landed and landless peasants travelled one or two times to this region to earn cash income.

There were a few masons who constructed homes with thick walls made of adobe bricks (laid up one on top of another and bound with a small amount of mud). Roofs were typically constructed of clay tiles supported by thick, heavy beams and rafters. Also, the thick walls were built relatively high and without any columns, and were thus quite unstable.

There were three main religions in the area: Church Catholicism, as represented by the church hierarchy and institutions; traditional Catholicism, as represented by the Indian hierarchy of *cofradias*; and various Protestant sects. The first, the Catholic Church, was dominated by priests and nuns from Spain. For the Indians, it represented a retreat from the traditional Indian religion: the leaders were mostly people who could read and write.

The second, traditional Catholicism, was a blend of institutional Catholicism and customs with origins in the Quiché culture. The *cofradia* was also a religious brotherhood whose explicit function was to guard and care for the saint images. They preserved the ceremonial customs of the Quiché. In Joyabaj, there were seven *cofradias*, each with ten *cofrades* (leaders) and their wives, who carried out secondary functions within the *cofradias*. There was a definite hierarchy, with each *cofradia* having a rigid internal structure. The men who attained the top positions were respected as elders among the Indian population. The final religious influence, Protestantism, existed principally in the towns of Joyabaj and Pachulum, and in a few rural Ladino areas.

In 1976, the health status of Joyabaj was precarious at best. The strain of seasonal migration, the climate changes and low wages combined to make malnutrition and malaria-like diseases endemic among all ages. The child mortality rate among the Indians of Guatemala was said to be as high as 150 per 1000.

The experience of the earthquake of 1976 brought some admirable consequences, because in that moment of anguish—of general grief—"all of us were brothers and sisters, we loved each other and helped each other with a surprising love. We forgot rancor, petty jealousies and enemies to share water, food, clothing and even humble homes and bedding."

III. PROJECT HISTORY AND DEVELOPMENT

In 1976, there were no local organizations prepared for earthquake relief. Groups, internal and external, which were already active in the area, were called on to modify their objectives and activities to respond.

The precursor to ALIANZA had been working in Joyabaj for three years prior to the earthquake of 1976. Since early 1974, there had been an active program in public health: instructing health *promotores* (extension workers) and midwives, as well as providing pre-natal orientation for women. The ALIANZA staff consisted of a physician, several midwives and a health program coordinator. The principal long-range goal was the incorporation of the program into a government-run local primary health care center so that ALIANZA could either withdraw or become part of the center. By February 1976, it was well on the way to achieving that goal.

From the beginning, ALIANZA staff had been clear that their guiding principle was "the improvement of the individual and community level of life." They also realized that such a program was ambitious under normal circumstances, and even more so under the chaotic situation following the earthquake. In 1983, ALIANZA was incorporated as a national institution, non-sectarian, and non-profit, which works towards the integrated development of the neediest Guatemalan communities.

Many agencies arrived to help Joyabaj after the earthquake. Those that arrived for a short time only were not well received. The national government assigned certain affected areas to certain agencies. Local groups felt that Joyabaj was the "most affected by the earthquake among all parts of Guatemala." While the same feeling was voiced in other localities of Guatemala, Joyabaj really was one of the most devastated zones. ALIANZA was to concentrate its work in the rural parts of Joyabaj, while government organizations and other PVOs would center their work on the two urban areas.

The program was to be implemented by the Save the Children Alliance, a joint effort of several agencies: *Rettet Das Kind* (Austria), Canadian Save The Children, *Red Barnet* (Denmark), *Redd Barna* (Norway), *Radda Barnens* (Sweden), Save the Children Fund (United Kingdom) and Save the Children Federation/Community Development Foundation (United States). The separate agencies would work through a unified local management team, under the direction of a single local coordinator and be organized as a new legal entity in Guatemala, the *Alianza para Desarrollo Juvenil Comunitario de Guatemala* (ALIANZA).

The Alliance agreed to work in the *Municipio* of Joyabaj as its target area after lengthy discussions with Guatemalan government agencies, with embassies and assistance agencies of each Alliance country, and with independent university and international relief experts. This project focussed on housing as an immediate need and used that as an entry into the longer-term development goals shared by the Alliance and the government.

ALIANZA was determined to respond to the "felt needs" of the people. The most critical need was anti-seismic housing. The project was designed to provide the materials at subsidized prices and the methods for the construction of light roofs and walls. Projects were developed within the community, rather than trying to import, in their entirety, pre-designed projects from other regions or situations. Local workers' teams provided both the labor and the design suggestions. Constant discussion of design issues led to confidence in the project and a feeling of community ownership in the final results.

Beginning with efforts to relieve the immediate needs for relief and reconstruction, the emphasis of the "Save the Children Alliance Joyabaj

Reconstruction Program" was to be gradually shifted to a more comprehensive development program, with projects to improve health and nutrition, education, productivity and rural infrastructure. ALIANZA did not want to fall into the trap exhibited by so many relief agencies: working for a short period of time during the immediate post-disaster assistance, then leaving suddenly with no ongoing local program in place. From the start, the five-year planning horizon of the project was critical. There were clearly understood long-term goals to strengthen the local institutions engaged in collective decision-making, self-help activities, credit and cooperatives, so that the communities of Joyabaj would become increasingly capable of self-sustained development efforts.

From an earthquake relief standpoint, the purpose was to encourage all the people in the municipality to rebuild their homes in accordance with basic principles of earthquake-resistant construction and to provide material assistance to those who were willing to undertake the necessary individual and collective initiatives to do that.

Other objectives included: 1) the training of individuals and families; 2) the organization of *comites pro-mejoramiento* (community improvement committees); and 3) the provision of community infrastructure: schools, bridges, local roads, and health clinics. The idea was to insert (to the extent possible) other community development messages into the housing rehabilitation and local education programs.

Housing Analysis

The housing damage caused by the earthquake was severe in the two urban centers. In Joyabaj, only four houses and a few public buildings survived. In Pachulum, about 80 percent of the homes were destroyed or damaged too severely to be usable. In rural areas, 70 percent of the houses either collapsed or suffered structural damage sufficient to make habitation hazardous.

In the immediate aftermath of the quake, few people built permanent houses. The majority built makeshift rooms for temporary protection through the rainy season, hoping to have more time, money and/or materials available when the rains ceased. Individuals and communities expressed a strong interest in using the best materials and techniques possible to avoid future destruction.

Several factors of the disaster were considered in designing the housing reconstruction program to respond to long-term as well as immediate housing needs. First, housing had failed not because the materials were inadequate, but because they were improperly used. The inexpensive adobe could be used in a more structurally sound manner.

Second, the use of tile roofs, for appearance, comfort, and status, had replaced traditional lighter roofs of straw. These heavier roofs were a major structural hazard in an earthquake, and lighter-weight materials, such as metal or asbestos cement would reduce that hazard.

Third, the evolutionary nature of rural housing had to be considered. Any temporary structure had to be built in anearthquake-resistant fashion, since it would remain part of the house, and not simply be a temporary shelter. Unless the frames were soundly constructed, new adobe walls would be built in the future weaker than the older walls and thus set the stage for the next disaster.

Phase One of the housing program was designed with three basic components: 1) training in the principles of earthquake-resistant housing, 2) building of demonstration houses, and 3) distribution of subsidized construction materials. Phase Two was designed as an outreach program to combine training follow-up, housing inspection and an opportunity to reach additional families in their villages, plus a review of credit arrangements, an evaluation of local committee performance and a needs assessment for long-range community development plans.

The Alliance chose to work closely with local organizations in the formation of a coalition called the *Comite Central de Reconstruccion Rural Joyabateca*. The *Comite* was composed of *Accion Catolica*, the *Liga Campesina* and the *Cofradia Indigena* (all local community development organizations). Throughout the Housing Rehabilitation Program, more than 75 percent of staff *promotores* were recruited from among Joyabaj residents. At the end of 1976, ALIANZA proposed the following goals:

Persons Trained	8,500
Buildings Constructed	85
Homes Built with Distributed Materials	4,000
Homes Inspected	1,500

During the first three months of the reconstruction program,[2] the materials distribution, the model house construction, and the training components were well integrated. Model houses served as the focus for storage and distribution of roof *laminas* (the corrugated, lightweight steel roof sheets used in anti-seismic construction) and a practical demonstration for the education of *promotores* and instructors. After three months, the following results were achieved:

Persons Trained	4,300
Buildings Constructed	12
Homes Built with Distributed Materials	None
Homes Inspected	None
Families Receiving *Lamina*	2,000

2. Summarized from "Reconstruction Program, First Report," ALIANZA, 1976.

The *lamina* had been distributed on both a cash and credit basis (subsidized at half the market price)—scrupulously monitored by local reconstruction committees and ALIANZA staff. A limit of ten *laminas* per family was set to provide the widest distribution of the materials and to allow families enough *laminas* to cover a small sleeping area temporarily. In 1977, the number of sheets was raised to twenty-four, enough for a typical forty-square-meter home.

A unique part of the construction training component was the presentation of courses specifically for women, often taught by a woman promotor or instructor. It was hoped that this aspect of training would develop into a sub-component that would address the health issues involved in the design and construction of homes (i.e.,smoke holes in the kitchen, raised fires, etc.)

Three factors were cited as reasons why the model house construction had fallen short of original expectations:

1. the estimated construction time was unrealistic;
2. there were problems in obtaining the community's share of materials; and
3. the planting season occupied most local labor, paid and volunteer.

The difficulties were due to certain process deficiencies and an initial unfamiliarity with the area and culture. Thus, more local *promotores* and builders were hired to spread the training/demonstration components more widely throughout the *municipio* on a regular basis, and an anthropologist was added to the professional staff to examine community-level impacts of the project components and to recommend modifications.

In March 1977, the chief goal of the Alliance Five Year Community Based Integrated Rural Development Program was articulated as: "to increase the ability of local communities to organize themselves into groups which can analyze a community's situation, find solutions inside or outside the community, and work together to achieve these solutions."[3]

The Joyabaj Reconstruction Program, a component of the larger program was intended "to encourage every person in the *municipio* to rebuild their homes using certain earthquake resistant materials and methods." This process was modelled on other programs which had been implemented elsewhere in Guatemala. A program review after one year revealed both problems and accomplishments.

---

3. Summarized from Charlotte and Paul Thompson, "Evaluation Report for the Save the Children Alliance Post Disaster Reconstruction Program—Joyabaj."

The problems revealed in the review were:

1. The educational process of a safe house design neglected to take into account differences in local literacy and income.
2. Labor and material costs were underestimated.
3. Traditional housebuilding roles (head of household vs. builder) were not clarified.
4. Anticipated first-year rebuilding did not take into account the local cycle of building, farming and seasonal migration.
5. The limited number of courses and demonstration houses was hardly sufficient to convince residents to choose new techniques.
6. Pre-disaster housing styles were not sufficiently analyzed or incorporated in the Alliance house.

The major accomplishments of the program were seen as:

1. Developing a network of local community organizations;
2. Communicating the basics of earthquake-resistant construction throughout the *municipio*; although real impact could not be measured since most families had not begun construction;
3. Employing staff who were representative of the region;
4. Building numerous visible model houses (local housebuilders and community members seeking *laminas* viewed the model houses used as warehouses as the best teaching tool, as long as they were in unfinished stages);
5. Establishing a workable construction materials distribution system.

However, several major defects of the project were reported:

1. Overambitious quantitative objectives for model structures, inspection visits and materials supply;
2. Requiring 100 percent compliance with earthquake-resistant standards; and
3. Excessive construction costs (The Alliance house, built completely to earthquake-resistant standards, cost almost double the amount of a traditional home).

After ten years, there were significant new results of the project. Anti-seismic homes had been constructed, local roads and health standards had been improved, and various government public service organizations had been established in Joyabaj.

Also, the road from Quiché was paved to Joyabaj. Urban streets are cobblestone or asphalt instead of dirt. The prime elements of an urban infrastructure—parks, markets, schools (public and private) and churches—have all not only been replaced, but also grown in number.

Socially, leaders, selected and trained through the project, were capable individuals, satisfied in the resolution of their individual and community problems. The community knows how to take care of itself. In the local idiom, people "*sabe defenderse,*" know how to fend for themselves. They have become adept at presenting social welfare projects of their own design to responsible government agencies. They learned the value of working in neighborhood committees. They learned to express their feelings better. This was especially notable among women, who had a much stronger role in community decision-making.

As a consequence of this community organization, the people had a real mayor for the municipality. Before, the mayor was formally elected, but had no political power whatsoever. Also, some locally recruited ALIANZA staff had become local leaders.

A terribly unfortunate negative consequence of these improvements in community organization should be noted. During the "Violence" of the 1980s, individuals who had developed their personal capacities during the post-disaster relief project were seen as troublemakers. Many were killed by the army and others sought exile in neighboring countries.

IV. DILEMMAS AND LESSONS FOR FUTURE PROGRAM DESIGN

Several lessons were learned through this project which might usefully be applied in other relief/development projects in Guatemala or other parts of the world.

Incorporation of Local People, Organizations, and Culture

There is a real opportunity to insure long-term development by incorporating the idea of eventual self-reliance at the start. In this project, the early and effective use of local staff at all levels led to an active development process with 100 percent Guatemalan staff. Even at the relatively high level of local participation in the project, some people still felt that there were too many *extranjeros* (foreigners) involved throughout the project. By 1985, the ALIANZA staff consisted of fewer than ten in the central office in Guatemala City and over sixty located in the program areas. All staff were Guatemalan.

Local political and social groups played an invaluable role in designing and implementing specific program elements. Ignoring such entities would have led to a much slower incorporation of the anti-seismic construction methods, or perhaps total lack of any incorporation. In addition, the project staff learned to refrain from trying to transfer already developed projects in their entirety from other parts of the country. The continued involvement of local people in decision-making was critical to success.

Fund Internationally, But Administer Locally

The example of the development of a local private voluntary organization, ALIANZA, to administer funds from several international NGOs has important implications for all relief/development projects. ALIANZA has now developed not only as an administrator of external funds, but has begun to solicit and receive funds from Guatemalans for their projects. This is self-reliance carried to its logical conclusion within a country.

Timetables and Long-Term Commitment

When a disaster occurs, the relief institution that is interested in integral development as well as emergency relief must clearly establish a timetable for the relief phase of their work so that there is an anticipated transition from relief to long-term work. The importance of making a long-term commitment cannot be overemphasized. In particular, political problems should not be reasons for leaving a project. The apolitical nature of relief and development must be paramount.

Involve All Sectors

Even as a relief/development project's leaders think and act regionally, implementors must not neglect any appropriate development sectors, i.e., educational, organizational, preventive health, small business development to combat unemployment, etc. The incorporation of health concerns into the anti-seismic housing design process, through the women's program, was a creative example of this idea.

While this project had an initial housing reconstruction focus, it was part of a much larger regional approach to rehabilitation and development. The various components of the entire project were able to adjust to regional nuances, rather than forcing the same solutions on different regional cultures. Staff always considered the region first and their particular sectoral specialty (health, housing, agriculture) second.

Train Local Project Staff

The ALIANZA program made as much of an effort to prepare its local staff as it did to train the recipients of the relief program. For instance, in the housing program, not only were local builders trained in anti-seismic construction techniques, they were also trained in how best to convey that information to the community. In many relief projects, the needs of the relief workers can be just as important as the needs of the disaster victims.

Keep Documentation and Reporting Manageable

In the Joyabaj project, ALIANZA originally set out to keep inordinately detailed and unnecessarily esoteric records of activities. While there were reasons for this information in the minds of national and international staff, local staff could not understand the needs nor could they find the time beyond their already packed work schedule. Forms went unfilled or incorrectly completed. Such record-keeping demands initially diminished ALIANZA credibility, until adaptations were made.

The People Claim Success

Perhaps the best lesson learned is from the brochure published by ALIANZA to describe their activities today:

When the best development programs are done, the People all say, "We have done it ourselves."

REFERENCES

ALIANZA, "USAID Housing Proposal," Guatemala, 1976.

ALIANZA, "Reconstruction Program, First Report," Guatemala, July 1976.

Alianza para el Desarrollo Juvenil Comunitario (ALIANZA), *Informe Anual 1985*, Guatemala, 1985.

Asturias Montenegro y R. Gatica Trejo, *Terremoto 76*, Cuarta Edicion, Guatemala, 1985.

Lawrence, Nancy, "Joyabaj, Background, Original Proposal," ALIANZA, Guatemala, April 1976.

OFDA/USAID, "Guatemala—A Country Profile," Washington, D.C., July 1982.

Programa de Actividades, Centenario de Joyabaj: 1887-1987, Guatemala, 1987.

Revista Folklorica Joyabateca, Año I, Numero 1, Guatemala, August 1987.

Thompson, Charlotte and Thompson, Paul, "Evaluation Report for the Save the Children Alliance Post-Disaster Reconstruction Program—Joyabaj," March 1977.

ACKNOWLEDGMENTS

This case was written in November 1987. In September 1987, a team from IRDP visited Guatemala and interviewed ALIANZA staff in Guatemala City, as well as some community members in Joyabaj. The *alcade*, or mayor, provided background information on the community. ALIANZA staff who were interviewed included both central office personnel and workers from the local area. Save the Children staff in New York and colleagues who had worked in other parts of Guatemala following the earthquake shared important insights.

The IRDP team was composed of Don Schramm, of the Disaster Management Center, University of Wisconsin-Madison, and Roberto Muj Miculax, an agronomist who had worked in nearby communities on relief and reconstruction projects after the 1976 earthquake. Roberto Muj prepared the initial report in Spanish and it was translated by Don Schramm, who also expanded on the material presented. The original Spanish summary document is available.

SPECIAL NOTE: Because of the volatile political atmosphere which descended on Guatemala in the late years of the last decade and even more from 1980 to 1984, no names are used in this case. Many individuals involved in the Joyabaj project immediately after the earthquake found themselves *personae non grata* during the period of the *"Violencia."* People who were interviewed spoke on the condition that they not be identified.

Chapter 15

LOCAL RESOURCE MANAGEMENT PROJECT
Santo Domingo, Albay, Bicol Region, Philippines

Project Implementing Agency:
International Institute of
Rural Reconstruction

Case Writer:
Mary B. Anderson

I. PROJECT BACKGROUND AND CONTEXT

International Institute of Rural Reconstruction

The International Institute of Rural Reconstruction (IIRR), founded by Dr. Y.C. James Yen, is located in Silang, Cavite, the Philippines. There are field offices and programs in Colombia, Ghana, Guatemala, India, the Philippines and Thailand. The work of IIRR is based on a "creed" (see Appendix A) which summarizes its philosophical approach to development work with the poor of the world. The basic premise of the creed is that peasant people have resources on which their development must be based and that the outsider may be a partner and facilitator in development but s/he is not a helper or developer since only the people can develop themselves. For several years, IIRR has implemented projects in Cavite, the Philippines, to 1) encourage active and meaningful

PHILIPPINES

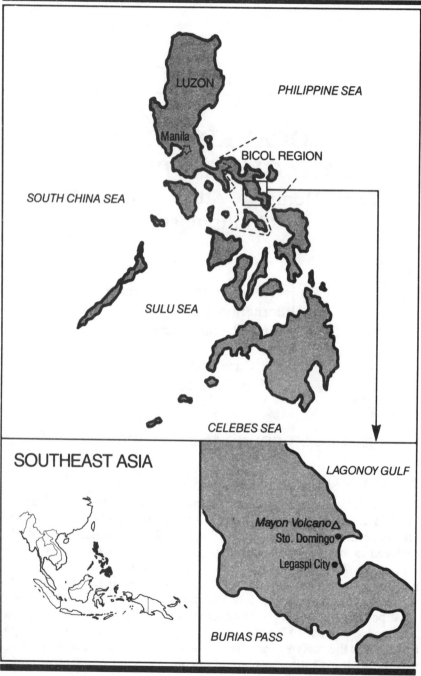

LUZON

PHILIPPINE SEA

Manila

BICOL REGION

SOUTH CHINA SEA

SULU SEA

CELEBES SEA

SOUTHEAST ASIA

LAGONOY GULF

Mayon Volcano △
Sto. Domingo ●

Legaspi City ●

BURIAS PASS

Map By Jerry Alexander

participation of the rural poor in development decision-making, and 2) to develop a responsive and relevant support system which plans and carries out development programs and projects that deal directly with the self-identified needs of the poor.

Initiation of Santo Domingo Project

In 1984, IIRR was seeking to expand its Cavite approach to some other area of the Philippines and, at the same time, the Government of the Philippines (GOP) was initiating a ten-year Local Resource Management program (LRM). With U.S. Agency for International Development (USAID) funding, the LRM was to be implemented in seven provinces. The GOP sought to involve four different private voluntary organizations as implementing agencies for LRM. IIRR was asked to take on the development of LRM in Santo Domingo, Albay in the Bicol region of southern Luzon. Because the government goals and objectives for LRM were similar to those on which IIRR operated its two-prong program in Cavite, IIRR agreed to do this work in Santo Domingo. The project was begun in September 1984.

Characteristics of the Project Area

Santo Domingo is located not far from Mt. Mayon, an active volcano which has a history of eruption every ten years. In addition, the area is typhoon prone, as is most of the Philippines. Santo Domingo is a municipality with thirteen villages. It extends east of Mt. Mayon approximately twenty miles. The distance between the northern and southern borders is about six miles.

Approximately 17,000 people live in Santo Domingo. While a few families are wealthy, the vast majority in the area is very poor. Most families survive on a combination of small farming, handicrafts, livestock raising and seasonal labor. Some also do commercial fishing. Most land is owned by a small number of wealthy land holders, and the poor rent the land they use, often paying one-third of their rice crop to the owner.

Santo Domingo formerly was the center of a thriving handicrafts business, started by a German who still lives in the area. A manager of the company absconded with most of the funds, and the market for handicrafts changed, demanding higher quality goods than were produced in Santo Domingo while prices dropped. Thus, the industry closed, and since no other industry has taken its place, the area has been quite depressed for a number of years.

For seventeen years, until February 1986, the same person had been mayor of the town. She comes from an extremely wealthy family; it is said that her family owns all the land of two villages. Her father was a judge, and her brother preceded her as mayor. She was elected upon her brother's death. After Aquino's election as president, this mayor was removed from office and the national government appointed a man who served for a year and half. He decided to run for office in the 1988 election (the first after the 1986 revolution), and another interim mayor was appointed by the national government. But another candidate was elected in January 1988 who took office during our visit to Santo Domingo in February. Thus, the project site has had four mayors since IIRR began to work there in 1984.

The New People's Army guerilla force operates in the hills near Santo Domingo and approximately every month, a body of someone whom they have killed is found in the roadside "dumping ground." Government security forces are wary of efforts to work with and organize village people.

The people of Santo Domingo have a few forms of traditional organization outside the political sphere. The church is, of course, important. People also cooperate on planning and running fiestas in each village, and they cooperate in small work groups when activities require more than one worker. This form of cooperative labor is called *bayanihan*.

Historically, Mt. Mayon has erupted approximately every ten years (in the eighth year of each decade). However, in September 1984, four years before the expected eruption, the volcano came, causing significant property damage and the loss of livestock and crops in some of the villages in Santo Domingo. At that point, the LRM project team was just finishing its training at IIRR headquarters in Silang. When they heard of the disaster, they wondered how they would start their village-based community development work, because many of the residents of the villages where they were going had moved out of these villages into evacuation centers.

The IIRR project is of particular interest to IRDP because it provides an example of a planned development project which was interrupted by a disaster. From the IIRR experience, we learn how their agency staff responded to the unexpected event and turned it to good developmental effect.

II. THE LOCAL RESOURCE MANAGEMENT PROJECT

Project Design

The Local Resources Management project was planned to "develop and test replicable approaches for organizing target beneficiary groups consisting of the rural poor to participate genuinely in the development process."[1]

1. Conrado S. Navarro, "People's Participation in Local Resource Management," *Rural Reconstruction Review*, 1985.

It was designed to work with beneficiaries in five of the thirteen *barangays* (villages) of Santo Domingo to help them identify their own problems and develop problem-solving skills, to plan, implement and evaluate plans and projects at local and higher levels. Ultimately the goal was to improve the social and economic status of beneficiaries through their own implementation of development activities. In addition, the project was intended to encourage local government units to respond to beneficiary participation and to involve local private voluntary organizations (PVOs) with rural beneficiaries in participatory development as well.

IIRR placed three full-time, experienced staff members in Santo Domingo during the summer of 1984 (before the volcano eruption) to begin to set up operations. Their first activity was a week-long survey of Santo Domingo to learn as much about the area as possible. They arranged a meeting with representatives of the national, regional, provincial and municipal governments in a workshop at IIRR to approve a final implementation plan for the project.

This team also recruited five individuals who would be trained to serve as full-time rural reconstruction facilitators (RRFs) in Albay. They hung posters throughout the region announcing these RRF openings and inviting people to arrive on a given day for interviews and tests. Over 500 people appeared!

Through a series of interviews (some group, some individual) and tests, ten people were selected. These ten were divided into teams of two and sent to live for ten days in five of Santo Domingo's villages. The IIRR staff observed their interactions with villagers in order to ascertain who was best suited to this kind of rural work. Finally, the ten were sent to the IIRR center at Silang for training. The plan was to hire the five best trainees immediately after this training and place them in the field. The other five would be ready as alternates if they were needed.

The recruitment criteria for the RRFs included: a willingness and readiness to live and work in the rural areas under difficult conditions; intellect, creativity, breadth and depth of development perspective; development experience; emotional maturity; soundness of mind and body; and skills in interpersonal communication and human relations.

After training in their assigned villages, the RRFs were to:

1. Conduct a participatory community survey in which they would learn as much as they could about each of the families in the village;

2. Convene a Key Informant Panel to classify each family according to its position in the community. The IIRR approach involves identifying the rich as group "A," the next tier of middle-income people as group "B," and the majority of the poor as group "C."

3. Begin to identify and work with "interest groups" from the poor group (C) who could get together to identify common needs (interests) and begin to learn to solve problems and meet their needs together.

It was assumed that each RRF would begin by getting one small interest group going and, once this group had achieved some success, move on to enable other groups to start. The IIRR approach is focussed on human development and accepts the fact that such a process may be quite slow. They, therefore, encourage the establishment of deep and strong relationships that build on each other. There is no pressure for fast "results."

Actual Project

The eruption of Mayon caused the evacuation of two of the five IIRR priority *barangays* (villages) so that they became ghost villages. The other three became recipients of the evacuees in evacuation centers, so they were also disrupted by the volcano. Three other *barangays* which were to have been second priority for IIRR's project also were severely damaged by the volcanic mudflows and were in need of relief assistance. IIRR decided to keep all ten newly trained RRFs on its staff and to begin its intended participatory development project by assisting in the immediate relief effort.

In Santo Domingo there existed a Municipal Disaster Coordinating Committee (MDCC) as a standing committee of the Municipal Development Committee. The MDCC included the social welfare, health, planning and education officers for the municipality, as well as representatives of voluntary and church agencies in the area. The mayor and his secretary also sat on the committee, the mayor serving as chairperson. This MDCC had designated the evacuation centers and organized the municipal social welfare, health, education and planning staff to distribute goods, provide health care and arrange for effective sanitation in the evacuation center. Because IIRR had established good relations with the municipal government in the initial stages of exploring and planning the LRM project, the staff were able to get the mayor to designate the newly trained RRFs as action coordinators in each of the evacuation centers. The RRFs who had originally been assigned to villages that were evacuated because of the volcano then became action coordinators in the centers that housed the people from those villages. They lived in the centers, received food rations, helped with the cleaning, etc., alongside the evacuees. (The RRFs who were assigned to villages not evacuated went immediately to live and work in those villages.) Thus, IIRR's new staff became part of the disaster response team of the municipality.

Almost immediately, the IIRR project team convinced the MDCC to shift people among centers so that they were with other families from their own *barangays*. In the rush of evacuation, people had simply gone randomly into the available centers. Two things were accomplished by this relocation. First, people were happier being with their own neighbors in these abnormal circumstances. Second, the IIRR project team was able to begin to establish rapport with people from the villages where they had been assigned to work on the LRM project. They began to talk with people about the project and its purposes even while they were still in the evacuation centers. They also started their first planned task—a participatory community study for each assigned village.

Because of their community development orientation, the RRFs constantly consulted the evacuees about problems, priorities, and solutions. This was unusual in the experience of the evacuees. Navarro, in his article about the project, quotes one evacuee as saying, "The other agencies never cared to ask us what we wanted. They just gave us what they themselves think we need. That made us feel like beggars. This procedure of yours is better. It enables us to express our own feelings and desires."

The people in the evacuation centers divided themselves into teams to clean, dig latrines, cook, care for children, etc. Very soon, the adult members of the families were able, in cases where the land had not been destroyed, to return to their fields during the day, but the volcano situation was still uncertain enough that they were encouraged to return to the centers at night. Every night the RRFs began to hold meetings or entertainment events (even a beauty contest!) in the centers. These provided a basis for building rapport both between RRFs and community and among the community people themselves, who had not previously spent much of this kind of time together. The meetings were, in fact, development seminars in which people were encouraged to work together on problem identification and problem solving. A high percentage of people attended these sessions because, as one staff person said, "it was the only show in town."

The MDCC initially thought that people would be in the evacuation centers for about two weeks, but mudslides (caused by rain after the volcano) made it impossible and unsafe for people to return home for two to three months. Some of the evacuees sought the help of the RRFs to start income-earning activities. The RRFs encouraged them to form "interest groups" to discuss their priorities and to organize themselves for carrying out the activities they chose. A couple of small projects were started including some handicrafts, weaving (a tradition in the area), and a small traders project in which people opened little sundries shops in the evacuation centers.

In fact, the people in the evacuation centers represented the poorer members of the village communities, since those in IIRR's groups A and B had other options and did not go to evacuation centers. Thus, by encouraging the formation of interest groups in the centers, and through the subsequent emergence of leadership among these groups, the RRFs were enabling the poor to establish leadership where they had not done so before. In the typical village environment, all local organizations (women's groups, youth groups and church groups) had been led by people who were economically and politically better off. Very often, the poor had not even participated in these existing groups. By the time they returned to their villages, the poorer groups who had occupied the evacuation centers had a new experience of selecting their own leaders, and the leaders had the experience of providing direction and receiving the support of their friends and neighbors. Everyone had joined in actions to solve immediate problems of living together in the close quarters of the evacuation centers.

When the evacuation centers were closed, the RRFs and evacuated villages packed up their goods and moved back to the villages. Here the RRFs continued with the plans they had made while at the IIRR training session in Silang. Because of the type of work they were doing, their work week was defined as including evenings, Saturdays and Sundays, the times when the village people were available for meetings and discussions. RRFs had Tuesdays and Wednesdays as their "free" days.

The RRFs initially developed interest groups around the need for clean water, and they were able to provide materials to install water pumps in suitable locations in each village. The experience of deciding where to locate the pumps, and of setting up a village-based organization capable of providing the necessary labor to install the pumps and, more importantly, the ongoing organization to maintain the pumps, gave these groups immediate successes in solving some common problem in their villages. The RRFs used their access to the material goods necessary to build these pumps as a *mechanism* to support their basic work in community organizing.

Meanwhile, those RRFs whose villages had not been evacuated were already at work on a community survey, the classification of the community into groups according to wealth, and the encouragement of interest-group formation.

In Santo Domingo, the villagers made an adjustment to the usual IIRR designation of groups A, B, and C. They felt that the degree of poverty in this area required that they name a group "D" as the poorest of the poor. The RRFs therefore focussed their efforts with both groups "C" and "D." In almost every case, the intense period of interaction in the evacuation centers caused the in-village work to proceed at a much faster pace than the RRFs expected. Rather than beginning one interest group at a time, villagers often started several groups at once. The RRFs who had begun work in the non-evacuated villages found that it took longer to establish rapport with people in their areas and to get interest groups initiated.

Examples of projects undertaken by interest groups included:

1. construction and installation of water-sealed toilets;
2. construction of footpaths to link remote communities to the village center;
3. carabao husbandry (first several bought with a loan to be repaid from sales of offspring);
4. handicrafts projects, mostly focussed on abaca weaving;
5. establishment of cooperative community stores;
6. piggery, both for consumption and sale; and
7. establishment of a rice mill within the *barangay* (planned and implemented by the spring of 1988).

In each project, the approach was to address the problems identified and the solutions worked out by the interest groups. The RRFs served only to help facilitate the groups; they did not offer solutions to problems.

In addition, the groups were encouraged to analyze the causes of their problems and to understand how their own situation was linked to the broader social and economic context. For example, in the handicrafts efforts, the villagers grew to understand that their own production role, while central, was less well paid than the roles of middle men, materials suppliers and marketers. In some cases, they found ways to take on these roles themselves in order to increase the income they received from their efforts.

In 1987, the IIRR team began to shift its working strategy. Finding that the community people were coming to depend on them too heavily, not really for solutions to problems which the RRFs assiduously avoided, but for continual motivation and encouragement, they moved out of the villages into either the Santo Domingo staff house or the nearby town of Lagaspi. At the same time, they identified indigenous volunteer facilitators (IVFs or VFs) in each village who were sent to IIRR headquarters for training similar to that given initially to the RRFs.

In some cases, the RRFs identified appropriate village leaders to become VFs; in others, the interest groups identified those who would become leaders. Because these were strictly volunteer positions, they had to be filled by people who could find time to take on such work. Again, however, most of the work was done in the evenings and on weekends when people were available to meet and work together. Otherwise, the criteria for selection were similar to those applied in the selection of the RRFs: dedication to the participatory process of working with rural people, maturity, experience in interest group activities, etc. The VFs ranged widely in age, from very young people involved in youth group organizing to quite senior people who had shown initiative and interest in this work.

September 1987: Typhoon Sitang

While Santo Domingo experiences a typhoon season each year, in September 1987 it was hit by Typhoon Sitang, the worst in many years (200 mph winds). Many houses, both those of bamboo and wood construction and a number of concrete block and tin roof construction, were blown down. An estimated one-third of all housing was destroyed. In addition, some of the community buildings constructed by village interest groups were destroyed and pigs, carabao and crops were killed. Much of the material progress made by the village groups was blown away in two hours. However, IIRR staff noted that the real work of the past four years endured the typhoon: the human development and social organization work.

After the typhoon, the VFs in each community were enlisted by the MDCC (again called into action) to identify those who suffered the most. The MDCC decided in this instance *not* to open evacuation centers. There was no continuing danger once the typhoon passed and people preferred to be in their own communities to begin the process of salvaging what they could and rebuilding houses as soon as possible.

The political situation in Santo Domingo was in flux. The campaign for the January election was soon to begin and the offering of relief supplies to those in need presented the mayoral candidates with a possibility of solidifying their village support. The *barangay* captains submitted lists of the "victims" based, in some cases, on political loyalty. The MDCC enlisted the LRM volunteer facilitators to validate these lists. When the VF lists came in, they were often quite different from those presented by the *barangay* captains. The ad hoc leadership of the MDCC, meeting outside the municipal hall and without the acting mayor present, acknowledged the greater accuracy of the LRM lists. One city employee was dispatched with the "corrected" lists to present to the mayor, and he was thereby constrained from using the relief supplies to buttress his own political strength.

The IIRR staff, and especially the VFs (with RRF support), were asked by two donating agencies to establish the priorities for who should receive housing materials and to carry out the actual distribution of these materials in the villages. In each village, criteria were set for designating who should receive such in-kind support. In all cases, those who were selected were families from groups C and D who had suffered complete loss of their houses and who had little or no employment. Often the families with more children were chosen.

In some cases, even after these criteria were applied, the need for housing support was greater than the available supplies. In several cases, a lottery was used to select recipients. This system was seen as equitable and no one felt cheated; each person had an equal chance of winning. We were also told of another case, in an earlier distribution situation, in which a meeting had been called of all those who met the criteria for receiving aid. At that meeting, leaders asked for "volunteers" to withdraw from eligibility. In enough cases, people actually did withdraw, indicating that their need was less than that of their neighbors. They were able to assert their pride in being able to give up outside help and to help themselves instead.

In one case, a community had chosen the people who were to receive housing supplies based on their own criteria. A Manila-based staff person from the donor agency then arrived to walk through the village with the VFs to observe the need. This staff person, in several instances, was so moved by the sight of flattened houses that, on the spur of the moment, she promised assistance to families whose names were not on the approved list. In each case, these were families with other houses or other resources known to the village-based RRFs and VFs. Because this outside staff person told the families on the spot that they would receive aid, other, needier families were bounced down on the list and in some cases did not receive aid.

The Situation in Early 1988

The plan in February 1988 was that, increasingly, the VFs would take over the village-based work and IIRR would phase out of the Santo Domingo area. The plan had always been to empower the poor groups in the *barangays* to identify, plan for and implement activities that would add to their social and economic well-being over time. Also, in early 1988 the IIRR staff was encouraging the interest groups to federate into village action committees, and these village-based groups would then collaborate on collective, municipal-wide activities. Through such cooperation it was assumed that the power of the people to effect the changes required for fundamental economic and social security in the broader context would be increased.

III. ANALYSIS OF CAPACITIES AND VULNERABILITIES BEFORE AND AFTER THE LRM PROJECT

During our last afternoon in Santo Domingo, we met with the IIRR LRM project staff and asked them to remember back to the time of their arrival. "What," we asked, "were the vulnerabilities and capacities of the people then? And, what were they even prior to the volcano eruption?" The staff group developed the lists on the facing page.

Their "before and after" analysis of vulnerabilities and capacities revealed the significant strengths of the IIRR/LRM project strategy. Taking as its focus the development of social and organizational capacities, the LRM project had a major impact on peoples' abilities to join together and work cooperatively in solving a number of problems. With such experiences, the villagers had a greatly increased sense of their capacities to affect and manage their lives and livelihoods.

Because of the disasters, first the volcano and later Typhoon Sitang, IIRR had been able to *use* the provision of material relief goods to encourage the development of this organizational capacity. When the volcano evacuees returned to their villages, IIRR provided materials to install water pumps, harnessing the energies of people to cooperate and organize around a material project.

IIRR/LRM took advantage of the volcano crisis to initiate organization among groups of villagers and, specifically, among the poorest groups. This was possible precisely because only these groups came into the evacuation centers; those who were better off had other options and were able to avoid the crowded and unpleasant circumstances of these centers. In addition, the evacuees had time on their hands and were collected in one place. LRM used this period of disruption to make significant headway in its organizing approach.

The vulnerabilities and capacities analysis revealed that the LRM project did not have as significant an impact on the physical vulnerabilities and capacities as it had on the two other realms. In part, this was because of IIRR's intentional strategy. The staff emphasized their belief that physical/material progress is only possible and sustainable when people are well enough organized to maintain the material advances they gain. If they were not strongly organized, any material progress could easily be cornered by strong individuals and the poor would not really be better off.

In part, the relative lack of progress in the material realm also reflected the physical reality of Santo Domingo. People do not own and control their land. They are subject to repeated physical disasters which destroy even what they have built. It has always been difficult to produce enough to create a margin of savings to ensure recovery from the impacts of typhoons and volcanic eruptions.

The IIRR team and the VFs recognized the difficulties of achieving real economic progress for the majority of the poor. Some of the small-scale livelihood projects undertaken by interest groups had failed. Peoples' skills in management remained under-developed, but the IIRR staff felt that there was a great deal of learning through the failed as well as the successful projects.

IIRR Team Analysis of Sto. Domingo

Capacities and Vulnerabilities Before Project
Physical Vulnerabilities
1. Volcano- and typhoon-prone area
2. No land tenure for most people; high rents for use of land; fields lost to volcano/mudslides
3. Prices of inputs to agriculture were rising while prices paid for the goods were falling
Physical Capacities
1. Skills in agriculture, handicrafts, fishing, etc.
2. Plenty of water; good soils
3. Plenty of people with industrious natures
Social/Organizational Vulnerabilities
1. History of failed cooperatives
2. Low expectations
3. Local government unresponsiveness to the poor
Social/Organizational Capacities
1. Traditional work groups called *bayanihan*
2. Active press which publicized social wrongs
Motivational/Attitudinal Vulnerabilities
1. Fatalistic attitudes on part of the poor
2. Superstitious beliefs
Motivational/Attitudinal Capacities
1. Resilience
2. Religious beliefs

Capacities and Vulnerabilities After the Project
Physical/Material Vulnerabilities
No change
Physical/Material Capacities
1. Great increase in skills
2. Ability to manage resources and increase in some (such as carabao, pigs, etc.)
Social/Organizational Vulnerabilities
Local government now more responsive
Social/Organizational Capacities
A great increase in local organization, interest groups, federated village-wide groups
Motivational/Attitudinal Vulnerabilities
Change from fatalism to hope
Motivational/Attitudinal Capacities
1. Ability to identify problems and solve them
2. Vigilance monitoring government/others' activities

Village people commented that their ancestors had been able to withstand and recover from the natural calamities in the area better than they. In early times, they neither received nor needed outside relief assistance. However, the population has increased, and the resource base has diminished (through repeated volcanic eruptions, and because of overuse of forests and fields) so that the people live on a smaller margin than previously. Everyone agreed that they needed to find some basically different way of organizing their economic activity if they were to be able to achieve real self-reliance in the future—self reliance in both normal times and times of disasters.

In the current political context, the only path for the majority of the poor to achieve any significant economic advance was through collaboration and federation. They felt that small village-by-village projects would be too easily subjected to co-optation by the wealthier factions. If enough people could achieve political solidarity through their community-based interest groups and, through federation, translate this into economic activity, it was felt that such gains could be sustained.

IV. DILEMMAS AND LESSONS FOR FUTURE PROGRAM DESIGN

The IIRR/LRM project raises a number of interesting issues and points to a number of lessons that can be said to have been learned, at least in this setting. Some of these are relevant in other circumstances and settings as well.

Emergencies as Opportunities

The most important indication from the Santo Domingo experience is that not only is it possible to "do development work" in an emergency situation, but *emergencies may offer opportunities* for initiating development work, that, without the crisis, would take more time or effort to get underway.

Specifically, when people are forced into evacuation centers, they are gathered in one place and have idle time that can be tapped. Both facts provide opportunities for organizing, educating, etc.

Santo Domingo also shows that it is often the poorest people who gather in such centers. Therefore, an agency which wants to target its work toward these groups may have special opportunities in such settings. Because the usually dominant groups are absent under these circumstances, there are significant opportunities for the emergence of new leadership, and agencies may find that these circumstances provide one of the rare opportunities for supporting such new leadership.

One of the field staff members in Santo Domingo analyzed it this way: "People's organization is a vital factor if you are to carry out relief and have it linked to development. Exposure to problem-solving in disaster situations and the development of skills in problem-solving are the most important factors in making the link to development."

"Victims" Have Capacities

In the Santo Domingo experience, the fact that even "victims" have a number of capacities on which development can and should be based is well confirmed. The evacuation center residents took leadership initiatives, started interest groups which later formed the basis for development activities in the villages, and even undertook economic projects within the centers. The capacities they had for undertaking these efforts were accentuated and reinforced by the IIRR approach.

Organizing Through Material Efforts

A physical project may be used as the means for furthering the social organization and motivational goals. The LRM approach was to organize people into interest groups, around specific (usually material) problems or needs that they agreed they shared. But organizing was the first priority in LRM's view. In the villages, however, the first consolidating activity was the installation of water pumps—a material asset. The tangible evidence of the pumps reinforced the groups' sense of effectiveness and cooperation.

Cooperative Relations with Authorities

The LRM project shows that, even in politically unstable situations, linking a project to government structures has important consequences for later effectiveness. By having early meetings with political people at various levels, IIRR staff established friendly relationships that they could call on when their field staff entered the area. In addition, they made and maintained very cooperative relations with the civil service staff of the municipality, ensuring their ongoing linking with government services and decision-making, but insulating themselves from alliances with any particular elected official. (In this case, this was particularly important since the elected and appointed officials have changed so many times in the life of the project.)

Balancing Close Association with Healthy Distance

Staff who work with villagers need to find ways to identify with the village people in the early stages of organizing; however, such identification may become a deterrent to self-reliance at later stages of development. At first, while the staff lived in the evacuation centers with the volcano victims, they both increased their awareness of what it feels like to be a "victim" and developed close contact with the villagers. Later, they lived in the villages where they worked. In addition, the LRM staff work week was designed to ensure that they met the people at the times and places where the people could meet. Also important to note, however, is the later LRM decision that staff should *not* continue to live in the villages after some point. When people seemed to be becoming too dependent on them, the staff moved into nearby towns and, at the same time, appointed and trained the local volunteer facilitators. This response was part of a strategy for ensuring that the village people, themselves, took and retained responsibility for their ongoing actions, preparing for the LRM project to end without losing the momentum and gains made during the project.

APPENDIX

IIRR Credo of Rural Reconstruction

Go to the peasant people
Live among the peasant people
Learn from the peasant people
Plan with the peasant people
Work with the peasant people
Start with what the peasant people know
Build on what the peasant people have
Teach by showing; learn by doing
Not a showcase but a pattern
Not piecemeal but integrated approach
Not to conform but to transform
Not relief but release

REFERENCES

International Institute of Rural Reconstruction, Project Documents (undated):
    "Consolidated Baseline Data and Community Studies of Villages in Sto. Domingo, Albay."
    "Local Resource Management Project: Beneficiary Participation Implementation Program."
    "The S.W.O.T. Analysis Technique,"
Navarro, Conrad S., "People's Participation in Local Resource Management," Rural Reconstruction Review, Voume VI, 1984.

ACKNOWLEDGMENTS

This case was written in February 1988. IRDP is grateful to the many IIRR/LRM people who made it possible for us to write this case. In the IIRR U.S. office, Robert O'Brien first brought the LRM project to our attention, and he made the appropriate contacts to ensure that we could visit the project. In Silang, at IIRR headquarters, the President, Dr. Juan Martin Flavier met with us and generously shared his sense of the history and accomplishments of the effort. Also we want to express our deep appreciation to Vice President, Antonio C. de Jesus and Program Director, Conrado (Ding) S. Navarro for meeting with us in Silang and both providing insight about the LRM experience and engaging with us on IRDP's approach. In Bicol, at the LRM Santo Domingo project, many staff gave generously of their time in discussions and in taking us into villages to meet participants in the project. We especially want to thank Rommel L. Manikan, LRM Project Director, for his assistance and friendship and, through him, all the other field staff and people of Santo Domingo.

Chapter 16

QALA EN NAHAL REFUGEE SETTLEMENT PROJECT
Eastern Sudan

Program Implementing Agency:
ACORD

Case Writer:
Peter J. Woodrow

I. INTRODUCTION

This case history will examine the project of Euro Action-ACORD (now called ACORD) in the Qala en Nahal Refugee Settlement in Eastern Sudan. The Qala en Nahal (QEN) case is of particular interest, since it allows an examination of how an ongoing development program was affected by a disaster, and how programming has been affected in the aftermath by the emergency response.

II. DESCRIPTION OF PROJECT CONTEXT AND CONDITIONS

Refugees in the Sudan

Sudan is the host country to many groups of refugees. About half are from Eritrea or Ethiopia, and a smaller number come from Uganda, Zaire, and Chad. Eritrean refugees have been arriving in the Sudan since the mid-1960s as a result of fighting between the Ethiopian government and those striving for the independence and/or autonomy of Eritrea. In 1984-85 significant numbers of new refugees arrived in Eastern Sudan as a result of

SUDAN

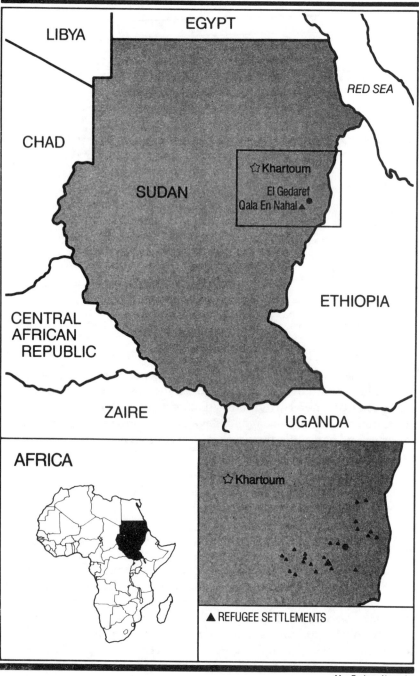

LIBYA

EGYPT

CHAD

RED SEA

SUDAN

☆ Khartoum

El Gedaref
Qala En Nahal ▲●

ETHIOPIA

CENTRAL
AFRICAN
REPUBLIC

ZAIRE

UGANDA

AFRICA

☆ Khartoum

▲ REFUGEE SETTLEMENTS

Map By Jerry Alexander

both increased fighting and severe drought and famine conditions inside Ethiopia. Eritrean refugees were joined by those from Tigray and from various political factions of the Amharic population.

Throughout this period, the government of Sudan maintained a policy of welcoming refugees despite the strain on its own resources. No refugee groups have ever been forced to leave. Since the establishment of a civilian government in 1986, however, local expressed resentment of refugee competition for unskilled jobs in the towns has resulted in public discussion of more restrictive policies.

In some instances, the Sudanese government provided land to refugee settlements. Between 1969 and 1983 the government of Sudan established seventeen refugee settlements of which Qala en Nahal is the largest and oldest. However, the amount and quality of land made available vary considerably, and the plots allocated to each family range from about 1 to 4.5 hectares. By providing land to refugees, the government adopted a policy to provide for refugees' basic needs without relying on the need for constant donations of food rations to sustain them.

All refugee programs in Sudan operate under the auspices of the Commission on Refugees (COR), part of the Ministry of the Interior. The United Nations High Commissioner for Refugees (UNHCR) provides funding and technical support services to many programs.

Background to the 1984 Drought and Famine

The drought, which affected crops throughout much of Africa, began in 1983 when a poor harvest depleted the few reserves that communities held. In many areas of Sudan the crop failed entirely in 1984, leading to famine conditions by early 1985. In the Qala en Nahal area, the 1984 rains were normal to good early in the season, but in August they ceased altogether and dry winds began. By the end of September, it was apparent that there would be very little yield from the sorghum crop. Unfortunately, similar conditions affected all of Sudan, and crops failed everywhere except in the areas of the largest irrigation schemes. The famine crisis was compounded by the movement of large numbers of people from their farmland to towns or roadsides where they sought water or food or both. The Nimeiri government initially tried to suppress news of the famine. Government policies did little to prevent hoarding and export of the few remaining grain reserves. Nimeiri was deposed in a *coup d'etat* in the spring of 1985, five months into the famine.

The Qala en Nahal Settlement

The Qala en Nahal Refugee Settlement was established in 1969. Refugees settled there during two main periods in 1969-70 and 1978-79, although there has been steady in- and out-migration since the settlement was established.

Qala en Nahal (QEN) consisted of about 400 square kilometers of land, or about 100,000 *feddans* (1 feddan = 1.04 acres or 0.42 hectares), of which some 74,000 *feddans* were cultivable. Most refugee farmers were allocated ten *feddans* although some, particularly later settlers, received only five or even 2.5 *feddans*. During its early years, about 20,000 refugees were settled in Qala en Nahal but population estimates in 1985 put the number at over 30,000 living in six villages. In addition, about 5,000 Sudanese lived in eight other villages in the settlement. These people, who originally came from Western Sudan, Chad, and Nigeria, have been settling in the area since the 1930s.

The refugee population was quite diverse and included Eritreans, both Muslims and Christians, highland and lowland groups, nomadic pastoralists, semi-nomads, settled farmers, and some urban tradespeople. In preparation for beginning their project, ACORD performed socio-economic surveys in 1981 which showed that 76 percent of the refugees were of rural origin. The vast majority, about 80 percent by one estimate, were nomadic and had never farmed before. Even those who had farming experience, had no experience with the soil or rainfall conditions found in QEN. The refugee population also represents diverse ethnic and language groups from Eritrea, including five major groupings (Asowarta 38%; Beni Amer 31%; Marya 11%; Barya 10%; and Tigrinya 2%) and small numbers from an additional seven ethnic groups (8 percent of the total).[1]

The soil in Qala en Nahal is deep clay and of moderate fertility. During the wet season it becomes very heavy with water. In the dry season large cracks, some up to two meters deep, open in the soil. Besides being difficult to cultivate due to the clay content, the soil is prone to heavy weed growth, an additional impediment to cropping. Mechanized cultivation has been found to alleviate the weed problem.

The area around the settlement was developed in the past twenty years for large-scale mechanized cultivation of sorghum and sesame. Depending on rainfall and soil fertility, yields have been good. Yields per *feddan* over a four year period are shown in Figure 1.

These yields (from ACORD reports) showed a vital link between rainfall and crop success. The distribution of rain over time during the season was also crucial. While total rainfall may have been adequate, in some years a large amount of rain fell at one time followed by a prolonged dry spell and crops were destroyed.

---

1. B.C. Spooner, *The Qala en Nahal Refugee Resettlement Scheme: Historical Review, Current Status, and Programme for Action*, Euro Action-ACORD, 1981, p. 57.

Figure 1		
Rainfall and Crop Yields in Qala en Nahal		
Year	Rainfall	Yield (sacks/*feddan*)
1981	1,000mm	3.00
1982	750mm	2.70
1983	500mm	1.00
1984	350mm	0.25

In addition to farming, many settlers have owned livestock. Included among the stocks were camels, donkeys, sheep, goats and cows. The larger flocks have not been kept at the settlement, but were moved to the river during the dry season and north to grassy plains during the rains. While the number of animals in the settlement varied with the seasons, a 1984 census undertaken by ACORD extension staff estimated the livestock populations as follows:

Cattle	16,620
Sheep and Goats	16,500
Donkeys	3,780
Camels	188

These animals used for transport and plowing also represented an important source of protein, and a form of savings. The livestock population has grown rapidly in recent years, and has become competitive with the human population for resources in the settlement.

Vulnerabilities of the Qala en Nahal Community[2]

The settlement of Qala en Nahal faced a number of problems that made the people vulnerable to drought. Rainfall has already been mentioned as crucial for crop yields. Qala en Nahal is in a border area between the semi-arid plains to the north and higher rainfall areas to the south, a high-risk area for farmers who depend on rain-fed agriculture.

2. This was one of the earliest cases written by IRDP and, as such, did not include a pre-project capacities analysis. The importance of the early assessment of capacities was learned through later project studies. The impact of the project on capacities is discussed later in the case.

Water for domestic consumption has been pumped from the Rahad River, about forty kilometers away from QEN, to distribution points in each of the villages of the settlement. This system was installed in the mid-1970s and has been subject to frequent breakdowns. In addition, the rapidly expanding livestock population living at the settlement puts added pressure on the system. Rain-fed storage pools called *hafirs* existed to supply water, but in insufficient numbers and with inadequate capacity for all livestock needs through the dry season.

Decreasing soil fertility and erosion were serious, but somewhat controversial, problems in the settlement. There was strong evidence to suggest that continued growing of sorghum, without fallowing or crop rotation with a nitrogen-fixing crop, resulted in severe depletion of the soil. On the other hand, the soil also appeared to be resilient and able to rebuild its fertility if left to natural processes. However, many farmers depended on their sorghum plots to feed their families and felt that they had no choice about which crop to grow.

Soil erosion was a particular problem in areas of the settlement that flooded each year and in areas immediately adjacent to small hills where swiftly flowing waters washed the topsoil away.

Land was a serious and complex problem in the settlement. Increasing population, due to natural growth and continued immigration, created an acute shortage of land. Those families who arrived in the late 1970s and later only received one to five *feddans* of land, in contrast to the original allocation of ten *feddans*. In this area, the average family of five needed ten *feddans* to produce enough to live on. Land tenure was also important for the refugee population in the settlement. Refugees held their land at the whim of the government and had no formal title.

Mechanization of farming presented a problem for farmers. While hand or draft animal cultivation was possible, the heavy clay soils and weed problem meant that mechanized cultivation was preferred. Hand cultivation required many days of back-breaking work to accomplish what a few hours of tractor plowing could do. However, mechanized cultivation depended on a fleet of well-maintained tractors, spare parts (imported), trained mechanics, and efficient management in order to ensure timely plowing during the crucial period just after the rains begin and before the land became too muddy to plow.

Credit was another problematic production factor for farmers in QEN. No credit was available through commercial or government banks. The informal lending system charged high interest rates and forced farmers to be dependent on the lenders. Farmers needed credit to pay for plowing, weeding, and seeds. Poorer farmers, who could not get credit, went without these inputs and faced lower yields.

Refugee participation in decision-making about the settlement was limited at best. Throughout his 1981 report on the QEN settlement, Brian Spooner pointed to the fact that refugees were seldom consulted on essential policy decisions regarding the settlement. The government Commission on Refugees, in its local, regional, and national bodies, made all important decisions. UNHCR also made decisions about the provision of funds for certain programs. The system encouraged the view that both decisions and material inputs were always provided from sources outside the control of the refugee community.

Early studies of the QEN community outlined the potential for considerable conflict between refugees and Sudanese villagers. These conflicts have not emerged in any dramatic way, probably in large part due to the fact that all services in the settlement were provided to both refugees and villagers. However, as resources become more and more scarce (especially land and water), the underlying difference in status and power could emerge as a problem. Mechanisms for mediating potential conflicts rely on COR or on local sheikhs.

The attitudes and motivations of QEN settlers were affected by these problems and by the way that the organizations in charge of the settlement dealt with them. Although, in general, refugees were poorly consulted on decisions which affected their lives, certain groups were systematically excluded from consultative processes. These included women, disabled people, younger adults and very poor people. Regular exclusion of these groups impeded overall development of the community. For instance, women's roles meant they dealt with the health and nutrition of the community, but they were not included in problem-solving and decision-making on these matters. Reflecting on the ways that refugees were involved in decisions regarding technology and management in the settlement, Brian Spooner made the following observation:

> The tested system of management has not provided refugees with an environment in which they can enthusiastically respond. It restricts any democratic involvement and progressive motivation to solve problems. Outside agencies and the Scheme [settlement] administration still promote ideas that refugees are lazy, uncooperative and not capable of self-management, thus everything must be done for them.[3]

Interviews with early ACORD staff indicated that a primary objective of the program was to "restore farmer confidence" in the viability of farming as a way of life in the settlement. The implication that the community had experienced a loss of faith in the basic source of productive capacity was supported by the figures on the number of *feddans* actually under cultivation as opposed to the number available.

3. Spooner, p. 121.

Spooner's report explored the reasons why farmers were not cultivating. Only 36 percent of the refugee households managed to cultivate all of their holdings, while 34 percent managed partial cultivation. Eleven percent of refugees did not cultivate any of the land allocated to them. People were discouraged with the agricultural process and had a sense that continued dependence on food rations was a viable strategy (food ration distribution continued through 1982).

III. PROJECT HISTORY AND DEVELOPMENT

Project Initiation

ACORD has been involved in refugee programming in the Sudan since 1976, and has been active in the Qala en Nahal settlement since that time. Early projects included assistance to health services, a poultry project, adult literacy efforts, and support of agricultural mechanics. However, ACORD's role was restricted to that of a funding partner only.

In 1980 ACORD was asked by the government of Sudan to expand its involvement in the settlement and, specifically, to take over management of the Tractor Hire Service (THS). Since 1970, under COR administration, the tractor fleet had fallen into disrepair and was poorly managed, resulting in erratic plowing and frequent breakdowns. These problems contributed to a general discouragement with farming in the settlement, and high percentages of land were left uncultivated.

With funding from the British Overseas Development Administration, ACORD provided twenty new tractors and repaired seven old tractors. ACORD also took over management of the THS, with authority to establish plowing schedules.

The ACORD Program

The basic aims of the ACORD program were:

1. To develop viable agricultural systems that would maximize potential benefits to all refugees;
2. To develop the agricultural capacities of the Scheme in an integrated fashion;
3. To involve an expatriate work program, if required, for a period of five years; and
4. To promote the organization and achievement of self-sufficiency and self-reliance among the refugee community.[4]

---

4. Spooner, p. 6.

By 1984, these general aims were described as follows:

The objective of EAA's (ACORD) assistance to QEN is to help lay the foundations for the long-run self-reliance of the refugee community and independence from external assistance by:

1. Promoting production methods with low import dependence and in particular encouraging the use of hand and animal cultivation methods as alternatives to tractors;
2. Achieving full cost recovery and independence of tractor hire and workshop activities;
3. Conducting agronomic research and extending useful results to farmers;
4. Relieving cash flow constraints on farming activities by providing credit;
5. Promoting practices which will prevent environmental deterioration which might undermine the scheme's longer-run productive potential; and
6. Transferring responsibility for managing refugee development programs from ACORD to refugees.[5]

Tractor Hire Service

The Tractor Hire Service provided new or repaired tractors, managed the service, and established an effective mechanics workshop. One of the first actions of ACORD was to divide the tractor fleet and assign tractors to the various villages, in five teams and later seven. Included was a team to handle cultivation of land held by local Sudanese farmers.

Since the "window" for effective cultivation is only about six weeks long, the main objective of the THS management was timely plowing of farm land. In the years after ACORD took over the THS, the amount of land under cultivation increased steadily. Figure 2 shows the number of *feddans* cultivated from 1980 to 1986.

An improvement was also made in the timeliness with which first cultivation of fields took place, although the actual period of cultivation varied depending on weather conditions. Most of this improvement can be attributed to ACORD's new management processes, particularly the greater participation by refugee groups in decisions. ACORD deployed tractors to village-based teams, including drivers and "checkers" from the villages, thereby transferring day-to-day management to local control. Basing the tractor teams in the villages meant that the THS was accountable to the farmers. Farmers were consulted about the method for determining the order of plowing. They decided that a strict lottery system would be best and that the lottery should be repeated each year.

5. Euro Action-ACORD, "An Information Document on the Qala en Nahal Agricultural Refugee Settlement," 1984, p. 1.

Figure 2: Cultivation Methods in Qala en Nahal			
	Feddans Cultivated by		
Year	THS	Hand	TOTAL
1980	26,000	*	26,000
1981	35,000	*	35,000
1982	37,000	*	37,000
1983	39,000	*	39,000
1984	31,000	21,000*	52,000
1985	32,200	32,300*	64,500
1986	39,000		

* Starting in 1984, ACORD provided credit to encourage use of non-mechanized cultivation methods. Earlier records of hand cultivation were not available.

Credit System

In 1984, ACORD introduced credit to support hand cultivation methods. The hand cultivation method in the settlement used a *seluka*, a long-handled tool with a spear-like head which was pushed into the earth with the foot. Because the *seluka* does not remove weeds, this method required the hiring of labor for weeding twice during the season. ACORD offered credit for weeding in lieu of plowing. They intended to increase the use of the *seluka* so that refugee farmers would not be dependent solely on mechanized plowing which required imported parts and fuel. ACORD offered eight Sudanese pounds for the first weeding and four pounds for the second, to be repaid at 12 percent annual interest.

The 1984-85 Drought and ACORD's Response

The 1984 agricultural season started off well with normal rains. More QEN crop land was put into cultivation than ever before. However, in August the rains ceased and a hot dry wind caused severe and early drying of the soil. An estimated 85 percent of the crop was destroyed, leaving the entire settlement with production of only 8,500 sacks for the whole year (of 80-100,000 sacks expected). This was enough for only one and a half months' consumption. ACORD staff worked with village leadership to assess the extent of the problem and to make a full report to COR and to ACORD headquarters, including a proposal for an emergency supply of grain.

As an organization dedicated primarily to development programming, ACORD was reluctant to get involved with relief efforts. However, it felt compelled to respond, partly in order to protect the gains that had been made during the previous three years of development program efforts. If relief were not provided, many farmers were likely to leave the settlement, undermining efforts to establish a stable agricultural economy. An ACORD report on the drought response quotes a local staff report as saying:

> When EAA began four years ago, people were apathetic and dependent on outsiders. Since then EAA has managed to change this attitude to a large extent. Whatever we do now must not allow the people of Qala en Nahal to slip back into a mentality of dependence.[6]

The ACORD consortium in Europe decided to go ahead with a relief effort, and staff from Sudan actually went to Europe to help raise the required funds (about US $1.7 million).

The relief effort took place in three phases:

1. Phase I: December 1984 - March 1985: Distribution of locally purchased grain to the most needy families.
2. Phase II: March - July 1985: General distribution of imported grain to all families to enable farmers to prepare for cultivation.
3. Phase III: July - December 1985: Continuation of general distribution throughout the growing season; implementation of grain security program.

After making the decision to provide relief food, staff soon realized that grain from European sources would take three months to arrive at the settlement. They managed to locate 3,000 sacks from a nearby Canadian Dry Farming Scheme, a large mechanized farm supported by bilateral aid. Buying mainly from this source meant that the purchase was not likely to inflate grain prices in local markets. Working with local sheikhs, staff decided to distribute emergency grain only to the neediest families during the initial period before the European grains arrived. Other families had to make do with the small amount of grain that had been harvested. Many local families shared grain with each other during this period and some sold livestock in order to purchase foodstuffs.

Throughout the relief program, there was close cooperation between ACORD and the sheikhs, who were the main leadership group in the community. In order to identify the families who were most in need, ACORD worked with lists that had been drawn up earlier in 1984 for the

6. Euro Action-ACORD, "From Development to Relief and Back Again: Euro Action-ACORD's Emergency Program in the Qala en Nahal Refugee Resettlement Scheme 1984-85," p. 5.

credit program. The sheikhs were asked to review these lists and add other families in need. About 850 to 900 families were identified, including elderly, sick, and disabled people, and families headed by single women. Prior to the arrival of European grain, ACORD undertook a survey of the entire settlement in order to obtain accurate estimates of the needs for each village and the area represented by each of the 207 sheikhs in the community. This was done within a one-week period at the end of February, 1985. From this census, the amount of grain required for general distribution to each sheikh's area was computed at 600 grams per person per day.

When the grain arrived on large trucks, it was distributed to the sheikhs who arranged for people to unload the sacks and transport it to the villages (using THS tractors in most cases). Because grain was immediately distributed, there was no need for constructing large storage warehouses. ACORD found that distribution went smoothly and equitably, largely because of the strong relationships with local people built up over the previous years of the program.

An additional aspect of the program during the second phase of emergency response was the purchase and distribution of seed grain to all farmers in proportion to their land area. Thus, even poor farmers could afford to plant again, in some cases with improved seed quality. The seed was provided on a loan basis.

Although Phase III saw a continuation of grain distribution, the new element was implementation of a grain security program. This program grew out of the credit program to support hand cultivation mentioned above. The first year of the credit scheme was the year of the drought and an almost total crop failure. ACORD deferred payment on the loans, and took payment in kind rather than in cash, for both 1984 and 1985 at the end of the 1985 season. The in-kind payment for the 1984 loan was pegged at the crop value as of the end of the 1984 season. This was greatly inflated due to the drought (i.e., a sack of sorghum which was worth 30 Sudanese pounds at the end of the 1983 season was worth 100 pounds in 1984 and about 25 pounds in 1985). The grain collected through this process was then put into storage in the villages as a buffer against the prospect of future drought or crop failure for other reasons. To this was added the repayments for seed loaned earlier in the season. Ten thousand sacks were stored in thirteen grain pits, enough to last the community three months in the event of another crop failure. The method used for the storage pits was a traditional local technique involving the digging of a pit and then sealing the grain with straw and mud. It was possible to store grain in this manner for up to two years quite safely. Low-lying villages used above-ground storage to prevent damage from flooding.

In Qala en Nahal the emergency program provided a ration of only grain, while other refugee communities also received oil, milk and beans. Therefore, QEN people were forced to find their own ways of getting other family necessities. They worked as day laborers out of the settlement, engaged in trade, or sold their livestock. The result was that although no one was starving in QEN, it did not attract large numbers of people looking for food. The relief program thus supported the long-term efforts at self-reliance of people already settled in QEN.

ACORD Program Since the Drought

Although studying and planning had started prior to the drought, ACORD afterwards significantly expanded their areas of involvement in the settlement. Many of the new efforts came as a result of demands from refugee groups during periodic meetings at the village level. In addition to the THS and credit programs which continued, new elements of the program included:

1.   An expanded agricultural extension program, and
2.   A natural resources program, including components dealing with water systems, forestry, soil conservation, and livestock management.

ACORD began to work toward a complete hand-over of the THS management to village committees. This was planned for two of the tractor teams in 1987, and the others would follow based on that experience. In a controversial move, much debated in ACORD meetings with the community, the price for plowing ten *feddans* was raised in 1986 from 2 Sundanese pounds to 6 pounds. This came closer to reflecting the real economic costs of maintaining the tractors and paying for fuel and drivers.

During the early years of its work, ACORD's agriculture staff helped to identify successful farmers and to make sure farmers learned from each other. In 1986 a new extension effort was implemented. The effort focussed on creating farming knowledge in the settlement, rather than depending on knowledge imported from other areas of Sudan or elsewhere.

Two sets of experiments were undertaken. The first was a series of tests of different techniques for sorghum production, including variations in planting methods and weeding repetitions. The second was a series of "village trials," in which each village experimented with a variety of types of sorghum, different fertilizers, and a variety of legumes, and tried various methods of crop intermixing and weeding to see their effects on the deadly parasitic weed plant, *striga*. The purpose of the trials was to provide demonstrations for farmers, to test different varieties of crops under the conditions in QEN, and to train village agricultural officers.

To address the long-standing water problem at the QEN settlement, ACORD worked with COR to refurbish parts of the old pumping system which supplied water for domestic use.

To solve the problem of water for livestock, ACORD provided funds for the creation of a number of new large, rain-fed catchment pools called *hafirs*. Some dry season vegetable production may also be encouraged using small-scale irrigation around the *hafirs*.

Forestry efforts in the settlement began in 1986, and included establishment of village woodlots (most of the trees on the settlement have been cut for firewood or construction); planting of shelterbelts around fields; planting on hills to prevent erosion and around *hafirs* to retard evaporation; and distribution of trees for planting in and around house compounds for shade or fruit. Some experimentation with cash crops from trees was also planned (the area has supported successful gum arabic production in the past).

ACORD's program became more comprehensive and integrated, extending beyond the fairly limited concentration in the pre-drought era on the THS. The program began to address the set of environmental factors to which the community was vulnerable.

IV. IMPACTS OF THE ACORD PROGRAM ON CAPACITIES/VULNERABILITIES

Physical/Material

The initial focus of the program was the improvement and management of the Tractor Hire Service. This was aimed at increasing the productive capacity of the community and guaranteeing a more secure source of food. However, ACORD staff emphasized that the primary objective of this program was to restore the confidence of refugee farmers in agricultural production, and affect their attitudes and motivations. Timely and reliable plowing was a crucial factor for improving the morale of the community.

Another aspect of the program was to improve skills in the community. Trained mechanics provided the community with crucial capacity for maintaining tractors.

Early assessments of the community noted that large proportions of the farmers were from nomadic backgrounds, unfamiliar with agricultural methods in the QEN setting. While in the early stages of the program, agricultural extension was limited to identifying successful farmers, subsequently ACORD took a more active skills development role. As detailed above, they took the interesting approach of generating knowledge in the settlement itself through agricultural trials, with potential for developing a greater capacity for experimentation. Village agricultural agents were trained as part of the process. All of these efforts helped to build the capacity of the community to deal successfully with the key activity of farming even as conditions change.

Later developments in the program began to address some of the broader physical vulnerabilities of the community, particularly those that relate to the environment: water, soil conservation, ground cover, trees, etc. In addition, the program has sought to stabilize and broaden the income sources of the community, through identification of drought-resistant strains of sorghum, crop diversification, livestock development, and exploration of agroforestry.

The drought relief program managed to sustain the gains made in terms of self-reliant agriculture, as evidenced by a continued increase in total land area under cultivation. In addition, the grain storage program promoted systematic planning against the possibility of future drought, reducing the community's dependence on outside assistance.

Social/Organizational

ACORD promoted village-based management of the THS, though those who ran it were ACORD employees and ACORD maintained ultimate responsibility for the service. In recent years, ACORD began the process of developing the community-based structures to take over actual decision-making and control of the tractor teams.

In other areas of the program, social/organizational mechanisms lagged behind. ACORD worked closely with the traditional leadership of sheikhs (also the officially sanctioned leadership through COR). When important decisions had to be made in the program, ACORD took care to meet in each of the six refugee villages—meetings which sometimes lasted four and five hours! These meetings were open and not restricted to participation only by the sheikhs. However, other groups that traditionally have been excluded from full participation in village affairs, particularly women, had no public voice in such meetings. Many of the poorest families in the settlement were female-headed and were thus left out of basic decision-making processes.

In interviews, sheikhs of two villages indicated that they felt consulted in ACORD decisions, but they felt that the final decisions were still ACORD's to make. In one village, the sheikhs knew that grain was stored for their possible use, but felt that it was ACORD's grain, not theirs. In a second village, sheikhs remembered being consulted about the type and site of storage and felt that actual use of the grain would be a joint decision between them and ACORD. However, they felt no group responsibility for the grain stores. The impression that the stored grain was "owned" by ACORD was probably reinforced by the fact that the storage sites were at the THS warehouses, the only secure places in the village.

Apart from this consultative process, the project did not encourage, in any systematic way, the formation of community-based committees or groups to take ongoing responsibility for managing development efforts. (Some of this may be attributable to COR reluctance to transfer control to refugee groups.) As it moved into more comprehensive programs as outlined above, ACORD planned to work more on forming refugee groups to take on specific long-term planning and development tasks.

Psychological/Motivational

Program reports indicated that farmer attitudes and morale improved dramatically in the five years of ACORD's efforts in the Tractor Hire Service. This is a clear indication of success for this part of the program.

However, it was also true, according to ACORD staff, that the attitude of looking for handouts persisted in the community. To the extent that refugees continued to look to outside agents for assistance through their difficulties, their commitment to strategies of self-reliance was low. The persistence of this attitude was confirmed in interviews with sheikhs in which they expressed helplessness regarding any steps they could take to prepare for future drought. In fact, they did not even mention the grain storage as a means of mitigating future famine until prompted by the interviewer. When asked what concrete actions could be undertaken by the community to help cope with a future drought, they had few ideas.

ACORD's program efforts helped restore confidence in agriculture as a viable means of livelihood, but, in general, refugees have not yet accepted active roles as community problem-solvers or initiators of self-sustained efforts to decrease their vulnerability to future disasters.

V. DILEMMAS AND LESSONS FOR FUTURE PROGRAM DESIGN

The ACORD program at Qala en Nahal is of particular interest because it is an ongoing development program that turned, in the face of an emergency, to a relief effort. The experience of ACORD in this period offers some lessons for future efforts.

Disaster as Development Opportunity

Agencies involved in development work in an area where disaster strikes may incorporate a response to the emergency into their ongoing work and, actually, improve their developmental impact in two ways: 1) by utilizing the opportunities posed by the urgency of disaster and 2) by refocussing their development work toward reduction of the vulnerabilities that led to the disaster. Often, development agencies view disasters as "interruptions" of their work and they resist getting involved in relief work. ACORD was rightly concerned about losing the progress made through its development work when the drought came. Because it had established working relationships with the local sheikhs and because of its knowledge of local capacities, ACORD was able to provide some rations during the periods of severe hunger. In addition, in the wake of a disaster which has strong environmental factors among its causes, there can be a heightened awareness of the ways in which the community is made vulnerable by such physical realities. The disaster, then, becomes an *opportunity* to work with members of the community to reduce vulnerability. This may be in the form of reinforcing (or reinstituting) traditional means for coping with periodic crises, or of evolving new societally supported mechanisms for coping.

In QEN, ACORD had already undertaken studies of the scheme's resources in preparation for additional program components. Many of these new initiatives were aimed precisely at the physical vulnerabilities of the community: dependence on limited varieties of a single staple crop, soil erosion, strain on water resources, etc. In addition, ACORD initiated a grain security project using traditional means for storage of sorghum.

The Dangers of Handouts

Development agencies that undertake relief must be very careful to avoid a damaging shift in their relationship with local people—a shift from "partners" to "providers." ACORD had tried, in the previous three years of program work, to minimize the image of the all-providing western donor agency. It limited the scope of its activities and concentrated on a crucial, agricultural activity. When it undertook a relief program partly to protect the advances it had helped make, ACORD ran the risk of altering the way the community viewed it. ACORD staff reported that refugee leaders became more insistent in their demands after ACORD provided rations and developed a sense that ACORD had the capacity to meet more of their needs if it chose to do so. During this period, ACORD had expanded the scope of its work into water supply, extension, forestry, and livestock management, thus reinforcing the image of an agency with considerable resources. When a community feels particularly and acutely vulnerable, its perceptions of an agency can alter considerably and quickly.

It is often *true* that the agency can command considerable resources. The challenge, therefore, is not to mask the capacities of the agency on the assumption that if the community knew the truth they would refuse to take initiative to solve their own problems, but to develop a relationship of mutual respect that supports and exploits the capacities of both in ways that are most fundamentally developmental.

Limiting Relief Aid

Agencies should consider what is the minimum input required to sustain a community through a difficult disaster period, and limit their relief to just the essentials if dependency is to be avoided. While this may, at first glance, appear harsh or punitive, it need not be. The so-called "dependency syndrome" is not created by refugee groups, but by the processes used by assistance agencies, even with the best of intentions, in trying to reduce suffering.

ACORD chose to provide only grain to the people of QEN. They viewed this only as "crop replacement"—offering only that which was lost due to the drought. In this way, ACORD treated the community as though it were already self-reliant in other things. Indeed, the increasing productivity of the settlement had led to a cessation of regular ration distribution in 1982 and a general increase in the amount of small-scale commercial activity in the settlement (local markets, etc.). People in QEN derived income from livestock, from trading, and from day-labor for other agricultural enterprises in addition to their crops. While each of these activities was also under stress due to the drought (the price of animals was quite depressed, for instance), there was no reason to suppose that the QEN settlers were totally destitute and to provide general food rations as occurred in other communities.

It would appear that by providing only the bare minimum, ACORD helped avoid a full reversion to the attitudes of dependency that had prevailed in the community prior to 1981. While there has been some lost ground in this regard as refugees demand handouts of various sorts, ACORD staff contend that the situation would have been much worse had a full-blown relief program been instituted.

Community Cooperation and Capacity for Relief Operations

For relief distributions to be developmental, outside agencies must seek out and then support the knowledge and capacities of local communities for identification of needs and distribution rather than assuming that all tasks must be done by the agency itself. Agencies with previous relationships to the community are in a good position to know and support such capacities.

ACORD recognized that the sheikhs of QEN were experts at arranging for distribution of goods among their people. For many years they participated in the distribution of rations, preparing lists of families and cooperating with the authorities to see that distribution went smoothly. ACORD took responsibility only for seeing that grain was delivered to a central point in the settlement. From there it was up to the sheikhs to receive it, transport it to their villages, and distribute it to each family. The alternative approach would have required that ACORD distribute rations to each village and to each family. In doing this they would have encountered less cooperation from local leaders and probably some resistance. More importantly, such an approach would have denied local capacity both to accomplish the task and to hold their leadership accountable for equitable distribution. The community had already demonstrated a capacity for exercising accountability through the THS village teams.

Emergencies as Opportunities to Work with Disadvantaged Groups

ACORD's ongoing development program concentrated on equitable provision of cultivation services to the entire farming community of Qala en Nahal, both refugee and Sudanese. With the introduction of the credit program, however, there was some differentiation among farmers, with poorer farmers being given "softer" loans. During the relief program, especially during the first three months, the most vulnerable families received grain first. At the beginning of the 1985 planting season, all farmers were provided seed grain according to the number of *feddans* they were to plant—a somewhat levelling mechanism. However, the poorer families were also those with few other resources (livestock, people to work as day labor, etc.) and therefore likely to suffer most severely during the year. Female-headed households were prominent among these.

In its work since the drought ACORD recognized a need to work more directly with the most disadvantaged groups, particularly with women. A challenge to taking on this work is that women have not been part of the regular consultation process that ACORD has followed in planning programs in the past and the traditional leadership in the community does not include women. Some of the new program directions include elements that could be of benefit to women-headed families, including irrigated horticulture, small livestock, and better agricultural extension aimed at poorer farmers, the most vulnerable to the dynamics of drought.

REFERENCES

Devitt, Paul and Ahmed Tahir, "Qala en Nahal Refugee Settlement: Preliminary Report on Water, Natural Resources and Livestock Development," Euro Action-ACORD, July 1984.

Euro Action-ACORD, "An Information Document on the Qala en Nahal Agricultural Refugee Settlement, Eastern Sudan," Prepared for the E.A.A. P.R.C. October 29.30, 1984.

Euro Action-ACORD, "From Development to Relief and Back Again: Euro Action-ACORD's Emergency Program in the Qala en Nahal Refugee Resettlement Scheme 1984-85."

Euro Action-ACORD, "Report on Grain Distribution in Qala en Nahal," 1985.

Euro Action-ACORD, "Qala en Nahal Refugee Settlement Progress Report - September 1985".

Euro Action-ACORD, "Port Sudan Small Enterprises Programme: Narrative Report for the Period 01/01/85 - 12/31/85".

Morris, N.G., "Qala en Nahal Refugee Settlement Water Supply: Preliminary Assessment Report," Euro Action-ACORD, February 1985.

Ogborn, James, "proposed ACORD Programme for the Management of the Mechanized Refugee Farming System in the Qala en Nahal Resettlement Area: Tractor and Land Management in the Qala en Nahal Resettlement Area," 1980.

Schulz, Michael and Schulz, Judith, "Port Sudan Small Enterprises Programme: Final Report of the Programme Design Phase 1982-1983," Euro Action-ACORD, 1983.

Spooner, B.C., "The Qala en Nahal Refugee Resettlement Scheme: Historical Review, Current Status and Programme for Action," Prepared for Euro Action-ACORD from and agricultural and socio-economic study, August, 1981.

Yuill, Robert M., "Discussion Paper on Euro Action-ACORD Involvement in the Qala en Nahal Refugee Resettlement Scheme," February 1984.

ACKNOWLEDGMENTS

This case was written in 1987. The author thanks several ACORD staff people who helped both by providing information about the Qala en Nahal project and by making arrangements for the field visit: Jacques Cuenod, Peter James, and Judy el Bushra in London; Iain MacDonald in Khartoum; Vernon Gibberd, Eyob Goitam and other project staff in Qala en Nahal. Appreciation is also extended to Mukhtar Hamour and to Fawzia Hamour of the Institute for Development Studies and Research who provided useful background and perspective on Sudan and to Higgo Abdel Wahid Higgo who assisted with gathering information and interpreting in the field.

Chapter 17

NOMAD PROGRAM
Tin Aicha, Mali

Project Implementing Agency:
American Friends Service Committee

Case Writer:
Peter J. Woodrow

I. INTRODUCTION

This case history is concerned with a program of assistance to nomads in Northern Mali who had been rendered destitute by the drought years of the early 1970s. In cooperation with the Malian government, the American Friends Service Committee (AFSC) helped establish a new nomad village called Tin Aicha.

The American Friends Service Committee began its work in Tin Aicha in 1974. Direct program involvement continued in the new village until 1980. Since that time, AFSC staff has been based in Goundam, continuing activities with nomad groups in the region and maintaining contact with Tin Aicha through occasional visits. On several occasions since leaving, AFSC has provided assistance to Tin Aicha for specific short-term projects, including assistance during the drought and famine of 1982-1985.

The Tin Aicha project is of particular interest to the IRDP because it shows how an outside NGO, working in close cooperation with a local government, assisted a population as they adapted to new circumstances forced on them by a catastrophic event, severe drought. The Tin Aicha case also provides an opportunity to assess the longer-term results of a program intervention by allowing us to see how the people responded to a second major drought in the early 1980s and how that response differed from their response in the 1970s.

MALI

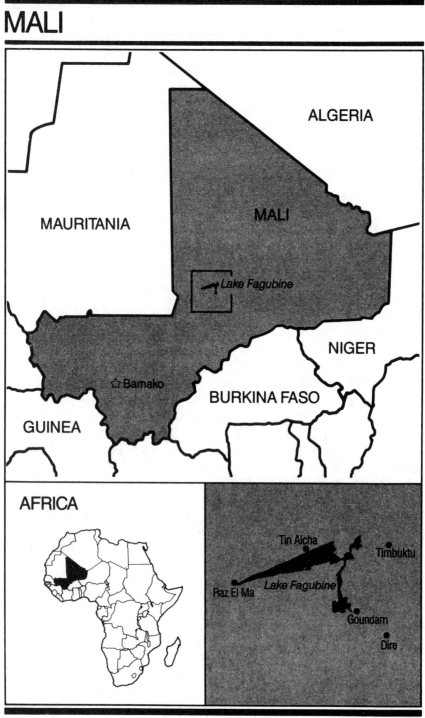

ALGERIA

MAURITANIA

MALI

Lake Fagubine

NIGER

☆ Bamako

BURKINA FASO

GUINEA

AFRICA

Tin Aicha

Timbuktu

Raz El Ma

Lake Fagubine

Goundam

Dire

Map By Jerry Alexander

II. DESCRIPTION OF PROJECT CONTEXT

General Conditions[1]

"The Sahel is a 3,000 mile strip of semiarid land in West Africa between the Sahara and the fertile savanna to the south. The word "Sahel" is Arabic for "shore" and refers to the edge of the Sahara "ocean." The Sahel stretches through six Francophone countries in West Africa: Senegal, Mauritania, Mali, Burkina Faso (formerly Upper Volta), Niger, and Chad. Its inhabitants are mainly nomadic or seminomadic, although many are also sedentary farmers who trade their grain for nomad livestock. The annual 50-150 millimeters of rainfall allows the survival of certain hardy breeds of grasses and small trees, which provide forage for the herds. During the cold months of December through February, temperatures can drop to 0 degrees Celsius (32 degrees Fahrenheit); during the hot, dry spring, temperatures reach 47 degrees Celsius (115 degrees Fahrenheit). The rainy season lasts from June to September and brings high winds and violent storms.

"The Republic of Mali is a Sahelian country located in the interior of West Africa. It is about 478,000 square miles in size (1,240,000 square kilometers) and has a population of about 5.7 million. Its topography includes savanna, the Sahel, and the Sahara. The region was conquered by the French in the 1890s and became that part of French West Africa known as the French Sudan. Mali became independent in 1960 and is currently governed under a one-party democratic system. The country is bordered by Mauritania, Senegal, Guinea, Ivory Coast, Upper Volta (Burkina Faso), Niger, and Algeria, and has no outlet to the sea.

"The Kel Tamashek are the most widely known of the nomads in Mali; the most numerous are the Fulani, although many Fulani are seminomadic. All the nomads share a culture and economy based on herding. Their animals turn a sparse, marginal environment into a productive region that has supported nomadic herders for nearly 6,000 years. Status, nutrition, mobility, and wealth all depend on the possession of animals—camels, cattle, sheep, goats, donkeys—and their care.

"Within the traditional society of the Tamashek are five distinct classes: nobles, vassals, *marabouts* (Islamic religious teachers), artisans, and servants. (The servants—Iklan or Bella—legally ceased to be slaves many years ago but their position in nomad society remains one of subservience).

---

1. The history of the early years of Tin Aicha included in this case is taken from a book-length description and evaluation of the effort written in 1981 after AFSC had concluded its full-time involvement with Tin Aicha. *Tin Aicha, Nomad Village*, American Friends Service Committee, 1982. Information about events from 1981 through June 1987 is based on a visit by the IRDP.

Occupations, social and religious rituals, and kinship patterns vary, but on the whole the nomad groups adapt to their environment in quite similar fashion.

"Although the nomads' pride and livelihood rely upon the ability to travel with their herds, it is not unusual for some to spend several months in one village or to leave some members of the family in one place, with a few animals, while the rest of the family travels with the main herd to richer pastures. Among some nomad groups, the higher classes in the society travel with the herds, and the lower classes remain behind, farming land that is owned by the upper classes.

"Most nomad groups circulate in a large "home" area, breaking camp before dawn, and traveling before the heat of noon. During the wet season, they move frequently; during the dry season, they camp near a well for as long as the pasture holds out, usually a matter of weeks. As the dry season progresses, they move from shallow, hand-dug wells to deeper wells. The distance between the camp and a well or water source is limited to about ten kilometers because small livestock must be watered every day; the distance between the camp and the pasture is limited to about twenty kilometers because the cows must return to the camp every day to be milked and to feed their calves.

"At the onset of the wet season, many nomads round up their animals to begin the month-long journey north to the edge of the Sahara—the salt earth, as the Tamashek call it. Here the animals can graze on salt grasses and drink water high in minerals, both of which are considered healthy for animals and for the humans who consume their milk. Also, since tribes tend to meet repeatedly in the same general areas every year, it is a time of celebration, with feasting, camel racing, wrestling matches, and courtship.

"Material goods, which must be light and durable, are limited to household necessities. They are therefore usually made of wood, and wood is the major non-food resource drawn from the environment. Aesthetic taste and material prosperity tend to be expressed by intricate decoration of functional items such as carved tent poles, bowls, and beds, woven mats, knives, and swords, rather than by the addition of superfluous goods.

"The tents are heavy and strong to withstand the high winds and driving rains of the wet season. During the dry season, straw huts, which are better protection from the heat than dark-colored tents, are generally built or rebuilt; tents are stretched, waterproofed, and mended. During cool, dry periods, the nomads camp near small trees and bushes which provide fodder for their goats. During the wet season, the tents are pitched on top of high dunes to avoid mosquitoes and water runoff; the hot, dry season also finds the nomads on top of high dunes to catch the breezes.

"Animals, as stated, form the core of nomad life, and a nomad's care and understanding of his herds is the key to his success. Cattle provide milk for souring, butter, and cheese; their hides are used for tents and sandals; and they are sold for large purchases. Sheep are slaughtered for sacrifice or celebration, they provide milk and butter, and they may be sold for small items. Their hides are made into pouches and wallets. Goats also provide milk and cheese and are sold to buy tea, sugar, tobacco, salt, and other small necessities; their leather is used to make water bags, milk churns, and cushions. Donkeys are used chiefly for transport, although their milk may be used for medical purposes. Horses are symbols of very high status and are generally reserved for respected elders. Dogs are kept for guarding the camp and the herds, and for hunting; they are rarely sold but often given as gifts. Camels transport the heaviest materials—tents, people, sacks of grain, slabs of salt. They provide fresh milk and are very rarely slaughtered. A large herd connotes wealth, but a large herd of camels is a special sign of prestige.

"The diet revolves primarily around milk and milk products. It is supplemented by wild and domestic grains, stored in sacks, in brick granaries in the town, and in secret caches in the sand where it is said to remain edible for two to three years. Animals are not regularly killed for meat, which is eaten only on special occasions (guests, for example, may have a goat or sheep slaughtered in their honor) or in times of dire need.

"There is a tendency in the West to regard nomadism as a throwback to humankind's primitive past, before the discovery of agriculture gave rise to sedentary civilizations. In the Sahel, however, nomadism is still the most efficient means known to date for exploiting this extremely marginal terrain. It should be viewed as a rational response to environmental circumstances and not as a refusal to progress to a settled lifestyle. Throughout their long history, the nomads have had a proud, generous, independent spirit and a cultural identity as extensive as that of any sedentary society. The events leading to the drought of 1968-1974, and the drought itself, threatened this heritage and the nomads' very survival.

Drought, Famine, and Relief

"Droughts have long been a fact of life for the sub-Saharan regions of West Africa. Poor harvests and acute famine were recorded in the Sahel from 1910 to 1914, and again in 1941-42. The conditions from 1968 to 1974, however, were without recorded precedent in the Sahelian countries. By mid-1972, the death toll for the nomads of the sub-Sahara had reached tens of thousands. Herds were so devastated that two million pastoral people had no means of subsistence. The social fabric of the family and clan in many cases was torn completely apart. The Sahelian nations, which had been slowly working toward economic independence after decades of colonial rule, saw their efforts destroyed in the space of three years as they once again became dependent upon other nations.

"Both natural and human elements contributed to the disaster. By 1968, changes in climate had dramatically reduced water supplies and had caused crop failures to the point that emergency measures were required to meet food needs. This, and the relentless encroachment of the Sahara wasteland southward, portended disaster. Yet most people ignored or dismissed these signs as temporary aberrations of cyclical phenomena.

"The potential consequences of certain human activities similarly were ignored. Decisions to raise cash crops for export ultimately affected the entire ecological balance of the region. The most fertile land, formerly used to grow staple foods for internal consumption, increasingly was used to grow cash and export crops—peanuts, for example.

"Further, the cash crops were produced in irrigated belts which traversed the nomads' traditional north-south migration routes, and the farmers prevented or limited access to the nomads' hardier dry season pastures. As farms encroached northward, the nomads who raised the nation's livestock were pushed even further north toward the desert. Many herders found it necessary to spend the entire year on marginal pastures which previously had been reserved for wet-season use. The rational, traditional balance between sedentary farmers and nomadic herders thus was disrupted.

"Another factor in the disaster of the 1970s was that increased rains in the early 1960s had caused improved health among humans and livestock, as had modern medicine and immunizations. The inevitable growth in human and animal populations created an increased demand for resources and insufficient attention was given to the livestock carrying capacity of any given area. Herds were augmented without safeguards against overgrazing, and large areas were stripped of protective vegetation. Foreign assistance programs further aggravated the overuse of marginal lands by funding the drilling of new wells, which lowered the water tables and caused the land around the wells to be completely denuded, as grazing herds, seeking water, traversed it again and again."[2]

In the years since the drought of 1968-74, the climate has not been kind to the people of the area. While there has been the occasional year of good rains, for the most part the rains have been average to poor. From 1982-84, severe drought again struck northern Mali, as it did most of the Sahelian region of Africa. Nomads, who had managed to reconstitute their herds, again lost most or all of their animals. People now speak of the drought as "permanent" and have begun to doubt if the nomads of the region will ever be able to return to their traditional means of livelihood.

2. End of quotation from *Tin Aicha, Nomad Village*.

Capacities/Vulnerabilities Analysis of Nomads
in Northern Mali

Prior to the drought of 196874, nomads in the Goundam *cercle* (the administration headquarters) of northern Mali followed the traditional coping mechanisms described above in order to survive the harsh conditions in which they lived. The common culture and values of this lifestyle represent important nomadic capacities but also vulnerabilities in relation to catastrophic events. A major capacity of the nomads is their proven ability to cope with a harsh environment, including periodic drought. Strong family ties and loyalties extending to their nomad "fraction" and ethnic groups meant that they had strong networks for achieving broad community goals. They are noted for pride, independence, dignity and religious unity and strength. They were able to move flexibly according to the needs of animals and people.

Traditionally, these nomads have been vulnerable to the vagaries of weather. Entirely dependent on rainfall for good pasturage and water for animals and people, they have faced chronic water shortages since the early 1970s. Many have lost herds, first in the early 1970s and again in 1983-84, and it is increasingly difficult to replenish these basic sources of livelihood under the conditions of territorial squeezes from the north by the encroachments of the Sahara desert and from the south by the increasing claims on land by sedentary farmers. They have few alternative sources of income, and rainfall shortages make agricultural activities also risky. Few nomads have adequate access to education or regular health care.

And while dedication to family independence and loyalty to fractions are assets in some ways, they also make it difficult to build cooperative structures for the common benefit of the nomad community as a whole, or to build a political power base to influence government policies. Also, the caste system and nomad fractions divide people and place them in rigid roles. Similarly, nomadic values are strengths but those that deem any kind of work besides animal herding as taboo or shameful for higher castes limit the options for livelihood.

In general terms, the Tamashek nomad groups of northern Mali are a population in forced transition—forced by both natural and human events. Almost fifteen years after the major droughts of the early 1970s, it is still debated whether the Tamashek nomads can re-establish a viable pastoral system even if the rains return. Despite yearnings for traditional ways, some Tamashek leaders question whether a return to the old ways is desirable, if the group is to build greater capacity to function in the changed economic and political system of independent Mali. One of the main points of the Tin Aicha experiment was to see if a different mix of income-generating activities and new ways of living and moving could be successful.

III. PROJECT HISTORY AND DEVELOPMENT

Project Exploration

The American Friends Service Committee is a nongovernmental organization (NGO) with headquarters in Philadelphia, Pennsylvania. It works on issues of justice and peace in the United States and on relief, development, and reconciliation internationally. AFSC representatives began to look for ways to assist people affected by the drought in Mali in 1973. In the course of their program explorations, they met with the *commandant* of the *cercle* of Goundam, who had been coping with an influx of five thousand people seeking refuge in a government relief camp in the town. By 1974, many of the refugees had left the camp, especially the farmers who were able to return to their lands once the rains had resumed. However, there remained several thousand destitute refugees who were mostly nomadic herders. Since their livelihood depended on rebuilding their animal herds, it was more difficult for them to start their lives again.

The Goundam *commandant* thought it important to help these nomads adapt to a style of life that was at least partially based on sedentary farming. He asked for volunteers from among the refugees to establish a village. One hundred families, about five hundred people, volunteered. The *commandant* granted them land which was officially unclaimed on the north shore of Lake Faguibine, about sixty kilometers north and west of Goundam. Each family received one hectare of land along the lake front. Thus, a new village was established and called Tin Aicha.

Project Agreements

The government of Mali agreed to provide some assistance to the new settlement, including seeds, health services, and transport to the site. When he met with AFSC representatives, the *commandant* asked if AFSC could provide technical assistance and funds for community projects.

Major decisions about the village, including planning and monitoring, were to be in the hands of an Interministerial Committee, with the *commandant* as administrator of their decisions. A smaller group in Goundam, including the AFSC representative and several local officials, was to oversee local project administration.

> AFSC agreed to provide a community development worker, live-stock for herd reconstitution, seed grain, medicines, agricultural and educational materials, a vehicle, and salary supplements for the project's civil servant personnel. The Malian government gave Tin Aicha its director, its agricultural and veterinary extension agents, two teachers and a school, a nurse and dispensary, a social worker, and housing for this staff.

The primary objective of both the Malian government and AFSC was the economic rehabilitation of Goundam's drought victims. The government tended as well to see project success as the sedentarization of nomads. AFSC, on the other hand, felt that improved health and education and new skills would stay with the nomads whether or not they remained settled.[3]

This was clearly a Malian project, so the role of the AFSC representative evolved according to the needs identified through her work with the community and with government officials in Goundam. The first AFSC staff person lived in Goundam but spent significant periods of time at Tin Aicha. She also trained a woman from Goundam as a social worker and several Tin Aicha women as health and nutrition aides.

Her initial role of providing continuity, leadership, and communication with authorities, including seeking support for the project from Bamako and regional headquarters at Timbuktu, became less important as the project became more firmly established. Thus, the second AFSC representative focused more on encouraging local leadership and building sustained relationships with local government services such as agriculture, health and education. In this second period a major element of the work was construction of Tin Aicha's permanent buildings which meant that this AFSC representative also devoted considerable energy to planning and implementation of these efforts.

In general, the role of AFSC was to work alongside the residents of Tin Aicha, to facilitate development efforts and to help integrate the project into normal Malian administrative structures that could sustain it in the long run. This involved helping Tin Aicha residents to identify and express their needs and desires and to communicate these to higher authorities to whom villagers had little or no access.

AFSC worked in the Tin Aicha community through 1980. After that, AFSC kept in close touch with the village and assisted with various specific projects, but moved on to work with other nomads in the Goundam region.

Project Implementation

The site chosen for the settlement on the shore of Lake Faguibine is among the most valuable farmland in the region. Faguibine is a seasonal lake, filling each year with the rainy season flood waters of the Niger River which flows through miles of channels into a series of four large shallow lakes, of which Faguibine is the largest. During the dry season, the water level drops such that only a small portion of the lake contains water. Over

3. Stephen Morrissey, "Tin Aicha: A Project of the Government of Mali and the American Friends Service Committee 1975-1980," on behalf of the International Institute for Environment and Development, London, 1987, p.12.

the past twenty years, the waters into the lake have been steadily diminishing, to the point that, in 1986, only about one-quarter of the lake filled, even at the height of the flooding.

The lake fronts are intensively cultivated when there is water. Cultivation follows the receding and rising waters. Fields run in narrow strips from the edge of the lake toward the middle. As water rises and recedes, the amount of land available for farming changes considerably. The yearly rainfall (average 140 mm) is not sufficient for rain-fed cultivation, so most of the surrounding territory is limited to herding.

By late 1974, the first one hundred families had arrived in Tin Aicha, established the village on the edge of Lake Faguibine, and begun cultivation. The first AFSC staff person arrived early in 1975. The interministerial committee felt that the project was going well enough that they approved the settling of a second hundred families later in 1975, although there was not as much farmland available for these families. They set up a second village not far from the first.

The people who came to Tin Aicha were those who had been most severely devastated by the years of drought. Some of them had been successful herders in the past, but many represented the poorer and less able families. The majority of the first group were Kel Tamashek nomads, largely from the Kel Antessar fraction. Only eight of the families were from the Bella caste who historically did agricultural work for their Tamashek lords. A significant group of the families were also Moors (traditionally a trading group). Most of the first group came from some distance away. The second group of settlers was mostly Tamashek from the Goundam area.

1978 Population of Tin Aicha:	
Ethnic Group/Origin	Number of Families
Moors from Goundam	1
Moors from outside Goundam	21
Bella from Goundam	1
Bella from outside Goundam	7
Tamashek from Goundam	110
Tamashek from outside Goundam	24
TOTAL FAMILIES	164
Families departed 1974-78	35
Women/girls	560
Men/boys	544
TOTAL POPULATION in June 1979	1,104

From Tin Aicha, Nomad Village, p. 63-64.

Government personnel arrived in the village by the end of 1975. These staff found Tin Aicha to be a difficult assignment since, except for the teachers who were themselves nomads, most had never worked with nomads or lived in desert conditions. The result was frequent staff turnover, which meant that the AFSC staff person provided an important element of continuity.

Agriculture at Tin Aicha

A key factor in the success or failure of Tin Aicha was the development of agriculture. The settlement was intended to provide an alternative source of income and food and to increase the options open to these nomad families. But, for many of the new residents of Tin Aicha, farming was a totally new experience. In fact, farm work was considered demeaning by Tamashek culture and only slaves were expected to engage in it. The many nomad families who owned farmland, and even lived part of the year on it, left the actual labor of growing crops to the Bella slave caste or to other paid workers.

> When Tin Aicha's first village began, the project's lakefront was divided into *soumboy* (strips two meters wide, the traditional land measure), and family fields were assigned a strip for every member. Closest to the lake, in wet, alluvial soil, the families planted rice. In a middle band, clay and sand, they planted sorghum. And farthest from the lake, in the driest and sandiest soil, they planted off-season crops (vegetables, beans, melons, and maize) which the rain would water.[4]

Despite efforts to secure additional land, the people of the second village never received the full amount granted to the first settlers. As a result, families did not have enough land to feed themselves entirely from farming. They were able to produce only about six months of their yearly food needs. As inexperienced farmers, they also had low yields at first..

For a time, a seed bank was organized from which farmers could borrow for planting and repay in-kind after the harvest. Eventually, however, farmers learned to store their own seed, and the seed bank was no longer used. The community also developed a grain bank in order to avoid the usurious interest rates of merchants who would buy the grain harvest at low prices at harvest time (when people were eager to sell to get cash) and then sell it back in the months before the next harvest. The grain bank enabled them to sell to the village cooperative, which stored the grain and sold it back at reasonable prices. But, the grain bank was undercapitalized, and though small sums were charged to cover maintenance expenses, the drought years of the early 1980s put it out of business. (See further discussion of the Village Cooperative below).

4. Morrissey, p.4.

Although the official rules of Tin Aicha forbade the hiring or use of other people to work the family's land, within a few years this became a common practice. By 1980, as many as a third of the families were hiring others to work their plots. This was particularly true of the Moors who had by that time returned to their traditional work as traders. Only the Tin Aicha families who had enough able-bodied members to divide responsibilities for farming and herding did not hire others.

Agriculture in Tin Aicha has been affected by the failure of floods in Lake Faguibine since 1983. The level of the lake has been falling since the 1950s, in what has historically been a sixty-year cycle.[5] The failure of rains in both 1982 and 1983 accelerated the rate of decline. The seasonal flood level in the lake did not reach Tin Aicha, so that lakeside farming was impossible. As the drought caused the loss of both agriculture and animals, a number of families were forced to leave Tin Aicha until the rains returned.

In 1986 and 1987, people tried intensive market gardening in the lake bed, using shallow wells for water. They sold these vegetables in the weekly market. The season for such gardening is short, however, which meant it served only as a temporary measure until the lake water would rise again.

The viability of making a livelihood in Tin Aicha in the long term is tied to the water level in the lake. If good rains come for several years and the lake rises, people can expect a fairly prosperous life with income from both herding and farming. A large government infrastructure project has received international funds to rehabilitate the Goundam *cercle* lakes. This project involves dredging the channels that feed the lakes from the flooding Niger River. If the scheme is successful, income from farming in Tin Aicha could become more secure.

An additional factor which affects the viability of farming for the community is the land tenure system. Even though the land was granted by the *commandant* no one has secure title. The *commandant* who started Tin Aicha has moved and two others have come and gone since then. Government priorities (or political demands) could lead to a reallocation of the valuable lands around the lakes, including those of the Tin Aicha farmers. This is, however, a problem faced by everyone, not just the Tin Aichans.

Livestock

The original concept of Tin Aicha was to mix farming with animal herding, for which the area is well suited, when there is adequate rainfall. In early 1976, animals were distributed to Tin Aichan families. Depending on family size, they received a maximum of three heifers and three ewes per family and were to repay the same number of animals in four years.

5. There has been no water at Raz El Ma (the *chef lieu* of the *arrondissement*) at the extreme western tip of Lake Faguibine since the early 1960s.

The Tin Aicha experience with livestock was frustrating and full of problems. Decisions made by the distant interministerial committee limited the options of the villagers. For instance, the animals for the project were purchased by an agent in distant markets rather than by the villagers who were, after all, experienced herders. As a result, the care taken in the purchase was inadequate and animals were lost in transit. The varieties were inappropriate in some cases, particularly the sheep which were southern merino instead of the hardier dama. Some animals were sterile or so young they could not produce offspring for several years. Repayment was, therefore, impossible. The government had refused to allow Tin Aichans to have goats because they damage trees and grass.

The Interministerial Committee felt that villagers should concentrate on agricultural activities, so they required that animals be kept in a communal herd and tended by paid herders. The animals were not managed as carefully as the villagers desired. Families, then, set up a system for rotating the herding responsibility. Later, they divided the herds into four groups which were tended by selected villagers who were paid. Ultimately, in 1978, the communal herd was disbanded, and individual families assumed direct responsibility for the care of their animals. The people changed dramatically the numbers and varieties of animals, opting for hardier goats rather than more vulnerable sheep and cattle. They chose goats because they do breed quickly, provide more milk, and are less expensive than other animals.

Many of the animals of Tin Aicha have suffered or died in the 1980s. Families who lost all of their herds in the drought of the early 1970s lost them again between 1982 and 1985. Some families managed to move their herds to the south in time, where they found sufficient pasture, only to see many of them die from disease. The goats that survived or were purchased after the worst period of drought were plagued by diseases in 1986-87.

Species	1976 Initial Distribution	1978 Census before Communal Herd Dissolution	Mid-1979
Cattle	383	533	295
Sheep	383	586	637
Goats			1,432
Donkeys			75
Camels			17

Animals in Tin Aicha:

From *Tin Aicha, Nomad Village*, p. 78.

By 1988, the pasture areas in the Tin Aicha region had not recovered from the drought years. Although some animals (particularly goats) could feed on vegetation in the lake bed, until there are several years of good rains in a row, herding on any scale cannot be supported.

Education

Education has been one of the most successful and lasting contributions of the Tin Aicha project. Malian nomads have the reputation of resisting modern education; part of the traditional nomad resistance to government schools was the fear that their children would be alienated from their culture. The teachers recruited for the Tin Aicha school, however, were themselves, Tamashek. Since the school is right in the village, children are not separated from their families as they would have been if only boarding schools in towns were available. In addition, villagers persuaded the Ministry of Education to provide a Koranic scholar to teach both the children and the adults in Tin Aicha. The presence of this *marabout*, as he is known, has supported the religious life and culture of the community.

Tin Aicha School Enrollment: 1975-87

Year	Grade: 1	2	3	4	5	6	7	8	9	Total
1975	73*									73
1975-76	42	33								75
1976-77	61	38	39							138
1977-78	48	43	34	26						151
1978-79	47	41	34	24	21					167
1979-80	48	45	58*		20	18				189
1980-81	61	43	32	30	21	10				197
1981-82	49	35	34	25	18	9				170
1982-83	45	25	30	18	15	8				141
1983-84	36	25	10	12	13	7	7			110
1984-85	28	22	18	17	14	8	10	6		123
1985-86	35	25	20	15	17	6	12	7	7	144
1986-87	35	29	18	18	15	7	16	10	10	158

* Grades 1 and 2 combined in 1975, 3 and 4 in 1979-80.

From *Tin Aicha, Nomad Village*, p. 88 and Ed Reed, AFSC, "Goundam Nomad Program Field Visit Report," July 1987, p. 36.

The Tin Aicha school provided a school lunch program, as do all Malian schools. The World Food Program gave the food, which was supplemented by vegetables from a village demonstration farm. This feeding program was particularly important during the drought years of 1983-85 as it helped sustain the families who remained in Tin Aicha.

The school started in 1975 with one class, adding additional classes each year until all six primary grades were included in 1979. With support from AFSC, a secondary school was added in 1982, eventually including 7th through 9th grades. Enrollment increased steadily until 1980 and then fell off during the difficult years of 1982-85 when some families temporarily left the area. It has been increasing again since 1985. The school has a high retention rate and a good scholastic reputation. Several graduates from the high school have gone on to the *lycée* in Timbuktu.

The Tin Aicha school proved a major element of stability for the community through the 1980s drought. Some even suggest that the community would no longer exist if the school had not been there. The leadership of the school has provided consistent leadership to the community, helping resolve conflicts and facilitate decision-making.

The significance of the secondary school in Tin Aicha went beyond the village. In the past, nomad students who wished to continue their studies beyond grade school had to leave their families and move to Goundam or Tonka, many kilometers away, to attend school. The dropout rate was extremely high. In contrast, retention of students in the Tin Aicha secondary school has been excellent and the number of students who have passed examinations to attend the *lycée* in Timbuktu has been at a rate higher than most other schools in northern Mali. The Tin Aicha school has provided education to nomad children in a nomad setting, helping to change parental and student attitudes toward education.

Throughout this period, AFSC provided modest subsidies to the school and direct assistance to the school canteen. While AFSC's help was extremely small in dollar terms (about $5,000 per year), its effects have been significant in terms of contributing to the viability of the school.

Fédération de Groupements Ruraux, the Tin Aicha Village Cooperative

Cooperatives in northern Mali have not been generally successful. Most were founded in the early 1960s with capital contributed by local populations. Many did not survive the decade. In the late 1970s, some were resurrected with government and outside funds, but their survival is still uncertain. They face fierce competition from local merchants; they are widely scattered in a region with very poor transportation; and they buy their goods from a state trading company which is itself only sporadically supplied.[6]

6. Morrissey, p. 10.

The cooperative in Tin Aicha has experienced numerous difficulties common to other cooperatives in northern Mali. The Tin Aicha cooperative was successful in the first years after its founding when the village was established. It later suffered and, finally, failed due to the drought. It began as a village store, supplying such staple goods as tea, sugar, cooking oil, lamp oil, soap, and cloth. By buying together, villagers were able to obtain lower prices on these goods. By 1978 it had become an official cooperative under the national cooperative service (*Fédération de Groupements Ruraux*), with an elected administrative council and a full-time manager hired from the village. Later, the cooperative also operated a seed and grain bank.

At its peak, the FGR cooperative was quite involved in a variety of activities. The following was written in 1980:

> It manages the monthly grain allotments to the village's civil ser-
> vants. It loans seed money to Tin Aicha's farmers, who repay in grain
> at the harvest. It manages the demonstration farm, which has become
> a communal field. It oversees Tin Aicha's livestock cooperative and
> village herd. These services have developed slowly. Each new venture
> is examined carefully by a population unwilling to take blind risks.[7]

The cooperative was forced to close its doors in 1983 when all of its operating funds were depleted because it could not collect on the credit extended to villagers who then lost their animals and had no crops as a result of the drought.

In 1986, AFSC provided funds to rehabilitate the store buildings. At the same time, ACORD (a European consortium of NGOs with extensive experience working with cooperatives in northern Mali) provided funds and technical assistance to restart the cooperative (a process still underway in 1987).

Construction of Tin Aicha's Permanent Buildings

For Tin Aicha's first few years, in part because no one knew if the community would last, the school, health dispensary, cooperative store, and civil servant housing were only straw mat sheds rather than permanent structures. In 1977 the villagers asked AFSC and the government to assist with the construction of mud and fired brick buildings that would help reinforce the long-term commitment to Tin Aicha. The building program was designed also to provide short-term employment and to train people in construction skills.

The basic structures were built from adobe bricks, and this was then faced with fired brick brought from Goundam. AFSC trucked in all the materials that had to be brought from elsewhere at great expense: palm trunks to form the roofs, gravel, cement, fired bricks, louvered steel doors and windows, paint, and whitewash.

7. Morrissey, p. 10.

None of the villagers had experience with construction. Therefore, AFSC arranged for professionals to come from Goundam to supervise and train them, twenty-five to fifty at a time. The village council selected the people to receive training. The first set of buildings—the school, the dispensary and the cooperative store—was completed by early 1980. A second set to house the secondary school was begun in 1981 and completed in 1983. The construction process had long-term secondary, beneficial effects that were not planned.

> From their experience, several workers emerged as qualified professional builders. Some local women developed pot and brickmaking skills. Local transporters (who carried adobe from the lakeshore to the building sites by donkey) had, by the end of the construction project, established ongoing businesses moving grain and commodities. And the buildings gave Tin Aicha a sense of stability and permanence, ensuring a long-term commitment from local government services.[8]

The Weekly Market at Tin Aicha

The Lake Faguibine area is served by a series of local markets around the lake. These markets provide a place for trade among Tamashek and Moor pastoralists, Bella farmers, Bozo fishermen and Sonrai merchants.[9] In 1976, a small market was set up at Tin Aicha and, by 1978, several of the larger merchants had set up regular business at this site. In prosperous times, the market has provided a place for Tin Aichans to sell their produce (vegetables, grains, and artisan products) and to buy goods not otherwise available locally. The market also provided regular transport and a source of news. Blacksmiths, potters, dentists, tailors, and butchers were attracted to the market. Tin Aicha's wells attracted herders to the market, and the only health dispensary and cooperative store on the north shore of the lake were also magnets, turning Tin Aicha into a center of commerce for the area.

Response to the 1982-85 Drought

Tin Aicha residents responded to the drought of 1982-85 in a number of ways. Thirty to forty families chose to stay in Tin Aicha throughout the drought, despite the lack of food for people or pasturage for animals and the fact there were few other options for earning income. The school was a major factor encouraging and enabling people to stay.

Some families, or parts of families, moved to major centers such as Goundam, Dire, or further south to Lere, Mopti or even Bamako. There they managed to find work using skills such as farming, masonry, well digging, etc. which they had acquired in Tin Aicha. Some stayed with relatives or

8. *Tin Aicha, Nomad Village*, p. 104.
9. *Tin Aicha, Nomad Village*, p. 92.

found help in refugee centers. Many of those who went south left their children in Tin Aicha with friends or relatives so they could attend school. Some individuals and, later, their families went to neighboring countries such as Algeria, Mauritania, or Ivory Coast to find work. Again, they used the skills they gained in Tin Aicha, and they sent funds back to their relatives in Tin Aicha.

These responses were significantly different from those of the families in the drought of the early 1970s. In 1973-74, many of the families ended up in refugee camps, destitute and without options. This time, a significant portion were able to retain some control by pursuing options as farm workers or semi-skilled laborers. These strategies were available to them largely because of the Tin Aicha experience.

Tin Aicha has become a home base, albeit a flexible one, for its permanent residents. People have developed systems that maintain something of their nomadic styles as well as a commitment to continuing life in Tin Aicha when conditions permit. Nomads have always shifted their base according to the demands of pasturage and water. This pattern remains, but the reasons for movement have changed as farming and other alternative income-generating activities have increased.

IV. IMPACT OF THE PROJECT ON THE CAPACITIES AND VULNERABILITIES OF NOMADS

The Kel Tamashek peoples of northern Mali have been forced by climate, economic events, and politics to face fundamental changes in their way of life in an extremely short period of time. People who a decade ago would not be seen with a tool in their hand tilling the soil now proudly demonstrate their ability to provide for their families through agricultural labor. Others have taken up other manual jobs.

Through projects such as Tin Aicha, nomads have developed new options for their livelihood. In this process, by all reports, the sense of shame and defeat they felt when faced with a loss of their traditional way of life has been replaced by determination and pride in their pursuit of multiple strategies for survival. These nomads are stronger in their motivation and attitudes, exploring new ways to live and creatively face the changes thrust upon them.

The main physical/material effect of the Tin Aicha project was to expand the income-generating options available to nomad families. Nomad families have expanded their knowledge and skills in agriculture. Almost accidentally, Tin Aicha residents gained other skills as masons, carpenters, and well-diggers: skills which proved extremely useful in the drought years.

The Tin Aicha school increased nomad children's access to education.

By providing the possibility of continuing on at the *lycée* in some cases, the project introduced other options for future employment for these children.

The FGR cooperative store provided a mechanism for supplying crucial goods at reasonable prices to Tin Aicha residents. It had difficulties, as reported, but through the subsequent rebuilding effort, the cooperative may be able to release people from dependence on merchants who charge extremely high interest and perpetuate the cycle of poverty.

The weekly market in Tin Aicha provided an effective outlet for selling and buying goods. Along with the water points, dispensary, and school, the market helped put Tin Aicha on the map as an economic entity. The health station, built with AFSC help, provided regular access to primary health care, a new situation for many nomad families.

In social/organizational terms, Tin Aicha became one of the most active population centers of nomads in the area. As a center of commerce, and education, it became an important center for articulating the needs and desires of nomads to various government authorities. When dispersed, nomad groups usually do not exercise this power; in Tin Aicha they have developed the ability to exert political influence.

V. DILEMMAS AND LESSONS FOR FUTURE PROGRAM DESIGN

Support of Peoples in Transition

NGOs can support a population that is in transition from a traditional economic base and lifestyle to a new means of survival. Throughout the world there are peoples in transition. For many of them, the pace of change has accelerated. Traditional means of living, with attendant customs, values, and social roles, have been destroyed or have become dysfunctional.

An external agency can be helpful in the transition process through several roles. It may cushion the effects of change by providing subsistence goods for a transition period, or it can help the people experiment with new ways of adapting. In particular, as AFSC did in Tin Aicha, it can open up options for people to earn their livelihoods in non-traditional ways. Skill training and education are particularly important in expanding people's options.

NGO Influence in Crises

Crises sometimes expand opportunities for small NGOs to exert influence on behalf of those it hopes to assist, even when larger and complex economic, environmental, social, and political forces are at work. Compared to governments, NGOs are small and usually insignificant in relation to the vast economic and environmental forces with which they hope to help people cope. In times of crisis (even "permanent crisis" such as the drought in northern Mali), opportunities for influence by such outside agencies are sometimes greatly expanded. AFSC found itself in a position to influence decision-making in Mali about the placement of a secondary school in Tin Aicha. By facilitating the movement of the papers through the government bureaucracy and providing materials for the construction of the school, AFSC affected the decision process. As a result, the long term viability of Tin Aicha as a community was reinforced.

Note that since there is a limited number of schools that can be built, other communities without outside advocates were at a disadvantage relative to Tin Aicha in gaining government approval for schools. This is truly a dilemma for an NGO: how to become better informed about the situation, but then to use the information gained in ways that are effective in the long term for the people with whom they work, while not, at the same time, putting other groups at disadvantage. NGOs must be aware of the ramifications of the influence they exert on behalf of some groups as it affects other groups.)

Skills Acquisition

Skills acquisition may be the most important capacity-building activity. Through the Tin Aicha program, in building the school, cooperative, and dispensary, many people learned the skills of mason, carpenter, well digger, etc. The program also introduced new skills in agriculture. In the subsequent periods of drought and famine, a number of families survived, not due to the institutions of Tin Aicha, but due to these skills.

Through the specific skills taught to specific individuals, the entire community learned that there are occupations other than animal herding which are viable and dignified work. For a nomadic population whose survival has depended upon their ability to move with circumstances, these *portable* skills were of equal or greater importance than the village itself.

Increase of Income Options

Efforts to increase the income options and to improve the economic stability of a group often have side effects in terms of the social fabric. When an NGO is involved in any activity that affects the work people do, such as skilled training or job creation, it should be aware of and careful in helping people deal with the impacts of these activities on access to, and control over, resources and on social and political power within families and across the society.

REFERENCES

Documents Cited Extensively:

American Friends Service Committee, *Tin Aicha Nomad Village*, Philadelphia, 1982.

Morrissey, Stephen, "Tin Aicha: A Project of the Government of Mali and the American Friends Service Committee 1975-80", on behalf of International Institute for Environment and Development, London, 1987.

Other Background Documents:

American Friends Service Committee, *"Etude Socio-Economique du Cercle de Goundam, Mali,"* 1982.

Negus, David, "AFSC Mali Nomad Program Progress Report", AFSC, 1985.

Negus, David, "Drought in Mali's 6th Region: 1982-85, AFSC Intervention in a Difficult Situation", AFSC, 1987.

Reed, Edward P., "Goundam Nomad Program Field Visit Report", AFSC, May 1987.

ACKNOWLEDGMENTS

This case was written in 1987. The author would like to express thanks to those who made the visit to Tin Aicha possible and who helped gather information and make contacts with the people living there now: El Mehdi ag Hamati, Oumarou ag Mohamed Ibrahim, Greg Comer, and the tireless AFSC driver, Garba Nhiga. Thanks also to AFSC staff in Philadelphia who facilitated the visit: Corinne Johnson, Ed Reed, Mohulatsi Mokeyane, Patricia Hunt and Cheryl McCool. The author is grateful to Stephen Morrisey and David Negus, former AFSC staff members in Mali, for their help in interpreting events and Tamashek culture.

Chapter 18

PROMOTION OF HEALTH CARE AMONG KHMER REFUGEES IN GREENHILL SITE B
Surin, Thailand

Project Implementing Agency:
Catholic Relief Services-Thailand

Case Writer:
Peter J. Woodrow

I. INTRODUCTION

This case history analyzes the work of Catholic Relief Services (CRS) with displaced Khmer people in the Greenhill Site B camp on the Thai-Kampuchea border. The program addressed the need for both medical and public health services among the Khmer population. It is of particular interest to IRDP because of its strong emphasis on training Khmer workers in various health-related positions. The Khmer people, regardless of their uncertain futures, will take these skills with them wherever they go after Site B.

II. BACKGROUND/CONTEXT OF THE THAI-KAMPUCHEA BORDER CAMPS

When the Vietnamese military entered Kampuchea in December, 1978, thousands of Kampucheans (Khmer) fled their country into Thailand. They were either pushed ahead of the retreating forces of the Khmer Rouge who were being ousted by the Vietnamese after four years of rule, or fleeing the fighting and the Vietnamese. By the beginning of 1980, there were an

THAILAND

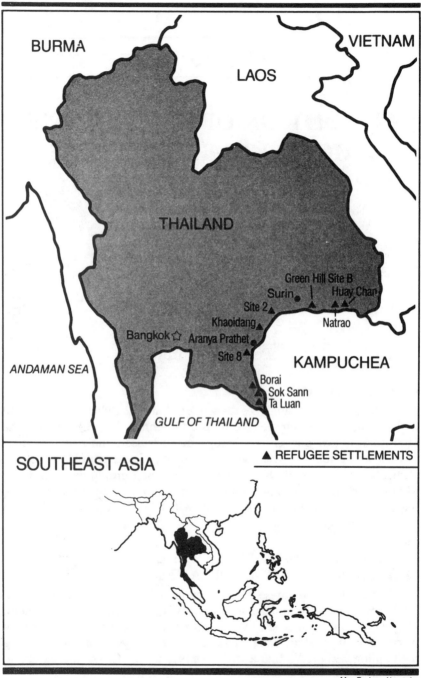

BURMA

VIETNAM

LAOS

THAILAND

Green Hill Site B

Surin

Huay Chan

Site 2

Natrao

Khaoidang

Bangkok ☆ Aranya Prathet

Site 8

ANDAMAN SEA

KAMPUCHEA

Borai
Sok Sann
Ta Luan

GULF OF THAILAND

SOUTHEAST ASIA

▲ REFUGEE SETTLEMENTS

Map By Jerry Alexander

estimated 500,000 to 750,000 Khmer refugees, either in official holding centers under the auspices of the United Nations High Commissioner for Refugees (UNHCR), or in ill-defined "border camps" which were on or near the border, often affiliated with various factions of the anti-Vietnamese resistance. Those in the holding centers were eligible for resettlement in third countries, but those in the border camps were not given official "refugee" status by the Thai government. The latter were designated as "displaced persons" who could not be considered for resettlement. Each of the border camps became affiliated with one of the anti-Vietnamese factions: the Khmer Rouge (the former government of Kampuchea, under Pol Pot and Kieu Samphan); the Khmer People's National Liberation Front or KPNLF, a more nationalist/rightist group under former Prime Minister Son Sann; and Moulinaka (*Mouvement pour la Liberation National de Kampuchea*), under the leadership of Prince Sihanouk.

These camps were also fluid with no fixed location. This flexibility was a necessity, as fighting between the various factions continued in the area.

During this period, it was a dangerous business to provide food or medical services in these border camps. Between 1982 and 1984 there were about 85 camp evacuations or relocations, many in the midst of active warfare. In 1984-85, a major Vietnamese offensive forced the evacuation of all of the border camps once again. This time, the Thai military allowed the establishment under their authority of more permanent camps farther from the border. These new camps, while considerably more secure, were also under both the control and protection of the Thai military. Thus, the relatively unimpeded trading activities, crossing of borders, and movement in and out by NGOs and others were no longer allowed. The Thai military strictly controlled entrance and exit from these new, closed camps.

Up until 1982, the task of providing assistance to the border camps (as opposed to the holding centers served by UNHCR and many other NGOs) was overseen by UNICEF. In 1982, a new entity, the United Nations Border Relief Operation (UNBRO) was set up under the U.N. Secretary General's Office. This operation was headed by the Special Representative of the Secretary General of the United Nations for Humanitarian Assistance to the Kampuchean People. UNBRO is responsible for providing services to the camps (often by contracting with NGOs); coordinating all U.N. agencies and other international entities involved; and, as far as possible, extending "protective services" to the camp populations (i.e., from hostile military actions, exploitation, Thai government interference, etc.). The main implementing agency for UNBRO was the World Food Program until, in early 1988, responsibility was transferred to the U.N. Development Program (UNDP).

By 1986, the population in the eight camps under UNBRO was approximately 250,000. Of these, about 41,000 were in Greenhill Site B which is allied with the Sihanouk forces. By 1988 the Greenhill population had grown to approximately 50,000.

Since the main source of income for people in the camps was the food ration distributed on a per capita basis by UNBRO, the question of population figures for the camps remained controversial and highly politicized. In addition, while most of the camp population were non-combatant women, older people, and children, the camps served as rest and recreation sites for soldiers from the nearby military operations. Many of these soldiers were actually registered with their families in the border camps, though they spent most of their time elsewhere.

Quite apart from the political controversies surrounding the real numbers and nature of the border camp populations, their connection to the military forces in the area had a profound effect on NGO programs. In addition to food and shelter, NGO programs in the camps offered medical services and, in some cases, training. NGOs trained medics to serve the civilian camp population, but these people were often drafted into the military. The first priority of the Khmer leadership was sustaining and furthering the military campaign. Potential and actual camp leaders were channelled into military roles, leaving few effective technicians or administrators to build community life in the border camps.

III. ANALYSIS OF CAPACITIES/ VULNERABILITIES AMONG THE SITE B POPULATION

Because we are interested in assessing the effects of the CRS program and other U.N. and NGO efforts in Greenhill Site B, it is important to know about the vulnerabilities and capacities of the camp people as they first left Kampuchea. However, because conditions in the border camps have changed so often and so dramatically since 1980, the summary below provides only a general picture of conditions in the border camps during the 1980-82 period.

The most important vulnerability that the Kampucheans faced as they came into the border camps was the threat of war. They constantly faced shelling and displacement. In addition, the disruption of both family and larger social structures had been extreme under the era of Pol Pot and the Khmer Rouge. Few community organizations were left; few survivors had educational or technical skills. The physical and social disruptions of these times had left their mark of psychological trauma. Fear, flight, and constant disruption meant that the people who arrived in the border camps were tired and discouraged and usually felt helpless in the face of the events in which they were caught up.

Still, the picture was not completely bleak. The women in the camps were strong and stable. The Khmer Women's Association was growing, and providing a channel for community activities and the rebuilding of social cohesion. There were also other skills and experiences which proved valuable for making the camp society work. Some people had served in administrative positions in the pre-Khmer Rouge period, and these skills emerged. Farming, artisan and trading skills still existed, so people were able to build houses from materials at hand and to plant small gardens when they were settled enough to do so. Furthermore, even after the traumas of the past and with the uncertainties of the present, the Khmer people had a strong will and determination that they, and their culture, would survive.

Particular problems, some mentioned above, emerged in the camps themselves. The flow-through of military personnel meant that the civilian populations were at risk, even in the camps. In addition, as noted, when leaders emerged or people acquired special skills, they faced conscription into the military where these skills would serve the cause. As in most refugee camp situations, there were no immediate means for earning income or for producing food, so all camp members were dependent on the provisions from the NGOs and under the control of the Thai government. It was in this setting that CRS took up work in Greenhill Site B.

IV. PROJECT HISTORY AND DEVELOPMENT

History of CRS Involvement in Greenhill Site B

CRS had been working with Khmer, Laotian and Vietnamese refugees and displaced persons since 1979. In 1982, the CRS staff who were involved in refugee programs numbered about sixty expatriates and 250 Thai workers, as well as more than 1,200 refugee workers. As the situation stabilized, especially in the camps along the Thai-Kampuchea border, CRS and all other NGOs working with UNBRO scaled back their programs.

Since 1982, CRS has been working under contract with UNBRO to provide health services to the population of Greenhill Site B. In the early years, since the camp was situated very close to the border, it was forced to evacuate and move numerous times. Since 1985, Greenhill Site B has been in a stable location about eight kilometers from the border. The new stability and security permitted a shift in CRS's approach from providing purely emergency and curative medical services to greater emphasis on prevention and public health education.

Program Components

The CRS program in Site B had two major components: medical services and public health, including a small dental program. In addition to facilities and services at Site B itself, CRS maintained a referral hospital at Kab Cherng (an older camp site some miles from Greenhill) for acute cases from the whole northern border area. CRS expatriate and Thai medical staff had access to Kab Cherng 24 hours a day, whereas they could only work in Site B during daylight hours.

Medical Services

The Greenhill Medical Center (GMC) included an outpatient department (OPD), inpatient wards, and a laboratory and pharmacy. In addition, there were obstetrics, TB/leprosy and dental programs. The staff of the medical program included six doctors, eight nurses, three pharmacy staff, a dentist, and two laboratory staff among expatriate and Thai personnel. They worked with thirty-six Khmer medics with three levels of training, Khmer nurses, and other Khmer health workers.

The day-to-day operation of medical services was provided by the Khmer staff with consultation and ongoing instruction from the expatriate and Thai medical staff. For instance, the OPD was run by Khmer clerical personnel, nurses and medics who prepared records, screened patients, took vital signs, diagnosed, and prescribed treatment. If a Khmer medic encountered a case s/he could not deal with, one of the fully trained doctors or nurses was called in for a consultation. Similarly, patients admitted to the GMC hospital were mostly treated by the Khmer staff, but CRS medical personnel provided daily consultations.

Within the GMC, the Khmer medics elected a Khmer Medical Committee responsible for personnel administration, with the assistance of the CRS medical staff. They set personnel policies and guidelines for behavior and enforced them among the Khmer staff of the GMC. Whenever Khmer staff were accused of inappropriate behavior of any kind, the Khmer Medical Committee investigated and made decisions regarding disciplinary action.

As with all positions among Khmer workers in the border camps, no direct salaries were paid, but workers were compensated with extra rations and, occasionally, with clothing or other useful articles. The trained health staff of the GMC, especially the medics, also enjoyed some prestige in the community.

Public Health Program

The goals of the Public Health Program were specified as:

1.   To raise the level of knowledge of preventive health care practices in order to increase Khmer self-reliance and responsibility for the reduction of preventable and contagious diseases.

2. To improve the health and nutrition status of the vulnerable population through preventive services.
3. To reduce morbidity from treatable conditions by increasing the case finding ability of Khmer health workers participating in all areas of medical and public health training programs.
4. To provide training and education to promote community awareness and implementation of better health care practices.
5. To provide appropriate nutritional management (treatment, referral, education) for related health problems.[1]

The public health component of the CRS program in Site B included activities in community health outreach (CHO), health education, maternal and child health (MCH), nutrition, and sanitation.

All the public health workers participated in a basic five-week training program covering general topics in health, sanitation, hygiene, nutrition, etc. They then received further on-the-job training in their specific assignments. Except in the maternal and child health program, there was little opportunity for more advanced training of the health workers, partly due to a rapid turnover of staff.

The community health outreach program compiled statistics on the general health status of the camp population, providing basic information to inform other public health initiatives. They were also responsible for screening new camp arrivals for health problems and undertaking campaigns in the community regarding specific health issues such as TB. They monitored the community to detect any circumstances or diseases which could threaten the general health among the population.

In the spring of 1988, there were 125 CHO workers assigned to one of the twenty-eight sectors of the camps. In addition, each carried specialized responsibility for a particular program area such as TB, water purity, etc.

The maternal and child health program was responsible for pre-natal care and teaching of pregnant women and for monitoring growth and health among children up to five years old. The program provided supplementary "dry pack" rations for pregnant women and for each child under three. The dry pack included a rice/mung bean mixture, eggs, sugar, vegetables, and fruit. In order to receive the dry pack, mothers were required to participate in nutrition and child care education programs run by the department. The MCH program employed eighty-one Khmers as of February 1988.

The nutrition programs concerned malnourishment among children in the camp. They provided supplementary and therapeutic feeding for children with acute malnutrition. As with the MCH program, parents participating in the program were required to take part in classes on a wide range of family health issues. In 1988, 118 Khmer workers ran the program.

1. "Public Health and Nutrition Programs," CRS-Thailand, 1987.

The Sanitation Program had responsibility for construction and maintenance of 3,000 latrines, 2,000 wells, and for disposal of trash, as well as other water quality projects.

Training

In addition to the Medical Services and Public Health Programs, the CRS program included a major effort to train Khmer health workers to work in the preventive or curative projects described above. The training components included:

1. *Basic Health Worker Training:* To train entry-level health workers (paramedics), teaching or reviewing primary school literacy and mathematics, basic sciences, human development, nutrition and hygiene. A four-month, full-time course.

2. *Khmer Nurse Training:* To train refugee nurses in a six-month course followed by on-the-job training for another six months.

3. *Medic Training:* To train three levels of medics: junior, intermediate, and senior. The medic training program was run by the doctors, pharmacists, and lab technicians. The junior course lasted six months, the intermediate level nine months to a year, and the senior level an additional nine months to a year. After initial training, the medics worked each morning in the OPD or hospital and continued training for three hours in the afternoon. As they worked in the clinics and wards, with the expatriate doctors, they also received practical assistance and instruction.

The training program was coordinated by one expatriate nurse and a Thai nurse. The Thai nurse ran the entry-level general course for Khmer health workers. Plans in 1988 included expanding the training for the public health workers, while continuing to support training for the medical staff. The training program involved courses for traditional birth attendants (midwives) who practice in the camp.

Another role of the training staff was to gather appropriate medical and training texts in various languages and to work with a border-wide health training committee to devise common strategies for the development of health services and standardized curricula for training workers of all levels. A significant part of this effort was to identify Khmer leaders who could begin to take more responsibility for health concerns so that management of health and medical services in the camp could be passed to Khmers. Because there were few educated Khmer in Greenhill Site B (or the other border camps), this was expected to be a long-term effort.

V. EFFECTS OF THE CRS PROGRAM ON VULNERABILITIES AND CAPACITIES

Social Organization: The Challenge

The CRS program with the border population began in a truly emergency situation with thousands of people coming to and across the Thai-Kampuchea border in extremely poor health. In addition, as camps were established, armed conflict continued, causing the frequent evacuation and relocation of the camps with consequent complete disruption of services, housing, and camp organization. Lives were lost and housing destroyed.

In these circumstances, CRS maintained close control of the health program, although, even during the years from 1982 to 1985 (the period of constant evacuations), CRS did train Khmer medical staff. Many of these, however, moved to other camps, disappeared, or were transferred to military units. Coupled with the scarcity of educated Khmer, the unsettled circumstances provided a difficult situation in which to support or encourage Khmer capacity to take on organizational or managerial responsibility for health concerns in the camps. In fact, most organizational energy seems to have been directed toward military and international diplomatic efforts, with the operation of camp life a lower priority among Khmer leaders with management experience.

After 1985, when the camps were relocated farther from the border, the situation changed somewhat. The Khmer Administration took on more responsibility for running the camps. In the health area, however, progress towards Khmer assumption of management responsibility was slow.

Within the CRS project, day-to-day operation of the program was primarily in Khmer hands. The Greenhill Medical center was essentially operated by the Khmer medics, nurses, and health workers, with the CRS Thai and expatriate staff serving as backup, trainers and overall coordinators. CRS encouraged the emergence of Khmer leadership in the GMC, and as noted above, the GMC Khmer Medical Committee took full responsibility for professional standards and discipline among the Khmer workers. The other programs in public health, nutrition, and maternal and child health also were operated by the Khmer staff with assistance from the CRS personnel.

Nonetheless, Khmer progress toward increasing their organizational capacity in the camps was slow. Results were mainly in terms of daily operations, but development of capacity for overall problem identification, problem solving, decision making, or management lagged.

Outside of the CRS program, in other areas of camp life, the Khmer increased their social/organizational capacities. The Khmer Administration took on increased responsibility for handling the distribution of extra rations to Khmer workers, a role that was earlier in the hands of CRS. The Khmer Women's Association initiated multiple programs in education and literacy, and developed an extensive organization at the base level throughout the camp.

On other levels the Khmers exhibited important skills for dealing with their situation. As with most refugee populations totally dependent on governments and camp administration for their supplies, they became adept at manipulating (in the best sense of the word) the system they lived in to meet their and their families' needs. Outsiders have frequently criticized these refugee tactics. However, these tactics represent extraordinary abilities to deal effectively with a system in which refugees have little or no power and few ways to gain resources.

Physical/Material Improvement

In contrast to the social/organizational realm, progress in physical terms was dramatic. The general health of the population improved markedly after 1980 when they were pictured as starving refugees straggling into hastily constructed camps. In early 1988, acute malnutrition in Greenhill Site B was below five percent (compared with eight to ten percent in other border camps, and twenty-five to thirty percent in 1982).[2]

There had been few serious epidemics, and outbreaks of typhus and pigbel had been controlled. These were remarkable achievements with so many people crowded into a small space. Sanitation was increasingly well organized, although, in some areas, the latrines continued to pollute drinking water sources. Efforts were underway to improve water quality, identify TB victims, and improve dental hygiene. Infant mortality had fallen to at least the level of the surrounding Thai villages and may have been better, although accurate figures were difficult to obtain.

In addition to these physical indicators, many Khmers were trained in specific medical service roles, as outlined above. These skills will stay with these people whether they remain in the camps or return to Kampuchea. In this sense, the CRS program contributed toward increasing the long term capacity of the Khmer population to deal with health issues, although the ability of individuals to make use of their skills will depend on political circumstances.

Two Approaches to Skills: Two Outcomes

CRS staff debated among themselves about how the Khmer staff should be trained. Some argued that the Khmer should be trained to be village health workers with broad integrated skills in both preventive and curative health. They noted that such workers would be able to function

2.   Chronic malnutrition persists with evidence of stunting among children.

independently in an imagined village setting in Kampuchea. Other CRS staff felt that the priority should be on improving the specific medical skills of workers so that they could take more independent responsibility for daily health services, especially in the GMC. They emphasized the importance of developing expertise in curative approaches. While the first strategy would increase capacity to deal with the longer-term future, the latter would increase capacity to deal with the immediate situation—which, it was expected, would persist for some time.

Psychological/Motivational Change

The CRS program had little direct impact on the psychological strength of the Khmer population. However, the stabilization of the camp, the improvements in health, and the regularization of food and other services improved the refugees' general outlook. By 1988, Khmer leaders were urging efforts oriented toward the future, including renewed focus on education of people to help rebuild Kampuchea.

On an individual basis, the CRS program benefitted the Khmer who have received training through the CRS program. Khmer medics and nurses were recognized and respected by their fellow country-people for the roles they performed. Graduation ceremonies of these trainees were presided over by well-known Khmer leaders.

A Potential Conflict

In order to promote health education, CRS required mothers who wanted the dry pack rations to attend classes. Some of the women seemed to resent these enforced learning settings, partly because they recalled the political indoctrination sessions under the Khmer Rouge. Attitudes and beliefs are important elements in the success of the program; if women resist health messages because they are associated with required activities, their capacities in this area will not be increased.

VI. DILEMMAS AND LESSONS FOR FUTURE PROGRAM DESIGN

Accountability and Competing Interests

In the context of the Thai-Kampuchea border camps, there were many parties with competing interests that have affected how programs were planned and implemented: the Thai government and military; the international community and U.N. agencies (UNBRO); the voluntary agencies and their staff (Thai staff vs. expatriate; field staff vs. central office); the various Khmer political/military factions fighting against the Phnom Penh government and Vietnamese forces; and the refugees themselves.

Each of these parties had a different set of interests regarding how the refugee population should be treated. The voluntary agencies were directly accountable to UNBRO through contracts, but they also had to build good relationships with Thai military authorities. Many agencies also felt somewhat accountable to the refugees themselves.

Within the voluntary agency, the interests and perspectives that staff held were different. Refugee workers, the locally hired national staff, the expatriate staff (further divided among Third World and European/American people), the country office personnel in a capital city, and the headquarters staff in the U.S. or Europe: each had a different viewpoint. In addition, in larger organizations, with more layers of supervision, there were differences in approach, philosophy, and implementation among the various layers. These competing forces created a confusing set of circumstances in which to attempt developmental programming among refugees. However, even within this constraint, agencies (including CRS at Greenhill Site B) have shown that positive progress towards development can be made.

Training

Even under the most adverse political situations where both agency and refugee actions are controlled by others (Thai security, UNBRO, etc.), an external NGO can carry out programs relying primarily on refugee capacities and can contribute purposefully to development through training programs for the refugees. The CRS program is a good illustration of the efficacy of education and training strategies in a refugee setting.

Even during the most disruptive period of the program (pre-1985), CRS was able to train Khmer medics to work in the program. Although many of these were diverted to the military, the skill base among the total population increased. Eventually, Khmer workers were able to run the Greenhill Medical Center on a day-to-day basis, a testament to the effectiveness of the training components of the program. Certainly if the refugees are able to return to their home communities in Kampuchea, these skills will be valuable, and will reduce vulnerability to health threats.

Management Skills

To train people in specialist skills is not the same as providing a situation in which they can develop community-based problem-solving and management skills; therefore an agency should be explicit about undertaking both activities if it is to have the greatest possible developmental impact.

Organization among the population in Site B remained weak and managerial skills few. Still, every community has some structure. In the case of Site B, community structures that could be used for public health promotion were the schools (some of which were entirely operated by the Khmer) and the Khmer Women's Association, which had pervasive organization, including a sub-office in each section of the camp (and women are generally in charge of family health, hygiene, and nutrition).

CRS chose to provide high-quality medical services and public health promotion and to train refugees to provide this care. This approach could be combined with working through the wholly-owned Khmer organizations to achieve greater self-reliance and community responsibility for health.

Refugee Capacities in All Areas

Just because refugees take over management control of one aspect of their lives in camps, it does not follow that they will do so in all areas. Each agency working in a camp must be independently committed to encouraging refugee responsibility—and must design its own delivery and training to encourage this—if it is to support and promote the capacities of the refugees in the sectoral sphere in which it has programs. At the same time, it is best if agencies agree on this approach so that they do not become unduly critical of each other.

CRS was accountable to UNBRO for its performance in Greenhill Site B. UNBRO, however, only began to encourage greater Khmer self-reliance in 1988. At that point, CRS had an opportunity to support the UNBRO shift and to engage more existing refugee groups in health promotion. Refugees had taken on other aspects of camp management, but continued to accept CRS's management of health care.

CRS cannot be faulted for not taking this approach from the beginning, as UNBRO itself only later adopted a commitment to Khmer self-reliance. Also, if the program moved vigorously toward promoting greater responsibility on the part of the Khmer, it is possible that some mistakes would have been made along the way—an unavoidable part of learning. CRS would have needed explicit commitment to a "risky" development approach with support from UNBRO in order to take such risks in the name of development.

REFERENCES

Catholic Relief Services, "Health Services Program," Background Information, Greenhill Site B, Thailand, 1987.

Catholic Relief Services, "Public Health and Nutrition Programs," Greenhill Site B, Thailand, 1987.

Jackson, Tony, "Just Waiting to Die? Cambodian Refugees in Thailand," Oxfam, July 1987.

Reynell, Josephine, "Socio-Economic Evaluation of the Khmer Camps on the Thai-Kampuchean Border,", Refugee Studies Programme, 1986.

World Food Program, "Summary Evaluation Report of WFP Involvement in the UNBRO Thai-Kampuchea Border Operations, " September 1987.

World Health Organization, "Health Conditions in the Kampuchea-Thailand Border Encampments," Report to the Kampuchea-Thailand Border of the WHO/UN Health Mission, January/February 1986.

ACKNOWLEDGMENTS

This case was written in March 1988. IRDP is indebted to people in CRS headquarters in New York, in Bangkok, and in Surin who made the IRDP site visit possible and provided helpful answers to incessant questions: Jeff Klenk, Joseph Curtin, Bill Rastetter, Denise Maguire, Tim Ryan, Doug Broderick, Gayle Miller, Lee White, Dr. Sakti Paul, Dr. Michel Laloux, Nancy Boyd, and a number of Khmer workers and leaders.

Chapter 19

NORTHEAST THAILAND PROJECT
Surin, Thailand

Project Implementing Agencies:
Canadian University Service Overseas
Thai NGO Consortium
NET Foundation

Case Writer:
Mary B. Anderson

I. PROJECT HISTORY AND CONTEXT

In 1979, a very large number of refugees began to move across the border from Kampuchea into Thailand. Many international agencies responded with emergency aid and sent their own staffs of relief workers to Thailand to administer the aid. Thousands of refugees were placed in camps under the United Nations High Commissioner for Refugees (UNHCR) with programs run by international NGOs.

CUSO had placed volunteers in Thailand since the 1960s and some of these volunteers had worked in the villages of Northeast Thailand. About a year after the major influx of Kampuchean refugees, CUSO went to UNHCR and offered to take on the administration of one of the refugee camps. In making this offer, however, CUSO set certain conditions. CUSO insisted that it be the only foreign agency in the camp and that the primary work be carried out by Thai NGOs; that the camp should remain relatively small—about 10,000 people; that the thrust of the work should be toward refugee self-sufficiency; and that work should simultaneously be carried out with neighboring Thai villages to ensure that the local people would not simply stand by and watch the refugees receive multiple services and benefits while they remained poor. UNHCR agreed.

THAILAND

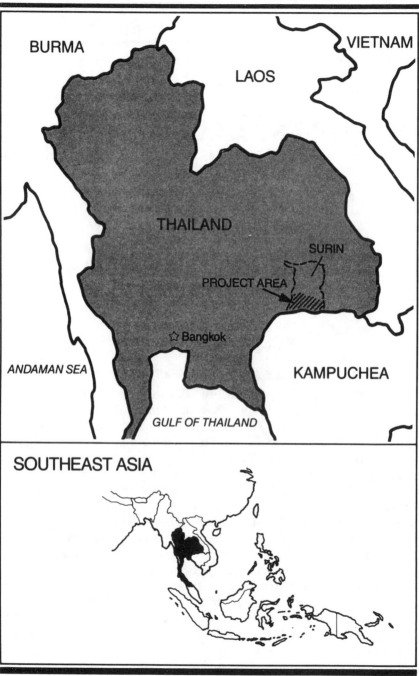

BURMA

VIETNAM

LAOS

THAILAND

SURIN

PROJECT AREA

☆ Bangkok

ANDAMAN SEA

KAMPUCHEA

GULF OF THAILAND

SOUTHEAST ASIA

Thus, in April 1980, CUSO began its work in Kab Cherng Holding Center, 400 kilometers from Bangkok. Kab Cherng was planned for those people who were most likely to return to Kampuchea, rather than those who sought settlement in a third country. Refugees who moved to Kab Cherng had been living in the largest camp on the border, Kao I Dang, which UNHCR had decided was too large and overcrowded.

The arrangements to work with Thai NGOs went forward as CUSO had stipulated. In the words of one of the Thai NGO leaders who was involved in setting up Kab Cherng:

> I was right there in Kao I Dang and saw the first Kampuchean refugees come across the border. We Thais are not so different from them, and we, from the Thai NGOs, thought we should help. But, whenever UNHCR had one of its "bidding sessions" where the different agencies would get contracts to carry out various functions in the camps, we [the Thai NGOs] would be turned down. This was always because we did not have enough experience.
>
> All the big foreign donors came in with huge amounts of money, the personnel ("experts") and the experience. All the discussions occurred in either English or French. But we wanted a role.
>
> When UNHCR decided to break up Kao I Dang, the time was right and finally our message had been heard. Not many donor agencies were willing to take the risk of involving the Thai agencies as co-equals, but CUSO was. So we began the operations at Kab Cherng as partners with CUSO and six other Thai NGOs.[1]

II. THE PROJECT: A THREE-PART HISTORY

The work in Kab Cherng which will be described below actually lasted only two years, and then the camp was closed. Because CUSO and the Thai NGOs also became involved with nearby villages even as they worked in Kab Cherng, however, a follow-up project, called the NET (NorthEast Thailand) Project (or NET I), was begun when the camp closed. This effort was planned to last for four years, but lasted six. In January 1988, NET II was to follow, extending work to new villages and run entirely by the NET Foundation, a new Thai registered NGO spawned through the earlier efforts. Through these stages CUSO's role changed. Under NET II, it provides the conduit for funds from the Canadian International Development Authority (CIDA) to the NET Foundation and deals in other ways with bilateral donors. In addition, CUSO has a role in strengthening the NET Foundation by training and staff support.

This sequence of projects provides an interesting case history of a transition from refugee camp work to local village work. This case provides

1. Personal interview (February 1988) with Dr. Malee Suwana-adth who was deputy director of the Population Development Association, the Thai agency that took the lead management role in Kab Cherng.

an example of working with refugees to help develop self-reliance. This case history is also interesting because it concerns the development of capacities of national NGOs with the support of an international NGO. For these reasons, CUSO and IRDP agreed that this project should be included among the case histories.

Kab Cherng

Kab Cherng housed about 8,500 people. It was much like other refugee camps in its requirements—food, housing, medical care and supplies, fuel, education, health services, activities for the refugees, etc. Its administration and programming were shared among CUSO and the cooperating Thai NGOs.

When it first decided to take on a camp, CUSO called a meeting of over fifty Thai agencies to invite their participation and collaboration. About twenty-five agencies sent representatives to the meeting, and seven agreed to become involved in running the camp. The selection of agencies was not complicated; they were simply the agencies that felt able and willing to become involved. Included was one very large, well-known population agency which took the lead management role as well as handling health programming and sanitation in the camp. Other agencies were specialists in formal and non-formal education, youth and women's activities, vocational training, and programming for children under five.

Responsibility was divided among the agencies according to program sectors. Housing was built before the refugees came, but, as soon as they arrived, a housing committee was formed of refugee representatives to help in any subsequent decisions about who should live where. Two schools and a small hospital were also constructed before the refugees arrived.

The approach of CUSO and its collaborating agencies was not to do anything *for* the camp residents that they could do for themselves. When the NGO in charge of education was having difficulty recruiting sufficient teachers from a Northeast Thai teacher training institute to meet the needs of the thousands of children in Kab Cherng, they went to the camp residents and asked anyone who had a minimum of 10 years schooling and who was willing to become a teacher to come forward. About two hundred people volunteered, very few of whom had ever taught before. The NGO arranged to train these people as teachers and schools were begun. Fifty-five Kampucheans became teachers and another two dozen acted as support staff for the schools.

Similarly, the resident doctor and nurse called for volunteers from among the residents to be trained as health communicators and hospital aides. The camp was organized with one health communicator for every ten houses and a second level of coordinator for every fifty houses. Other training programs were established based on a) the expressed desires of the refugees for skills they wanted to learn and b) the abilities of refugees to train each other. In every instance, the staff were able to find someone within the camp who had the requisite skills to train others.

One story is told of an old woman who came to camp headquarters to ask whether there would be any program for women. She was assured there would be handicrafts. She then said, "I can weave," and she volunteered to teach others. The staff agreed that this would be a good idea, and they began to scour the neighboring villages for the right kind of loom for her to use to teach. However, because they were afraid that the looms in use in Thailand would be different from the one the Kampuchean woman knew, they wanted to arrange to take her with them to look at these looms. The Thai security forces would not allow the woman to leave the camp. While the staff were still trying to make the arrangements to get permission for the woman to visit the villages, she went to the people in the camp whom she knew were carpenters and got them to make a loom to her design. Staff were surprised and delighted at her initiative. This loom and others for students were built, and the lessons began. The first items that the people wove were mosquito nets for their own use. They then wove the traditional fabric that they wear, again for in-camp use. Finally, they began to weave for export.

Some activities were planned which involved local village residents as well as refugees. The camp hospital was opened to people from the area who had no other health facility, and often as many as a thousand villagers a day showed up for care. In addition, when a camp pond was to be constructed, the staff organized a group of villagers to join the refugees in digging it and it was built just outside the camp so that the villagers could share it. Whenever possible, Kab Cherng staff bought food and other supplies from the neighboring villages and local merchants rather than going through Bangkok merchants as the administrators of many other refugee camps did. In order to prevent local inflation due to Kab Cherng's demand, the staff spread their purchasing out across a number of villages in the local area.

The governor in Surin, the province where Kab Cherng is located, was also committed to increasing the self-reliance of the area. While he had no control over the operations of the refugee camps in his province, he was able to refuse any development aid to the villagers which, he felt, would leave them with half-finished projects that they could not complete. He consistently set a standard for programming that relied primarily on resources which were in the area, and which would help the people develop a skill or activity that would last after the donor agency had left. This influence helped the Kab Cherng administration in its attempts to involve local people and rely on village supplies. It was even more important when NET I began.

Such stories of reliance on the expertise and experience of refugees themselves, are, by now, familiar ones. Kab Cherng was, however, one of the first camps to adopt an approach designed to avoid dependency among the refugees. It did so partly because of CUSO's fundamental development mandate and ideology and partly because the residents of Kab Cherng were destined to return to Kampuchea rather than settle in another country. It did not make sense to import expertise since their own capacities were all that the refugees would have to take back with them when they returned home.

In addition to the goal of creating the conditions in which the refugees could be as self-reliant as possible, CUSO also had the additional objective of relying on and increasing the capacities of the Thai NGOs. While there were some problems of coordination among the quite disparate group of Thai agencies, the joint collaboration in Kab Cherng was essentially successful in providing the agencies with an opportunity to gain experience that strengthened their work in general. However, when the NET I Project followed, some problems emerged which are discussed below.

No follow-up of any kind has been done with the residents of Kab Cherng camp. Some did return to Kampuchea and others moved to other holding centers. It is impossible to know to what degree they learned skills in the camp that served them and increased their self-reliance when they left the camp.

NET I Project

The full name of the NET Project is "Toward Self-Reliance in North East Thailand: Integrated Village Development on the Thai-Kampuchean Border of Surin Province." The project was planned to last for four years from May 1981 to May 1985. Building on the collaborative experience with Thai NGOs in Kab Cherng, the NET project involved one governmental agency (the Community Development Department of the Ministry of Interior), and seven Thai NGOs (the Chao Surin Association, the Education Society of Thailand, Friends for All Children Foundation, the Harry Durance Foundation, the Holt Sahathai Foundation, and the Population and Community Development Association. The Girl Guide Association of Thailand was also involved but withdrew after about two years.) These agencies not only had different areas of specialization; they also had very different approaches to their work, ranging from the provision of goods and services to a commitment to fundamental grass-roots development.

The plan of the project was to work in fifty-three villages (later reduced to fifty-two when two villages merged) chosen either because of their size and poverty (under 100 households and therefore too small to receive regular governmental services and support) or because they were "principally affected villages" which had been disrupted by movements of people due to the conflict on the Thai-Kampuchean border. In some cases, these villages were affected because they were, themselves, forced to move by the war; in other cases, they received other displaced villagers. The villages were in three border districts of Surin Province: Kab Cherng, Sangkha and Bua Chet. The population included about 30,000 people or about half of the total population in the specific areas where the project focussed.

The agencies which had collaborated in Kab Cherng each chose the number and locations of villages (in clusters of three) for which they would take primary responsibility. They were responsible for placing a resident development officer (RDO) in each village for which they took responsibility. These workers were to become general community development workers, rather than the sectoral specialists that the agencies had provided to Kab Cherng. When the RDOs felt that they did not have sufficient knowledge about things that the villagers identified as areas of need, the workers could call on others in the NET project who had the requisite expertise.

With the expansion into the villages, NET had to increase its staff. Some of the group which had worked in the holding center at Kab Cherng remained and others were recruited. Also, a more elaborate administrative structure was required to coordinate the staff and activities in multiple villages. The project proceeded in three phases, starting in fourteen villages and expanding over the four years.

For each group of eight to nine villages, there was a village coordinator (ViC) and, over these, a provincial coordinator. Above the provincial coordinator was a CUSO project coordinator and, finally, a board of directors. Each RDO was selected by his/her NGO. Each NGO, not surprisingly, had slightly different recruitment procedures and selection criteria. Thus, the first team of RDOs was quite varied in experience and approach and, to complicate matters even more, when they joined NET, they were accountable to two "bosses"—their own NGO and the NET Project.

The NGOs that worked together in the Kab Cherng Holding Center had a good experience and were ready to collaborate in the more elaborate job of rural development in the surrounding Thai villages. Their impetus to cooperate grew directly out of the relief operation in which they had been involved. They had gained experience in project management and collaboration, and they had become very aware of and knowledgeable about the needs of the Thai villages as they had travelled and worked in the area. As noted above, they had from the beginning included a focus on the neighboring villages in their relief work. In the eyes of Thai authorities the success of Kab Cherng proved that these groups they knew nothing about (NGOs) could do good work. The area was sensitive politically and militarily, and the Thais needed to be persuaded that NGO work was not subversive.

The shift from the refugee camp to village work required a fundamental commitment, on the part of the collaborating agencies, to change their operational approaches. By engaging in this project, they were adopting a village development strategy unfamiliar to most of them. Few, if any, of the agencies actually realized the seriousness of this commitment or, in fact, really made it.

In retrospect, everyone with whom we spoke felt that the method of dividing up the villages, organizing the NET administration and lines of responsibility, and selecting and placing the RDO staff were not adequately thought through. There was considerable turnover among staff in the early months, and a number of conflicts arose among the NGOs and between the NGOs, NET and CUSO due to mixed lines of communication and responsibility. For the purposes of this case, since we are not concerned with project evaluation, it is not necessary to recount here all of the problems that ensued. However, the problems encountered in redeploying staff from emergency work to village development raise issues about relief and development approaches that will be considered below.

NET II

NET II is now an operational village development program run by a newly registered Thai NGO called the NET Foundation. The original collaborating NGOs are no longer directly involved, although several representatives of these agencies sit on the NET board and some continue to provide technical support to the project. When the conflicts of management and accountability arose during NET I, the solution that was finally worked out required the staff to switch from their original employing NGOs to be employed by NET. Thus, by the time NET II began, the individual NGOs did not have operational staff in villages.

CUSO's involvement in NET II has lessened and changed. They provide one staff person whose (partial) job it is to monitor and report on the project for CIDA (which is providing funds) and to arrange other types of support to NET, mostly focussed on training. She has other responsibilities for CUSO with other projects.

NET II is extending village work, with RDOs, into new villages in Surin Province. The villages involved in NET I have been classified into three groups with approximately one-third of the villages in each group: highly successful and self-sustaining; somewhat successful and requiring some more support; and very weak requiring intense future work. NET is ending its work in the villages that are successful and where the work is self-sustaining.

The procedure which NET followed for withdrawal from direct work in these villages is instructive. In each case, the RDO who was responsible began a conversation (negotiation) with the village long before the planned departure about the purpose, timing and conditions of the proposed withdrawal. It was clearly communicated that NET was only a supporter and catalyst; the villages were helped to understand that they themselves, should and could be responsible for their efforts without outside help.

In one instance, the village requested a one-year extension for NET support and received it, with clear plans about how and when the NET withdrawal would occur. The village leaders with whom we spoke were pleased with the process.

NET has two teams who are responsible for follow-up with the villages that are on their own. They make occasional visits and see their role as continuing a friendship and encouraging ongoing activities.

III. ANALYSIS OF CAPACITIES AND VULNERABILITIES

It is impossible to assess the changes in vulnerabilities and capacities of the refugee group with whom CUSO and the Thai NGOs worked since there has been no follow-up with them. However, the design and structure of the camp, and the stories told by those present as well as in written evaluations, indicate that every effort was made to rely on the existing capabilities of the refugees for managing their own affairs. In addition, every activity of the camp involved training refugees in new skills which, it was hoped, would serve them later.

Kab Cherng was widely known in Thailand for the lack of violence or mistreatment the refugees encountered from the Thai authorities. In part, this resulted from the early and continuing efforts to relate the camp to the surrounding villages. The Thai security people were, in fact, local villagers and these relationships, therefore, had an immediate impact on the security forces' intervention with refugees. In addition, the Kab Cherng refugees set up a complete system for self-discipline with explicit norms for behavior and sanctions. The Thai security forces learned to respect these.

Our analysis of vulnerabilities and capacities will focus on two groups: 1) the Thai NGOs (and their staff) because CUSO had as one purpose the increased capacities of these agencies; and 2) the villagers with whom CUSO and its collaborators began working when Kab Cherng opened, and where NET I and II have continued to work.

Thai Collaborating NGOs

There is no doubt that the Thai NGOs developed experience, and a track record, in the programming and management of refugee camps. This experience is recognized by UNHCR and the Thai government, and these

NGOs are now regularly chosen to take on similar functions, independent of international agency involvement, as needed. Thus, their capacities for this kind of work were substantially increased.

However, the experience of attempted collaboration in NET I was not so positive. The assumption that the Kab Cherng camp experience provided a sufficient base for undertaking village community development work was proven wrong. First of all, work in the camp was very different and required different skills from those required in the villages. Second, some agencies and staff not involved in Kab Cherng joined in the village effort so patterns of collaboration did not exist. Third, the decision to start in several villages at once overburdened the project administration. Both CUSO and the Thai NGOs shared the decision to proceed as they did. It is easy to see now that the administrative and staffing arrangements, rather than supporting a process by which the capacities of NGOs would increase, were a formula for disunity and difficulty.

The attempt to use some of the staff who had worked in specific sectors within the camp as village-level community development workers did not take sufficient account of the differences in style of work required by the change in locations and emphasis. Specialists had been effective in the camps while generalists were needed in the villages. NET carried on extensive training and follow-up with village-level staff. Meetings were held every two weeks. However, many of these early NET staff (both those with camp experience and those recruited by the individual NGOs for NET I) were not prepared for village work in terms of background, ethnicity, language, experience, education or cultural awareness. The villages were very "foreign" to them. It is not surprising that there was a very high staff drop-out rate in the first months of NET.

The NET II outcome—a newly registered and operational Thai NGO—represents new Thai competence in village development work. However, changing the styles of the collaborating NGOs that had no previous experience in village work proved difficult. This was due in part to the fact that no formal mechanism was created by which the field staff transmitted their learning back into the institutions. Where individual staff people *did* develop abilities for village-level field work, they retained it individually. Sometimes the agencies did not also gain from this.

The Affected Villages

The basic physical vulnerability of the villages arose from their location on a border that was continually disrupted by war. This disruption continues (as of mid-1988) so that people who have been moved before may be moved again when security considerations require it. Each move disrupts lives and economic activities. Each time they move, the people have to start anew in arranging every aspect of basic living.

This physical reality (vulnerability) means that people live with a great deal of uncertainty. They are not able to plan (for example, to make improvements in their land) with any assurance that they will be there a few months, or years, later. Such uncertainty has a negative impact on people's sense of control over their lives and on their motivation to plan and invest.

People who were moved by government order from their affected villages into new areas complain that the lands they have been allocated are insufficient. In one village we visited, the people felt they "could do nothing" for themselves because they faced such a severe land shortage. (In spite of this "belief", they had managed to organize a number of village activities, including construction of a community center, a water buffalo project and latrine construction, among others.)

The problem that villages identified as a lack of land could be understood as a problem of a lack of knowledge and/or resources to make the land that is available productive. In this particular village, the people said that they each have eight *rais* in this new area; however, they claimed, these eight *rais* are not able to produce what one *rai* produced in their former village location. Inadequate water is a continual problem in the whole area, and land tenure remains uncertain for many people.

These physical facts—war and the threat of war, inadequately productive land and uncertainty about tenure, and inadequate access to water—set the context for all activities that NET has undertaken. In addition, the disruptions and dislocations in their lives have left people disgruntled with their new circumstances and uncertain about the returns from any economic investment activities they might undertake.

NET began by focussing on the villagers' needs. The approach was intended to help people organize themselves around specific issues and, together, to devise a strategy for meeting their common needs. NET projects have involved a number of physical activities including buffalo husbandry projects, latrine and other building construction, improved farming methods, revolving funds, and rice banks. One staff person pointed out, however, that these physical projects serve as a "front" for the real purpose which is to increase the people's abilities "to plan and carry on by themselves."

The villages in this area of Thailand have strong leadership traditions. People believe in, are loyal to, and seldom challenge their leaders, and leaders hold their positions for many years. NET staff pointed out that this system may be either a liability or an advantage in terms of change and development. When the leadership is forward-looking and able to support people's efforts to improve their capacities, the fact that it is unquestioned is an advantage. When it is self-serving and not really interested in seeing the people's lives improve, it is a major impediment to NET-style organizing. NET staff have found both situations in the villages where they have worked.

In our village visits, we found one area in which the people were having particular difficulties. They expressed discouragement with their plight and felt that they could do nothing until, and unless, the government gave them more land. In this area, the leadership had consistently misappropriated group funds when they had been collected. Perhaps the sense of dependency on other, outside agency decisions was a reflection of these unfortunate experiences.

In another village, the traditional leader had fled the village when they had been forced by war to move. New leadership had emerged. While the experiences of evacuation, starting over in a new area, then moving back to the original village had thoroughly disrupted these people's lives, they expressed their conviction that these experiences had strengthened them. Through this disruption and adversity they had learned to work together and to accomplish things as a group. They also noted that the support of NET, both with some staff and with some resources, had greatly helped them gain a sense of their own abilities to cope and affect change.

In the third village we visited, we were also told that the crises they experienced in moving their village had helped to unify the people. "Before the rich went their own way and the poor theirs; now we have systems for helping the poor. We are more cooperative," said the headman. He claimed, and the elders sitting with him agreed, that the main role that NET played in helping them was to provide access to ideas and agencies with which they had no previous contact. This village had been, they claimed, "closed up." NET brought contacts with government, other villages, and new ways of doing things. This introduction to others seemed more important to these villagers than the physical resources involved in some of the NET projects.

When I asked the village group with whom I was meeting, "But what if you have to move again?" they laughed aloud and shook their heads. "If we have to move, we have to move," they said. "But, every bit of knowledge and every experience we have gained stays with us." They said that they could start similar programs everywhere no matter where they moved "until the day we die."

IV. LESSONS LEARNED FOR FUTURE PROGRAM DESIGN

Developmental Approach to Refugee Work

It is possible to take a developmental approach to refugee work. The first important lesson demonstrated by this case is that a developmental approach and philosophy *are* relevant to refugee work. Some agencies now base their approach to working with refugees on the assumption that the refugees have many skills and capabilities. When CUSO and the Thai

NGOs began in Kab Cherng, they were pioneering this approach. Their commitment to self-reliance made a difference in the ways they dealt with the acquisition of supplies, the establishment of health and education programs, and the management of the camp.

Support for Development by an External NGO

An external NGO can support development at several levels, but sheer limitations on time and energy may affect the possibilities of pursuing development at too many levels at once. This case illustrates the several levels at which an international agency can have a developmental impact, whether working in an emergency or not. CUSO intended two such impacts: 1) with the Thai NGOs and 2) with the refugees. Later, NET extended its developmental work to the affected villages. Examination of the multiple levels of development work by CUSO, and later by NET, raises the potential for contradictions and competition among goals. In the early days of NET I, when staff were struggling to find the way to do village-level work, the organization spent most of its energy and time on coordination, staff support and inter-staff and inter-organizational communication. Little energy and time were left for village-level development. At that stage, there seems to have been a direct conflict between developing staff and NGO capacity and developing village people's capacities. With more planning and forethought, such contradictions could have been reduced and complementarities enhanced. For example, slower phasing in of the number of villages where staff worked would have allowed more integration of staff training and support with village-level activities.

Skills Acquisition Focus

The CUSO/NET experience shows that it is always possible to focus on skills acquisition, but that, in different circumstances, the skills that will benefit people differ. The project provides an excellent lesson about working with populations in flux. Both the refugees and the affected villages suffered from basic disruptions to their lives and livelihoods and from uncertainty. In both cases, the program strategies emphasized the acquisition of skills—organizing, problem-solving and tangible production skills. These are portable and are not lost when additional moves become necessary. One CUSO person pointed out that, with refugees, the focus often must be on training in individualized skills since there is no certainty that, when people move, they will move together. Each refugee, or refugee family, needs to be able to leave the camp with skills he/she (or they) can use. With villages, the strategy should be to develop community skills. For a sustainable development impact, community-based problem identification and solving, and cooperative planning and implementation of projects are important.

REFERENCES

Research and Development Institute, "Report on the Process and Impact Study of the NET Project in Surin, Northeastern Thailand," Khon Kaen University, Khon Kaen, Thailand, March 1985.

Sundhagul, Malee; Wonghanchao, Warin; Ressler, Everett; Pongsapich, Amara, "Development of a Self-Help Assistance Programme for Displaced Cambodians: A Pilot Project (1980-1981) Report of the Project Evaluation," For CUSO/Thailand, February 1982.

The SVITA Foundation, *Toward Self-Reliance in Northeast Thailand: Integrated Village Development Along Thai-Kampuchea Border of Surin Province (The NET Project): An Evaluation Report of the Mid-Term Review*, For CUSO Thailand, April 1983.

ACKNOWLEDGMENTS

This case was written in February 1988. Many people helped with the arrangements for writing this case and with the process of gathering the information about the project. We wish to thank Paul Turcot of CUSO, Canada who provided important background. In Bangkok, CUSO Director, Gerald van Koeverden was helpful with his insights and in freeing his staff for support of IRDP's work. Chanida Chanyapate, who is CUSO's liaison with NET, deserves special appreciation for the many arrangements she made for relevant appointments in Bangkok and with the field staff in Surin. She also was generous with her own time and ideas.

Many staff and villagers shared time and ideas with us in the Surin area. We thank them all. Greatest thanks, however, go to Kowit, the Program Field Coordinator of the NET II project and Kanchit, the Coordinator of the Farmers' Training Centre in Surin for their special contributions to our understanding. Thanks also go to Dr. Cherdsak Choomnoom who served as interpreter for this case history.

Appendix A

ANNOTATED LIST OF
ADDITIONAL IRDP CASE HISTORIES

Cases #1 through #11 appear in this book. The cases listed below will be available after the fall of 1989 from the Disaster Management Center, University of Wisconsin, 432 North Lake Street, Madison, WI 53706. Cases are in English unless otherwise noted.

#12: Jalalaqsi Reforestation Program
Location: Jalalaqsi Refugee Camp and town, Somalia
Implementing Agency: Africare
Case Writer: Ann K. Qualman
Sectors: Refugees and reforestation
Description: The program engaged refugees in efforts to address deforestation and dune destabilization resulting from the presence of refugees in the area.

#13: Qorioley Refugee Development Project
Location: Qorioley Refugee Camp, Somalia
Implementing Agency: Save the Children Federation (USA)
Case Writer: Christopher M. Harris
Sectors: Community development, forestry, agricultural development and irrigation
Description: The program worked with refugees in a camp setting on development efforts in several sectors and with several nearby refugee-affected communities.

#14: Community Development for Settlers in Sablaale
Location: Sablaale, Somalia
Implementing Agency: ACORD (formerly Euro Action-ACORD)
Case Writer: Mary B. Anderson
Sectors: Agricultural development
Description: The program worked with people resettled to Sablaale from drought-affected areas to develop agricultural self-sufficiency.

#15: Sheik Banane Cooperative Development
Location: Baidowa, Somalia
Implementing Agency: Sheik Banane Cooperative
Case Writers: Mohamed Hassan Farah & Christopher M. Harris
Sectors: Multi-sector development
Description: The case describes efforts by a well-unified religious community to build resistance to periodic drought under the leadership of a charismatic sheik.

#16: Ogaden Refugee Returnee Program
Location: Hararghe Region, Ethiopia
Implementing Agencies: World University Service Canada, in conjunction with UNHCR and the Ethiopian Relief & Rehabilitation Commission
Case Writer: Ann K. Qualman
Sectors: Water supply, food distribution, health
Description: The program assisted refugees returning to the Ogaden, providing food, secure water supply and health care as people attempted to reestablish their lives and economic activities.

#17: Karkora/Um Gargur Refugee Program
Location: Karkora & Um Gargur Refugee Camps, Eastern Sudan
Implementing Agency: Save the Children Federation (USA)
Case Writer: Peter J. Woodrow
Sectors: Health, sanitation, community development
Description: The program encouraged refugee initiative and community development, trained health education workers, provided health services, and improved sanitation.

#18: Kordofan Supplementary Feeding Program
Location: Northern Kordofan Region, Sudan
Implementing Agency: CARE-Sudan
Case Writer: Ann K. Qualman
Sectors: Nutrition, food aid, women's program development
Description: The program began during emergency stage of famine relief training women to operate village feeding stations, and later turned to development programming among these women.

#19: Cereal Banks in Senegal (in French with English Summary)
Location: Central and Northern Senegal
Implementing Agencies: SOS Sahel, Church World Service, Catholic Relief Services
Case Writer: Hady M. Ly
Sectors: Food security and development
Description: The case examines the use of cereal banks as a strategy for increasing food security in drought-prone areas of Senegal. Three different agency programs are compared and contrasted.

#20: The Drought Years in Northern Mali: Rehabilitation and Development in the Context of Rehabilitating the Cooperative Network in Northern Mali
Location: Gao Region, Mali
Implementing Agency: ACORD
Case Writer: Mark Nieuwkerk
Sector: Agricultural and fishing cooperatives
Description: The case explores the interaction between intermittent drought and efforts to revive economic cooperatives among farmers and nomads.

#21: Volcanic Eruption and Mudslide: The Relief of Armero
Location: Armero, Colombia
Implementing Agency: Catholic Relief Services
Case Writer: Ronald S. Parker
Sectors: Housing reconstruction, small enterprise development
Description: The project provided assistance for rebuilding homes and credit for (re)starting small businesses for direct "victims" of the Armero disaster and people in surrounding communities.

#22: The Relief of Sequential Disasters: Earthquake, Tidal Wave and Floods
Location: Tumaco, Colombia
Implementing Agency: Foster Parents Plan International
Case Writer: Ronald S. Parker
Sectors: Emergency reconstruction aid and community development (health, education, small enterprises, etc.)
Description: The PLAN project promoted development in an isolated coastal community struck by repeated disasters.

#23: Drought Relief and Rehabilitation of Agricultural Production
Location: Porcon, Cajamarca, Peru
Implementing Agencies: Equipo para el Desarrollo Agropecuario de Cajamarca, with support from Catholic Relief Services
Case Writer: Donald Schramm
Sectors: Agricultural production
Description: CRS funded efforts by EDAC to rehabilitate damaged irrigation infrastructure as part of a larger multi-sectoral program.

#24: Agricultural Reconstruction after El Nino
Location: San Pedro de Morrope, Lambayeque, Peru
Implementing Agencies: Centro de Estudios Sociales Solidaridad, with support from Oxfam Canada
Case Writers: Donald Schramm & Daniel Torrealba
Sectors: Emergency agricultural relief and rehabilitation
Description: A Peruvian agency worked with local rural communities to help rehabilitate agriculture, including irrigation and credit systems.

#25: 1987 Earthquake in Ayora Parish

Location: Santa Rosa de Ayora Parish, Ecuador
Implementing Agency: Catholic Relief Services
Case Writer: Ronald S. Parker
Sectors: Housing reconstruction, technical assistance, and loans
Description: The project worked with communities damaged by the 1987 earthquake, supporting housing loans and technical education and using food-for-work to support community projects.

#26: Urban Earthquake Rehabilitation

Location: Colonia Bethania, Guatemala City, Guatemala
Implementing Agency: Foster Parents Plan International
Case Writers: Donald Schramm and Roberto Muj Miculax
Sectors: Health, housing reconstruction, small business development, education
Description: The project began in 1976 with housing reconstruction following a large earthquake, but continued and expanded into a community development program.

#27: Reflections on NGO Post-Earthquake Projects in Mexico

Location: Mexico City and Jalisco State, Mexico
Implementing Agencies: Mexican NGOs with Canadian NGO partners
Case Writers: Robert Thomson, edited by Maureen Hollingworth
Sectors: Housing reconstruction, day care, small enterprise development
Description: This case examines the experience of eleven projects funded through Canadian agencies and implemented by Mexican NGOs, drawing on an evaluation which used the IRDP framework.

#28:Projects Supported by Oxfam America in Rajastan and Gujarat States

Location: Mada, Dungarpur District, Rajastan State; Godhar, Panchmahals District, Gujarat State
Implementing Agencies: Social Work and Research Centre (SWRC) in Rajastan and Social Action for Research and Tribal In-Habitants of India (SARTHI) in Gujarat, both with funding from Oxfam America
Case Writer: Mary B. Anderson
Sectors: Agriculture, hydrology, soil and forest conservation, small enterprise development, primary education
Description: The case discusses the experience of two projects, each of which works with people in rural districts severely affected by several years of drought, engaging in multiple strategies to increase the capacities to cope.

#29: Drought Prevention and Development in Rural Orissa
Location: Mayurbhanj District, Orissa State, India
Implementing Agency: Lutheran World Service-India
Case Writer: Peter J. Woodrow
Sectors: Water conservation and irrigation, health care, agricultural development
Description: The case describes how an ongoing development project works on disaster prevention efforts in two rural subdistricts by reducing vulnerability to drought.

#30: Typhoon Rehabilitation in Lapu-Lapu City
Location: Lapu-Lapu City, Cebu, Philippines
Implementing Agency: Norfil Foundation
Case Writer: Peter J. Woodrow
Sectors: Health and nutrition, day care services, leadership training, small enterprise development
Description: The project works with people affected by a severe typhoon but addresses the long-term problems of poverty, ill health and unemployment.

#31: A Long-Term Approach to Drought in Thies
Location: Louly de Bretegne, Thies, Mbour, Senegal
Implementing Agency: The African Network for Integrated Development(RADI)
Case Writer: Ronald S. Parker
Sectors: Community organization, agricultural development
Description: The project worked with drought-prone communities, organizing irrigated communal vegetable plots, improved marketing systems, cooperative stores, and a para-legal project.

#32: Food Self-Sufficiency in the
Villages of Bamba Thialene (in French)
Location: Central Senegal
Implementing Agency: The Action Committee for the Development of the Bamba Thialene Zone
Case Writer: Moussa Ba
Sectors: Agricultural development, credit, natural resources conservation, community organization
Description: The case describes the formation of a grassroots NGO and its subsequent efforts to combat drought and deforestation.

#33: Fuel-Efficient Stoves for the Sahel (in French)
Location: Cercel de Kati, Koulikoro Region, Mali
Implementing Agency: Association d'Etudes de Technologies Appliquées et d'Aménagements en Afrique (AETA)
Case Writer: Amadou Bocoum

Sectors: Community development, natural resource conservation
Description: The case examines the diffusion of fuel-efficient stove technology as a means of slowing deforestation, and reducing women's daily labor.

#34: An NGO Coordinating Council: Famine Relief in the Sahel
Location: Mali
Implementing Agency: Comité de Coordination des Actions des ONG au Mali (CCA/ONG)
Case Writer: Ronald S. Parker
Sectors: Inter-agency coordination, creation of indigenous NGOs
Description: The program began as a response to the needs of agencies working in famine relief. The case describes how the CCA continues to coordinate NGO development efforts in Mali while attempting to search for better formulas for North/South collaboration.

#35: Using Unemployed Young Professionals in Drought-Prone Rural Villages (in French)
Location: Bamako, Mali
Implementing Agency: Groupe Jeunes
Case Writer: Adama Diawara
Sectors: Water, employment, training, community development
Description: The program trained unemployed professionals to work with rural villages in drought-prone areas, providing the youths with their first jobs, and the villages with dams and water systems.

#36: Development in the Cercle de Niafunke: An Integrated Approach to Drought and Famine Relief (in French)
Location: Niafunke, Tombouctou Region, Mali
Implementing Agency: Association Malianne de Recherche-Action pour le Dévéloppement (AMRAD)
Case Writer: Mariam O. Touré
Sectors: Animal herd recovery, water, literacy, agricultural development, community organization
Description: The case examines an indigenous NGO's use of integrated development to help extremely remote communities achieve food self-sufficiency.

#37: Helping Nomadic Populations During Drought (in French)
Location: Gao, Mali
Implementing Agency: Tassacht Association
Case Writer: Baba Abdou Dicko
Sectors: Agricultural development, community organization and animal husbandry
Description: The program worked with nomad communities to restore their herds, and facilitated a transition to agriculture for those willing.

#38: Organization Building with Traditional Structures
Location: Yatenga Province, Burkina Faso
Implementing Agency: SIX-S
Case Writer: Ronald S. Parker
Sectors: Community organization, soil and water conservation, agricultural development, small enterprise development
Description: The case describes community development efforts based on village-level organizations called *groupments naam*. These now operate in several countries, and provide work in the dry season for farmers in the drought and famine-prone Sahel.

#39: The Use of Credit with Peasant Organizations in Burkina Faso (in French)
Location: Bobo-Dioulasso, Burkina Faso
Implementing Agency: l'Union Coopérative d'Epargne et de Crédit Burkinabé (UCECB)
Case Writer: Guillaume Badoit
Sectors: Savings and Loan Cooperatives, agricultural development
Description: The case describes the creation of a national federation of credit cooperatives and its experience with financing food self-sufficiency in drought-prone areas.

#40: Yako Regional Development Committee (in French)
Location: Yako Region, Burkina Faso
Implementing Agency: Comité de la Dévéloppement de la Région de Yako (CDRY)
Case Writer: Bernadette Pallé
Sectors: Agricultural development, community development, food security, credit, irrigation
Description: The case describes the efforts of an indigenous NGO to build resistance to periodic drought and famine. Emphasizes the results of integrated development and community organization.

#41: Self-Help Housing in Popayan (in Spanish)
Location: Popayan, Colombia
Implementing Agency: SENA
Case Writers: Julio Castro, Carlos Salazar, Ronald S. Parker
Sectors: Housing, community organization, training
Description: The case describes efforts to teach earthquake-resistant housing techniques, and to organize self-help groups to build safe homes.

Appendix B

BIBLIOGRAPHY

We have listed below some of the people on whose work we have relied in carrying out this project. This bibliography is suggestive only; it neither includes all the important books and articles in the field, nor does it include all of the useful items written by these particular authors. We provide it here both to acknowledge our debt to these individuals, and to give the interested reader some indication of other sources which are helpful.

Brodhead, Tim and Herbert-Copley, Brent, with Lambert, Anne-Marie, *Bridges of Hope?: Canadian Voluntary Agencies and the Third World*, Ottawa: The North-South Institute, 1988.

Chambers, Robert, "Project Selection for Poverty-Focused Rural Development: Simple is Optimal," *World Development 6:2*, February 1978, pp.209-19.

Clark, Lance, "Promoting Refugee Participation in Assistance Projects," Washington, D.C.: Refugee Policy Group, 1987.

Cuny, Frederick C, *Disasters and Development*, Sponsored by Oxfam America, Oxford: Oxford University Press, 1983, and "Refugee Participation in Emergency Relief Operations," Washington, D.C.: Refugee Policy Group, 1987.

Currey, Bruce, "Coping with Complexity in Food Crisis Management," Bedford Park, South Australia: Food Crisis Management Institute, The Flinders University of South Australia, n.d.y.

Disaster Management Center, University of Wisconsin, *Disaster Management Program*, a series of self-study courses in disaster preparedness, mitigation, and response. Disaster Management Center, University of Wisconsin, 432 North Lake Street, Madison, WI 53706.

Forbes, Susan and Copeland, Emily, *Making Ends Meet?: Refugee Women and Income Generation*, Washington, D.C.: Refugee Policy Group, 1988.

Fruhling, Pierre, ed., *Swedish Development Aid in Perspective: Policies, Problems and Results Since 1952*, Stockholm: Almsqvist and Wiksell International, 1986.

Glantz, Michael H., ed., *Drought and Hunger in Africa: Denying Famine a Future,* Cambridge: Cambridge University Press, 1987.

Hagman, Gunnar, (with Henrik Beer, Marten Bendz and Anders Wijkman), *Prevention Better than Cure: Report on Human and Environmental Disasters in the Third World,* Stockholm and Geneva: Swedish Red Cross, 1984.

Harrell-Bond, B.E., *Imposing Aid: Emergency Assistance to Refugees,* Oxford: Oxford University Press, 1986.

Hyden, Goran, *No Shortcuts to Progress: African Development Management in Perspective,* London: Heinemann Press, 1983.

Kent, Randolph C., *Anatomy of Disaster Relief: The International Network in Action,* London: Pinter Publishers, 1987.

Korten, David, "Micro-Policy Reform: The Role of Private Voluntary Development Agencies," Working Paper No.12, Washington, D.C.: National Association of Schools of Public Affairs and Administration, August 1986.

LeComte, Bernard, *Project Aid: Limitations and Alternatives,* Paris: Development Centre of the Organisation for Economic Cooperation and Development, 1986.

Mason, Linda and Brown, Roger, *Rice, Rivalry, and Politics: Managing Cambodian Relief,* Notre Dame: University of Notre Dame Press, 1983.

Minear, Larry, *Helping People in an Age of Conflict: Toward a New Professionalism in U.S. Voluntary Humanitarian Assistance,* New York: Inter-Action, 1988.

Overholt, Catherine; Anderson, Mary B.; Cloud, Kathleen; and Austin, James E., *Gender Roles in Development Projects: A Case Book,* West Hartford: Kumarian Press, 1985.

Rodale International, "Regenerative Agriculture in the Third World: Building on Capacity Not on Need," International Ag-Sieve, Premier Issue, Vol. 1, No. 1, Emmaus: Rodale International, May-June, 1988.

Timberlake, Lloyd, *Africa in Crisis: The Causes, the Cures of Environmental Bankruptcy,* London and Washington, D.C.: Earthscan, the International Institute for Environment and Development, 1985.

Torry, William I, "Social Science Research on Famine: A Critical Evaluation," *Human Ecology,* Vol.12, No.3, 1984.

Wijkman, Anders and Timberlake, Lloyd, *Natural Disasters: Acts of God or Acts of Man?* Washington, D.C.: International Institute for Environment and Development, 1984.